A Postcard from Joseph

A Postcard from Joseph

Clif Cormier

VANTAGE PRESS
New York

FIRST EDITION

All rights reserved, including the right of
reproduction in whole or in part in any form.

Copyright © 2002 by Clif Cormier

Published by Vantage Press, Inc.
516 West 34th Street, New York, New York 10001

Manufactured in the United States of America
ISBN:0-533-14172-9

Library of Congress Catalog Card No: 2002091181

0 9 8 7 6 5 4 3 2 1

Contents

Foreword   vii

One	Louisiana in the Depression—1937–1938	1
Two	The Marine Corps Beckons—1938–1939	11
Three	The Seventh Platoon–1938	19
Four	Home on Leave—1939	29
Five	Louisiana Revisited—1940	40
Six	Iceland and Beyond—1941	55
Seven	The Third Marine Division—1942–1943	70
Eight	Up the Pacific—1943	101
Nine	Crossroads of the Pacific—1943–1944	118
Ten	The Marianas Landings—June–July, 1944	129
Eleven	Iwo Jima: Black and Red Sands—February 1945	143
Twelve	Reunion with Cara—1945	163
Thirteen	The New Civilian—1946	188
Fourteen	Prelude to Korea	199
Fifteen	The Forgotten War—1950–1953	216
Sixteen	The Peacetime Corps—1953–1959	231
Seventeen	Camp Lejeune: Farewell to the Corps—1959–1960	255
Eighteen	A Time in the Sun—1962–1985	280
Nineteen	The Turbulent Years—The Sixties	296
Twenty	The Golden Years—1986	312

Foreword

Paraphrasing the old jokes about aging that pop up on your e-mail: You know you're getting old when you want to write a book about yourself. The itch got to me when a couple of my friends put their life experiences down on paper. Their efforts were chronological diaries at best, intended to be of interest to grandchildren and perhaps future generations of their families. My hope was to make my story of a more general interest. Do it now, I was advised, before it's too late. After twenty-two years with the *Gainesville Sun*, I figured my writing days were over, until I read a couple of best sellers dealing with people of my generation, notably Tom Brokaw's *The Greatest Generation*.

I knew I could never put words together as does the likes of Brokaw, but in my lifetime, I had knocked about in some unusual places, acquiring a few interesting experiences along the way that might be of interest to readers.

I first intended to limit the scope of my story to a youth growing up during the Great Depression, who joined the marines to escape the bleak future of his poverty-stricken rural Louisiana town. Then I got talked into continuing past the war and my military career and into my second calling as a newspaper journalist by Helen Gilbart, my volunteer editor and counselor. Helen was an English teacher at the college level who has written and edited textbooks. As the project began, I fed chapters to Helen, not just for her to clean up my grammar but to get her opinion. If I had gotten back a lukewarm endorsement, I probably would have folded. On the contrary, Helen not only praised my efforts but continually offered encouragement and inspiration. So I know that I have at least two interested readers, Helen and my wife Dorothy.

From my years of experience writing about others, I shunned the use of the first person and adopted the pseudonym Joseph, my middle name, as the central character.

I have also used fictitious names in several instances, including family members, not that there would be any embarrassment but because I preferred it that way. After a bit of persuasion, my wife Dorothy adjusted to being Cara, shortened from O'Cara, her ancestral Irish family name. Annie, my daughter, is really Leslie Ann. Ornas and Clarissa are fictitious names for my parents, very similar to their real names in pronunciation. A couple of names of my Marine Corps boot camp buddies were also inventions necessitated by my lack of recollection. Unfortunately, the Marine Corps was not able to provide me with a roster of my boot camp platoon.

Lake Tarsa is a fictitious name that originated with one of my young cousins who could not pronounce the name of our town. So are the Mamatou River and Dennings made-up names. My friends and relatives in Louisiana will have no problem recognizing the deceptions. Other than those, my story is entirely factual told to the best of my recollections.

With apologies to politically-correct readers, I have used the language spoken in the time frame of incidents, particularly the "n" word for black people and repeated references to Japanese soldiers as Japs, which was what everyone called them during the war.

I am indebted to a score of friends and old acquaintances who helped fill in the gaps and provided valuable recollections. It was through Al Mount, a retired master sergeant, that I learned of the fate of Bobby Adkins, my San Diego sidekick in the 10th Marines.

Bobby was doused with gasoline and incinerated on Palawan Island in the Philippines after suffering nearly four years as a prisoner of the Japanese. Mount and Adkins had guarded the beaches of Corregidor, were taken prisoner with the surrender of the fortress, and survived the infamous Bataan Death March.

This cruel and inhumane treatment of American prisoners of war will forever remain a shameful black mark on Japan except that their history books remain mute about the incident.

Roy Conway, who served as my office clerk at Cubi Point in the Philippines during the mid-fifties, provided useful details about the shooting of Private Benjamin Bolt while on sentry duty. Conway corresponded from Stratford, Texas, up in the panhandle of the state. I am also indebted to Sam Jones, Bill Brown, and George

Green who organized and presided over reunions during which useful facts emerged among the tall tales.

Hugh Cunningham, my journalism professor at the University of Florida and later a colleague at the *Gainesville Sun* when we worked together with Hugh's laboratory classes at the newspaper, offered this encouragement. "You write well. Tell your story."

Jean Chance, a coworker at the *Sun* in our beginning years of journalism, provided valuable information about the fatal airline crash at the Gainesville airport. Chance, who then was Jean Marshall, reported on the disaster with me. She is, and has been for a long time, a professor at the UF journalism college.

Ed Johnson, my boss during my entire career with the newspaper, offered some insights I had misplaced in my recollections. Ed completed his newspaper career as a political correspondent for *The New York Times*. It is his opinion that the events during the decades of the 1960s and 1970s were the most dramatic in the *Sun's* history.

I have attempted to relate some of these as I was involved. Bob Tartaglione, the circulation manager and my former golfing partner, came through with interesting particulars and insights from his end of the newspaper business.

Finally, were it not for the marvelous recollections of Dorothy, many of these pages would be blank. I pestered her relentlessly and picked her brain for nuggets of information.

I vaguely remember reading about a magazine whose zany editors wrote headlines and then set about creating stories to fit. In a way this is how this tale came to be. My love affair with the Marine Corps began with a colorful recruiting poster in the post office. It depicted two marines raising the Stars and Stripes over a tropical fortress with a squadron of battleships cruising the blue water in the background.

When I enlisted in New Orleans, the recruiters gave me a postcard to send home.

Ironically, the picture on the card was the same as the poster. I wrote a brief note to my father and mother and mailed the card. Many years later, Dorothy found the card, somewhat mutilated, among my mother's shoe box of family photographs. The card now reposes behind a faithful reproduction of the flag-raising that hangs over our fireplace mantle and which graces the cover of this book.

This is my humble story of "A Postcard from Joseph."

A Postcard from Joseph

One
Louisiana in the Depression—1937–1938

The ground convulsed spasmodically with each explosion, spraying Joseph's back with dirt. Shards of steel that could slash a man in half whistled overhead. His shallow trench in the center of airfield number 2 had been gouged from dried, unyielding clay, nowhere deep enough. Except for the airstrip, Iwo Jima was mostly coarse black sand, put down ages ago by Mount Surabachi. Always visible, the extinct volcano stood broodingly a couple of miles to the west, 500 feet high. Once again it was smoking, this time from puffs of white phosphorus shells and black TNT.

Now and then snipers' bullets thudded before ricocheting off with a scream. His G.I. watch said 8:15. He had lost track but believed it was the twenty-fourth of February, 1945. D day plus five.

For the time being, he was on the hottest piece of real estate on the island. A warrant officer, known in Marine Corps terminology of the time as "Marine Gunner," Joseph had waded ashore the previous afternoon, accompanied by a radio operator and a field telephone wireman, past the D-day carnage and mangled landing craft and amphibious tractors. He led an improvised forward observer (FO) team so hurriedly scraped together on the navy transport, he hadn't even learned their names.

His orders were to find the 2nd Battalion of the 21st Marines and replace Lieutenant Millsaps, who had been hit the night before and nearly bled to death before he could be carried out. His scout sergeant had been killed. Good guy, Sergeant Gregory. He'd been Joseph's ordnance assistant maintaining the howitzers back in New Zealand before volunteering as an FO.

Hunching their bodies to make smaller targets in the sights of Jap Arisami rifles and Nambu machine guns, the three raced across the hard-packed dirt strip, zigzagging and occasionally hurdling over marine bodies.

He would forever remember the blackened flame thrower, incinerated by his own exploding tank of deadly jellied fuel.

The three had followed close behind an infantry company that made a heroic—all but suicidal—charge across the airstrip and seized a dirt promontory some forty feet high, left standing when Jap bulldozers had cut bisecting landing strips.

Charging into enemy trenches with bayonets and small arms, the grunts of the 21st routed the Japs and seized the bluff. The 21st had driven a wedge into the heart of General Tadamichi Kuribayashi's Japanese defenses.

Early the following morning, the decimated 21st was ordered back to regroup. The 3rd Marine Division's 9th Regiment had been landed and would relieve the 21st. Trouble was the poor bastards of the 9th were hopelessly pinned down in open ground across the airstrip by the unrelenting fire. Their unsoiled utilities and clean camouflage helmet covers told they were not long off the ship. Fresh meat for the grinder, thought the Gunner. The 9th could only wait for the firestorm to abate. Inching forward on their bellies, some men pushed slender wooden poles with bundles of TNT tied to the end. Hopefully the charges would make it into the mouth of a Jap cave before detonating.

A screaming voice interrupted a lull. "Where's the goddamned artillery support? We're getting the shit cut out of us."

Standing over the foxhole was Lieutenant Egan, a lanky, fiery redhead who appeared immune from shell and bullets. Yesterday he had taken over when his company's second C.O. had been killed.

He was right, the artillery support was missing. Joseph's wireman had connected one end of lightweight "combat" wire from a reel to the switchboard at the infantry battalion command post in the rear. He had paid the wire off the reel while crossing the airstrip, but it had been cut either by shells or tank treads. Frantically, they cranked the field telephone but got only the empty feel of an open line. And the radioman couldn't raise the battery of 75s, or anyone else back on the beach, with his screeching field radio, no doubt an army reject.

Mercifully, relief appeared out of the bright morning sky. Angels, no less, those stubby navy Hellcats that swarmed off the decks of carriers standing out to sea.

Their rockets screamed terrifyingly before slamming into the Japs, only yards away. Some launched napalm bombs with fireballs that seared the tortured earth and sent up plumes of black smoke.

Under cover of the air strike, the 21st staggered back across the airstrip, passing through the long skirmish line of the forward moving 9th. Companies that had entered the battle with 200 men retreated with half that number. So ended his first day on Iwo. There would be twenty more.

* * *

Home in Lake Tarsa was a vague memory. The youth, Joseph, hadn't been thinking of war when the Marine Corps recruiting poster in the post office caught his eye. It held the promise of adventure, flashy blue uniforms, admiring girls, travel to exotic lands. It offered an escape from the miasma of the Great Depression in Louisiana. The poster kept coming back in his mind.

Joseph's schooling had an inauspicious beginning in a one-room country school. Frightened by the older children, he walked home less than an hour after his mother had taken him in the buggy with old King in the harness.

Next was the parochial school in Texas, where a nun failed miserably in communicating with him. "Write your letters on the line," she would beseech him. So Joseph would make his letters straddle the line, each letter protruding halfway above and halfway below the line. Again and again she would urge him, ON THE LINE. And again and again he would repeat his mistake. Generally, Catholic schools are noted for academic excellence but it never occurred to this novice to say, "Make your letters sit on top of the line," which would have registered. It was only after Joseph stole a glance at another pupil's tablet that he grasped the meaning of "on the line."

The discipline demanded by the sisters left a strong mark on him, in the true sense. They were different from his Aunt Bonaventure, a kindly Dominican nun in New Orleans. A hint of sadism must have lurked behind the hooded wimple of one sister, the impression stemming from an incident on the playground. While on yard duty at recess she stationed herself on an imaginary line separating the boys' side from the girls' holding a buggy whip. While chasing an errant ball, Joseph suddenly felt the stinging lash of the nun's whip around his bare ankle. One look at the nun with her whip poised to deliver a second lash sent him scurrying back to the boys' side.

Like most boys his age, Joseph was a dreamer. It never occurred to him what he would do after his schooling. In the seventh grade at Lake Tarsa, from his desk in the third-floor classroom he had a view of the lake and the opposite shore. His mind would be immersed with thoughts of paddling across the lake and exploring the other side while Miss Delauney lectured on adverbs and adjectives. More than once he suffered the embarrassment of being called on in the middle of a fantasy.

Louisiana public schools had never been noted for academic excellence, and they became even worse in the Depression. One year, there was no money to pay teachers for the full nine-month term, so the state declared a school "holiday" after seven months.

Joseph's grades were in the mid-range, and would have been much worse but for the proddings of his mother and father. Neither Clarissa nor Ornas had gone beyond the fourth grade, so they were determined that their son would finish school. His sister Mae dropped out from the sixth grade. "What do you want to be, a bookkeeper?" Ornas would ask encouragingly, bookkeeping, or any white collar occupation being looked up to in rural Louisiana.

"Cowboy," Joseph would usually answer, much to the chagrin of his father.

Finally, it came to pass on a hot June evening. He sat on the stage, uncomfortable in a new mail-order, charcoal-gray suit. It had needed alterations but arrived too late to send back. Clarissa had done a reasonable job of shortening the sleeves and cuffs. She was good at her old, foot-driven Singer. Of the nineteen graduates only six were boys. In a somnolent drone, a state politician from Baton Rouge, sweating under the armpits and crotch of his white linen suit, delivered an uninspiring moral imperative. The culmination of Joseph's schooling seemed like a bad dream.

Social activities for youngsters in those days of want were lacking. Girls tended to date boys three or four years older, and then marrying early, leaving the younger boys to find other diversions. For Joseph and his buddies, a favorite pastime was watching the Saturday night dances at the Bucket of Blood on the highway to Dennings. They never went to actually dance, they didn't know how;

neither did they have the price of admission. So they'd crowd the open windows of the ramshackle dance hall that smelled of uncured cypress and watch. A two- or three-piece Cajun ensemble provided the music with accordion, violin, and sometimes a guitar and an iron triangle. The operator, a bald little man with a nasty temper, maintained decorum with a fat nightstick.

Troublemakers suffered split scalps and nasty headaches if they resisted his entreaties to quit the premises. Major differences and grudges were settled outside with knives. Cuttings were frequent. The dance hall was an eponym of those bloodlettings. The combatants would begin the duel with insults and then out would come the switchblades. Like gamecocks with steel spurs, they'd circle each other warily, their thin blades flashing under the dim light of the utility pole. There would be a brief flurry of slashes aimed at the stomach, and at first blood the battle was ended. Mostly the result was a superficial wound, but occasionally an intestine would be seen protruding from one's shirt. Sheriff's deputies always arrived after the battle.

In his first summer out of high school, the only work Joseph could find was in the rice fields. For four bits a day, he waded through knee-deep water, yanking out indigo weeds while keeping a wary eye out for snakes. Years later, big-shot farmers and corporations, enriched by healthy federal subsidies, hired airplanes to spray the fields with DDT that killed the weeds and the snakes and the birds and, eventually, some field hands.

The fall harvest paid better, but the labor was demanding. Reaper-binders, drawn by teams of horses or mules or occasionally a tractor, took to the fields of chest-high ripened grain. Rotating paddles on the reapers gathered the stalks and forced them into a row of cutting teeth.

The severed stalks were gathered, tied into bundles, and dumped onto the clean-cut swatches of stubble left behind. The invention of Cyrus McCormick's nearly 100 years earlier was still state of the art with Louisiana rice growers. Complete mechanization would follow after the Second World War.

Joseph's Cajun ancestors had brought in the first rice from South Carolina—one of their stops en route to French Louisiana following their expulsion from Nova Scotia. Slaves from Madagascar had first introduced the grain to the New World. In the lowlands of Louisiana, the Acadians planted small quanties by hand for their own consumption. Yankee farmers arriving from the midwest discovered a profitable circumstance about Louisiana's soil that enabled rice to be grown commercially, using mechanization. The impervious subsoil of clay not only held the irrigation water necessary for the rice to grow in the summer months, but was firm enough to support heavy farm machinery at harvest time.

When the work of the reaper was done, field hands followed with pitchforks and built shocks by standing the bundles with the grain ends up to dry in the hot month of September.

Come threshing time, the farmer would pray for continued dry weather. A hurricane or prolonged rainy period could soon rot the grain and leave the farmer with nothing but unpaid bills and a bank always ready to foreclose.

If all went well, a thresher would be towed to the field, a long boxlike machine of galvanized metal pulled by a farm tractor. With its snout attached to blow the straw into a stack, the apparatus resembled a trumpeting elephant. Power was supplied by a tractor turning a steel drum that spun a long belt attached to another drum on the thresher. It turned gears and wheels inside the elephant, activating steel teeth that separated the grain. It was the ultimate in farm mechanization at the time.

In October, wagons pulled by teams of mules would head into the fields. A field hand would snatch sheaves from the shocks and fling them upwards to be speared by the wagon driver with his own pitchfork and stacked into the bed of the wagon. As the last sheaves were lifted off the ground, sometimes snakes would slither out. Or rats six inches long scurrying to escape the piercing tines of the pitchfork.

As the stack on the wagon grew taller, the man on the ground had to fling the bundles ever higher, ten or fifteen feet up. When loaded, the wagon would be driven to the thresher and the sheaves fed onto a conveyer and into the belly of the machine, which swallowed whole bundles, stripped them of grain, and blew out the hay to form a haystack, where cattle and horses would munch through the winter.

The thresher could never be let idle. Its hungry maw set the work pace of the field crew. Sore muscles and blisters notwithstanding, the sheaves had to keep coming without interruption—tomorrow might bring rain.

Joseph alternated with the other field hands between working on the ground and the wagon. Ornas, his father, sometimes worked at the thresher. His job, which paid the best, was sewing the filled sacks. It was work that combined brawn with dexterity. Wearing a canvas apron holding strands of hemp and sailmaker's needles, he would attach a large gunnysack to the feeder pipe catching the stream of grain. As the sack filled with some 200 pounds of rice, he would swiftly attach a new bag and drag the first a distance away where he would quickly sew the mouth of the pregnant sack. No time could be lost, for there was always a filling sack to attend to.

Several years before, Ornas farmed his own rice on his father's extensive lands close by the lake which supplied irrigation water. A succession of crop failures from salt water intruding out of the nearby gulf, plus bank foreclosures on loans, would eventually drive Ornas with his family all the way to East Texas with their belongings in a Model T truck.

There he found work of the worst kind, in an oil refinery laboring besides Mexican migrant workers. After a year, Ornas moved his family back to Louisiana but would never return to farming. He'd met with too many disappointments. Like the year he lost his best team of mules to anthrax. *Le charbon* they called it in French. The child Joseph had watched as the dead mules were pushed into a deep pit, doused with crude oil, and set afire. The smell of burning oil and animal flesh had nearly made him vomit.

The youth's own career in the fields was cut short by a blister from a pitchfork. It was on the finger that held his LTHS class ring. He awoke one morning with the finger so swollen he couldn't remove the ring.

In pain, he walked to Dr. Heinen's house, which was also his office and clinic, on the lake at the other end of town. The doctor was a little gray-haired man, his small stature providing grist for jokes made by the town's smart alecks:

"Have you heard? Doc Heinen is suing the town."

"No shit. What for?" the other redneck would bite.

"They built the sidewalks too close to his ass."

What the good doctor lacked in height, he more than made up with compassion and generosity. Toting his little black bag, he made the rounds of the town and along the rutted roads of the countryside in a black sedan, delivering babies and ministering to the sick, often pro bono or a promise of payment.

Daubing the throbbing hand and finger with alcohol, he warned in his strained voice, "This will hurt a little." No numbing drug. The youth clenched his teeth and tightened his sphincter as the shiny lancet sliced into the end of the finger releasing a gush of blood and pus.

The ring has got to come off, the doctor said, otherwise the whole hand would become infected. With a pair of wire cutters he severed the constricting fourteen-karat gold band, poured an astringent on the incision, bandaged it, and cautioned to keep it dry.

That recruiting poster kept surfacing in Joseph's mind. One day he went to the post office and copied the address. On a penny post card he wrote to the marine recruiting office in New Orleans asking for details and waited.

Several days later, his reply came in a brown government envelope. It held a questionnaire, a dental chart, and physical examination form to be executed by a physician. The physical was easy, with Doc Heinen probing his thin body here and there. The dental part was another matter, what with several teeth in need of fillings.

Old Doc Percy was the town dentist, as well as the veterinarian. He rode to and from his work on a big roan mare. His office upstairs in the bank building was a scary room, with evil-looking implements and pliers for extractions. A stained porcelain cuspidor stood next to the arm of the leather chair. A pulley holding wires with coarse drills on the ends dangled overhead. On the floor, a foot treadle, like that of a sewing machine, provided the power for the drills. The place reeked of medicine and disinfectants.

With heavy breath smelling of alcohol, the old dentist probed Joseph's teeth and at length made a cost estimate of filling the cavities and rendering them acceptable to the marines. The few dollars was more than the youth or his father could hope to come up with. But, continued old Percy, he could drill the cavities and fill them with cement at half the price. "That way," he added, " when you get there, they'll take out the cement and put in some real fillings with silver."

Agreement reached, the drilling began, without novocaine. More than once he would bolt almost out of the chair when the dentist's old burrs struck the raw end of a nerve. The ordeal finally over, he staggered down the wooden stairs with a mouth full of cement-filled teeth.

The medical forms completed, there remained another step, parental consent, as he was not of age. Reluctantly, Clarissa, his mother, signed the document on the rolltop desk of Mr. St. Germaine, notary public.

He awaited word from the marines, with misgivings about having started the process. The corps was not wanting for even a very few good men. In 1938, the strength of the entire Marine Corps was less than 20,000. It was smaller than the New York City police department.

With mixed feelings, he read the notice that he had passed the preliminary examinations and was to report to the recruiting office in New Orleans in two weeks.

It was in mid-February, a rainy period, when the bullfrogs in the swamps croaked lustily after females and the crawfish began to surface from the muddy bottoms of the swollen bayous.

Maurice, the husband of Joseph's sister, was a good frogger. He had accompanied Maurice a couple of times, fascinated by the rays of the miner's lamp on Maurice's hat, which pierced the dark and gloom of the swamp. It illuminated the eyes of frogs and other creatures half-submerged in the murky water. Wading stealthily towards his blinded quarry, Maurice would reach down, clamp his thumb and finger around the eyes, and lift up long-legged amphibians ideal for the frying pan. Into a croaker sack they would go. Sometimes the green eyes would not be those of a frog but of a snake which Maurice would drop like a hot potato.

*   *   *

Dennings, the parish seat, straddled a set of shiny rails of the Southern Pacific going east and west. He had often watched the trains go by, the big locomotives belching smoke and steam and the engineer leaning out of his cab yanking on a cord that made the whistle scream. He imagined being in one of the green coaches that flashed by, headed for a distant city, but had never ridden in one.

In Lake Tarsa, there was only a spur line with a single rusted track to Lake Charles. Once in a while, a locomotive would come in pushing a freight car or two. Sometimes on holidays, the engine would bring in a single coach to be filled with Negroes headed for an excursion. Dressed in their Sunday finery, they would laugh and joke and slap one another on the back. The Depression never seemed to bother them. After all, they had never benefited in even the best of times.

When the D&L Brewers, made up of white baseball players from Dennings and Lake Tarsa, folded for lack of interest, the Negroes took over Rainbow Park with games of their own. The players were much more animated than their white predecessors, and what they lacked in skill was made up with spirit. Their Sunday games had all the trappings of a holiday. The fans dressed in church clothes and women sipped pink drinks from tall glasses in the grandstand, where the seats were made of uncured lumber that exuded pine pitch under the broiling sun.

Games began with the selection of an "empire" and some poor disinterested chap would be coaxed from the grandstand as arbiter. Fights were rare but vicious. Joseph had witnessed one that began as an argument at home plate and ended far out in right field with one of the participants suffering a fractured skull when struck by a baseball bat.

Joe Louis had begun his ascendancy to the world's heavyweight boxing championship, and clots of blacks gathered on the little grass neutral grounds that divided Main Street to hear the blow-by-blow from the old Philco in the window of Bailey's barber shop. When Louis knocked out his white opponent, which was usually the case, they prudently held their cheers. But when safely back within the confines of "coon town," their whoops could be heard for miles, much to the annoyance of the white folk.

Two
The Marine Corps Beckons—1938–1939

The day arrived, and late in the evening, the three of them drove to the depot in Maurice's old Chevy pickup. The silence of the trip was broken occasionally by Ornas's inquiries. "Are you sure you want to go?" "Yes," he would answer, mustering his strongest voice.

A drowsy stationmaster sold him a one-way ticket to New Orleans on the twelve o'clock train. With heavy heart, he hugged Ornas, shook the hand of Maurice, and waited for the train to come to a stop. Only a few of the green imitation leather seats in the dimly lit coach were occupied. He took an empty seat near the window and stared vacantly into the formless night as the train gathered speed. He dozed off and on, awakening when the conductor called out approaching towns.

He dreamt fitfully on and off, coming to each time the train whistle wailed its warnings at forlorn road crossings. The first light of dawn revealed only swamps and bayous with stands of cypress and tupelo bare of foliage but weighted with long hanks of gray moss.

He thought of the time he and Erv Miller had gathered moss by the sackful in hopes of selling it as stuffing for mattresses and easy chairs. It had to be cured by being immersed in water a long time and then rinsed and dried. Their curing pit was a hog wallow at best, and none of the stuff ever achieved the qualities that moss buyers demanded.

They tried picking cotton, but at two cents a pound, it was backbreaking and unrewarding. They would pick from sunrise to sundown and at the end of the day sadly watch the scales at the weigh-in barely reach forty pounds. To augment the weight, they resorted to stuffing green boles in their crocus sacks and sometimes even pissing in them. They were caught at it red-handed, actually wet-handed, when the suspicious foreman reached his arm in Erv's sack. He withdrew it with a disgusted look, wiped his wet hand off on his trouser leg and told them not to come back.

Erv was older and had been in the Civilian Conservation Corps camp, one of Franklin Roosevelt's make-work programs for youths. The CCC was a quasi-military organization run by National Guard officers. Erv still wore parts of his olive drab Army issue uniforms. The two shared a passion for baseball. Erv taught him how to read the major league box scores and what all the abbreviations in agate print stood for. While hanging out in town on summer evenings, they would filch a *Beaumont Enterprise* from the newspaper rack, spread it out under a street light, and with June bugs buzzing about, catch up on the previous day's action in the big leagues. They would first search for the box score of the New York Giants, a favorite team because they had a Louisiana player named Mel Ott, who was leading the league in home runs. Erv was also a good fishing buddy.

They found a productive fishing hole in an old logging canal that ran into the lake. Erv would spit tobacco juice from his chaw on a squirming worm and extend his cane pole outward with the hook and worm swaying back and forth. At a precise moment, he would drop the bait through a small opening in the hyacinths. Within seconds, his pole would bend and he would deftly lift out a flopping bass or a large perch. They seldom came home without a string of fish.

The failed moss gathering was but one of many enterprises people tried in the Depression. One year, his uncle Amos and another chap heard there was a market for cabbages. They planted two acres of cabbages on a farmer's plot with a promise to share profits. The crop was a success but there were no buyers. However, there was cabbage on the table every day until the harvest ran out.

The train whisked through willow swamps, causing the supple trees to sway as in a summer tempest. New Orleans was just ahead. At the station, he got directions to the federal building where the Marine recruiters had their office and started walking. He passed an open market with stalks of bananas hanging from the ceiling like hog carcasses. Not only was he hungry, but he remembered what old Doc Heinen had told him about the need to put on weight. "Eat some bananas before they weigh you." He bought and ate three ripe ones.

It was the day after the Mardi Gras celebrations, and the streets of New Orleans were littered with parade debris and empty beer and whiskey bottles. And the street car benches were taken by human debris sleeping off hangovers.

One such celebrant was stretched out on the floor in the doorway of the recruiting office, which had not yet opened. He was a husky, blond youth from Chicago wearing good clothes. He had spent all his money on women. "Now's as good a time as any to join the marines," he quipped. There were three other candidates that day, all of them bigger than Joseph. One of them said he had heard they would take only one recruit that week. Probably not me, Joseph thought, eyeing the strapping candidates. Two were from Mississippi, one of them talked about his prowess on the football field. He was big enough for the game.

During the Depression, the Marine Corps didn't have to beat the drums to find their few good men. For the private's pay of twenty-one dollars a month, clothing, and three square meals a day, there was no shortage of applicants. They came from the red clay farms of Georgia and Alabama. There were poor Irish youths from the slums of Boston and New York, Slavs from the tough neighborhoods of Chicago, and out-of-work Italians from San Francisco. There were always some running from bad marriages and illegitimate babies.

The five were ushered into an unheated room with white-tiled walls and told to strip down for physical examinations. Two of the recruit candidates were quickly eliminated, including the football player. Flat feet. The Chicago fellow appeared uneasy as the doctor, with a frown on his face, listened to his heartbeat. It came down to the last two. Joseph was disbelieving when the examining physician told him he was the only one acceptable, although a tad underweight. "They'll put some meat on those bones in boot camp," he said. So he would not only get silver fillings in his teeth but meat on his bones. Already, he liked the marines.

He was issued two meal tickets for the Chalmette Grill two blocks down the street and told to return at eight that evening so the colonel could swear him in. Taking the oath, he mispronounced corps, calling it corpse, and was swiftly corrected by the colonel.

They gave him a postcard to send home. It was a colorful depiction of Marines hoisting a billowing American flag over a tropical fortress. A squadron of battleships steamed on the distant sea. He scrawled a message to his parents, saying he was a "full-fledged" marine headed for California. In boot camp he would realize how far he was from being full-fledged. It would be years later before he would learn from his sister Mae, who was older, how devastating the arrival of that postcard had been to his father and mother. They were brokenhearted. All along, they had thought he would be coming home. His sister had married young and as the only remaining child in the household, he had enjoyed the love and sheltering of devoted parents. Though they struggled to make ends meet in the hard times, he always had decent clothes and occasionally a few coins to spend on movies and candy.

Recruits enlisting in the South were usually assigned to boot camp at Parris Island, South Carolina. To his surprise, he was given a choice between Parris Island and San Diego. Without hesitation he picked the latter. Much later he learned the wisdom of his choice. While boot camp discipline was much the same at the two bases, the South Carolina weather could be hot or cold. The base was surrounded by a salt marsh and infested with mosquitoes and sand flies. Its isolation made it a perfect place to produce tough marines. San Diego, on the other hand, had an ideal climate, and the city's bright lights were just outside the gate of the marine base.

A sergeant escorted him to the train station and handed him an envelope containing his orders and a set of tickets for the train. First class: a Pullman berth and meals in the diner. Boarding the train, he felt the same apprehension as the night before in Dennings. He wished one of those other guys had passed the physical so he wouldn't be alone.

After crawling into his upper berth, he removed his shoes and sweater, but not his shirt and trousers. He had never slept among strangers, and the occupants in the berths were concealed only by cloth drapes. What's more, some of the passengers were women. He was not about to be caught indecent in case of an emergency. He tried sleeping, but the train bounced and lurched too much. Late in the night, he heard a conductor announce Shreveport. All the time he thought he was traveling back towards Dennings.

As the train again got underway, he dressed and found a seat in the adjoining coach. Curiously, he watched the morning ablutions in the tiny men's washroom. Two well-dressed Chinese were shaving. They spoke perfect English to his surprise and talked of places like Walla Walla, which he knew was not in China but in the state of Washington. The only Chinamen he had ever seen were in the movies, and they wore clothes like pajamas and talked in singsong phrases.

All day the train labored through Texas. The terrain changed. The trees were stunted and outcroppings of rock poked through the freshly plowed fields. Not at all like Louisiana. In the distance, he saw remote farms, cattle ranches, and occasional oil derricks. After another sleepless night in the jostling berth, he arose as the first rays of the morning sun bathed the top of a mountain close by, the first he had ever seen, and he gazed in awe. His chuckled to himself, thinking of his childhood cousins who used to talk of wanting to go west and roll down a mountain.

This one was barren and hostile with only rocks and dried mesquite. "I like my mountains with trees on them," a passenger on the next seat observed. *Hell,* he thought, *a mountain is a mountain, and this is a pretty good one.*

In El Paso, the passengers wandered around in the expansive Spanish-style station, serenaded by a duo of Mexican guitarists under huge sombreros and attired in colorful native dress. Mexicans were usually bad guys in the old cowboy flicks he watched on Saturday nights in the rat-infested theater in Lake Tarsa. His childhood heroes of the silver screen were Tom Mix, Hoot Gibson, and Bob Steele. Often the films had been scratched and abused by projectionists, so the screen always appeared like it was raining. He didn't think much of Gene Autry. Too much singing and not enough action.

Los Angeles was the terminus of the Southern Pacific. The end of the continent. He wandered about the white stucco station waiting for the train to San Diego, his eyes searching fruitlessly for Hollywood movie stars. Off a news rack he read headlines that reported flooding in Southern California. On the train approaching the coast, he had seen rushing rivers but assumed that was normal. In a short time, those "rivers" in the California desert would become dry gulches again.

On the short run to San Diego, the tracks followed close by the coast. Giant waves rolled over broad beaches. Under trestles along the way, swollen streams emptied into the ocean, carrying not only brown silt but also rafts of citrus fruit washed from groves at the foot of the coastal range. A sea of oranges floated out as far as the eye could see, resembling the rays of a setting sun reflecting off the water.

San Diego appeared much like he had imagined. A few tall buildings and listless palm trees hovering above the red-tiled station. He removed his sweater. A corporal dismounted from a green pickup truck with a canvas top and motioned to him. Funny how they recognized a recruit without even seeing his orders. In silence they rode to the Marine Corps base only a couple of miles down Pacific Boulevard.

A sentry in forest green trousers, khaki shirt, and fore-and-aft cap waved the truck through after briefly studying Joseph. They drove through streets bordered by neatly manicured lawns lined with eucalyptus trees and emerged into an enormous asphalt parade ground.

Immediately facing the parade ground and the bay in the distance was a long row of tawny, two-story, Spanish-style stucco barracks with red tile roofs. For two years one of those barracks would be Joseph's home. The last one on the row was the receiving barracks. The corporal led him inside where a balding, avuncular-looking sergeant was seated at a desk at the entrance to the squad bay, reading a newspaper. *About Papa's age,* thought Joseph, *though not as handsome.* Silently, he accepted the orders identifying Joseph as a new recruit.

He spoke in a gentle voice, apparently sensing the discomfort and loneliness that engulfed Joseph. He would again be alone for a while, the first recruit reporting for the 7th platoon of 1938. The old sergeant issued him a bath towel, blanket, sheets, and a pillow case. He showed him how to make up his bunk then marched him to the mess hall a block away. Joseph was no stranger to being marched, having learned in the Boy Scouts. Once at a field meet of Scouts in Lake Charles, he had been a finalist in the O'Grady Says drill.

He sat apart from the Sixth Platoon, in khakis, eating platters of fried liver and onions. He stole curious glances at their red, sunburned faces that contrasted with the whiteness of their skinned heads. Some had badly chapped lips with the skin about to flake off. Those closest to Joseph quietly chorused, "You'll be sorree." He already was.

The following day, in trooped a small band of recruits, two from Chicago, a couple from San Francisco, and one from Seattle. Joseph was elated in meeting his first marine buddies. They exchanged cigarettes and lit up. As he was already a "salt" by having been there a whole day, they bombarded him with questions. He was filled with relief and reassured by the camaraderie. The bonding had begun.

More recruits joined them with each arriving train until the squad bay was almost full. Three drill instructors (DI) appeared to lay claim to the platoon. The first was Sergeant Staley, the platoon leader, a manikin of perfection in his starched khakis, perfectly blocked campaign hat, and shiny shoes. He wore a single row of campaign ribbons, the legacy of pursuing guerillas in the jungles of Nicaragua. His pleasant clean-shaven face and steely blue eyes seemed to suppress a smile. Here was a marine to admire and emulate.

Private Cameron, on the other hand, appeared to have forgotten how to smile. His square ruddy face bore an uncompromising look, and he had a habit of compressing his lips before shouting a command. His sunburn and chapped lips were like those of the 6th Platoon recruits. It was rumored that Cameron had busted out of the Naval Academy in Annapolis, for what, nobody knew. Or dared ask.

The third DI was Corporal Arneson, a blond Adonis in uniform. He had the graceful build of an athlete, with sloping shoulders and long arms. His eyes were slightly crinkled, giving a hint of a fun-loving nature. He had played college football in Oregon and would continue to play for the base team. Staley would be the father figure, one who could be counted on to keep Cameron's latent, sadistic nature in check. Arneson was a macho role model to envy.

When the last of the Seventh's forty recruits had checked in, they were marched to the base barber shop for regulation haircuts. There was little waiting for any of the six chairs. Eager barbers fell upon them with buzzing shears. Soon the floor was like an autumn lawn in need of raking. An attendant's broom pushed the mass of civilian hair of all hues and forms into a waste can. The recruits stole glances of themselves in the mirror and recoiled in humiliation. They felt like inmates. Already, the Corps was making a point. Everybody would be the same.

From the barber shop, they marched to the quartermaster building to be issued clothing and uniforms. They got six sets of white underwear, the drawers with but two buttons and adjusting tie strings on the sides. The crew neck, T-style undershirts were popular items.

A tailor took measurements for the outer clothing and a young second lieutenant observed the fittings, either nodding approval or ordering a different size.

World War II movies and newsreels of Army inductees showed recruits in baggy, oversized uniforms. Not so with Marine recruits. Everything had to be the exact fit.

They each got four sets of khakis with web belts and fore-and-aft caps, a set of forest green uniforms with matching fore-and-aft caps and black "fair leather" belts with heavy brass buckles. Later, they would hear old China hands in the base slop chute brag about how they had used their belts in Shanghai street brawls with soldiers of other foreign legations. The belts made lethal weapons when wrapped around the fists and the buckles swung at the heads of French "frogs" and British "limeys."

They were issued a pair of black high-top street shoes and white cotton socks. Topping it off were brown cavalry-style felt campaign hats with a leather chin strap that was worn around the back of the head, not under the chin. Where was the flashy blue uniform with shiny brass buttons and white hats? They groaned in unison when the sergeant in the clothing room cackled, "You won't be needing blues where you're going."

The new-smelling clothes were dumped into a heavy canvass seabag and toted back to the barracks. On the way, they stopped to shop at the PX, using coupon books which would come out of their first paycheck. Following a required shopping list, they bought toiletries, shoe polish, and cleaning kits for their rifles yet to be issued. Also, a scrub brush, known as a kiyi, laundry soap, and a galvanized bucket.

Three
The Seventh Platoon—1938

Morning began with the platoon falling in for roll card. Joseph learned that Marine NCOs, however much their military know-how, weren't the most articulate in pronouncing names. In fact, mispronunciations were the rule, particularly with surnames not of Anglo origin. Victims of fractured ethnic names rarely complained, fearing a rebuke questioning their Americanism. When Joseph's French family name was anglicized, he merely answered, "here, sir."

It was not that he was ashamed of his ancestry. He dreaded being inflicted with the nickname "Frenchie" or "Cajun." The word Cajun, a corruption of Louisiana natives of Acadian ancestry, was not yet in vogue outside Louisiana and East Texas. To be called a Cajun among Cajuns was an acceptable, if not welcomed greeting. To be called one by an Anglo, especially a "Texien," was generally considered a pejorative and usually meant to be. It was not until recent years, when a New Orleans chef burnt a fish filet marinated with fiery peppers and dubbed it "Cajun style" that the name became widely associated with Louisiana cooking. Joseph's mother Clarissa was a classic Cajun cook, but she had an even hand with the hot stuff. *Justment.* Her gumbos, courbouillons, crawfish étouffes, chicken fricasees, fried catfish, and jambalayas were beyond compare, yet she never set anyone's tongue aflame with spices.

Most educated Louisianans of Acadian ancestry shunned the corruption of Acadian into Cajun except in jocular situations. Their ancestors had migrated to the New World from Normandy in the early 1600s, settled in Acadia, now Nova Scotia, and prospered.

In the state's zeal to silence the French language in schools, Louisiana textbooks omitted any history of the Acadians, who represented a major segment of the population. What Joseph knew about his ancestors had been learned after finishing school.

According to the Rev. Msgr. Jules O. Daigle, a historian of the Cajun culture, the French government sold out the Acadians to the British in the 1713 treaty of Utrecht. From that time, the Acadians were harassed and persecuted by the British. In 1755, the Brits began uprooting the Acadians from their homes and prosperous lands and deporting them. They were herded aboard leaky, rotting ships and dumped like so much ballast in seaports from New England to the Caribbean. "Scattered like dust and leaves" was the way poet Henry Wadsworth Longfellow described the diaspora. Their crime was refusing to renounce their Catholicism, become Protestants, swear fealty to George II, and agree to take up arms against the French. *Non, non, jamais,* they responded. In New England, the rebellion of colonists was heating up, and the Brits feared having French enemies at their backs while dealing with unruly Americans.

In *le grand derangement,* as it came to be known, some escaped the death ships only to be hunted down in the forests and shot like animals. Their homes and crops were torched, and families purposely separated. It was genocide, yet the barbaric eviction and banishment was given no place in American or English history books. Scant knowledge of the fate of the Acadians came in *Evangeline,* the romanticized epic of Longfellow.

Small wonder that the thousands who made it to Louisiana, at the time under Spanish rule, sought refuge in the backwaters as far as possible from anything British.

They lived in isolation for more than a hundred years, clinging to their French culture and resisting American ways. Encroaching American settlers mocked them for their rustic simplicity, lack of education, and their Acadian dialect. By the First World War, families slowly began to adopt American ways and send their children to school.

Many abandoned their traditions and taught their children to speak English only. Joseph's family remained solidly French. He spoke scant English when he began his schooling. His cousins, however, were brought up speaking English only. He and his sister Mae were the only ones among nineteen grandchildren who could speak to their grandparents in French, the one language the elders knew.

Sometimes little Joseph would get an appreciative pat on the head from his grandpa and a quarter might slide out from the old man's pocket into the boy's hand. When he was older, his grandpa gave him horses to ride.

* * *

The 7th Platoon joined the other boots doing close order drill on the parade ground. The grinder, it was called. Hour after hour, day after day, they were drilled either by Private Cameron or Corporal Arneson. Before long, their faces turned red from the sun and their lips began to crack.

Sergeant Staley made cameo appearances but mainly stayed in the background, observing not only the recruits but the instructors as well. The marching drill of that time consisted of a set of complicated maneuvers somewhat like those of high school and college marching bands, though on a smaller scale. Squads right, squads left, squads right about, to name a few, required each man to count and measure his steps and pivot one way or the other. The platoon would emerge in a different formation and in a straight line if done properly. It was impressive to watch as bodies went milling past bodies, exchanging positions without colliding and with a moving thicket of rifle barrels weaving above their heads.

One day while executing a squads-right-about Joseph collided head-on with Private Bishop. In a chain reaction, the whole platoon became a comic jumble. " 'Toon halt!" shouted Cameron.

Swiftly identifying the source of the screw-up, he pounced on the two, grabbed them by the neck, the stacking swivel in DI talk, and bashed their heads together. Campaign hats went flying. "Shit heads," Cameron screamed. "Think, dammit, think." The platoon tittered while perversely enjoying the moment. Neither Joseph nor Bishop blamed the other for the misstep. It was done but was a lesson not forgotten.

The basic drills had begun without arms, but soon they were marched to the base armory to draw rifles. The old, reliable bolt action, caliber .30, 1903 Springfield would be the marine's alter ego from that moment. It would be his best friend, trusted and pampered like a bride. In fact, he might be made to sleep with it if it were neglected or abused in any way. He memorized its serial number like his own birth date.

The rifles emerged from storage crates coated with sticky Cosmoline preservative. At the paint shed, they drew a ration of benzene in their buckets. Back in the barracks they fieldstripped the rifles, following step-by-step instructions by the DIs, using their footlockers as workbenches. Into the benzene bath went the parts to be dissolved of grease, then lightly oiled and reassembled. The process of fieldstripping and reassembly was repeated several times. Then the lights were turned off, and they were made to do it in darkness. With the lights turned back on, there were some whose rifles had the comic look of Rube Goldberg contraptions. This triggered a tirade of scatological name calling from Cameron and more instruction for the unfortunate ones.

The discipline wore on nerves, and occasionally scuffles broke out between recruits. Private Hughes, the biggest man in the platoon, began to assert his bulk, pushing and shoving smaller men out of his way. In the mess hall, he hogged the platters of chow.

One day while the platoon was picking trash from the dunes near the bay, Hughes threw Private Crane to the ground for apparently no reason. In an instant, there was a melee of bodies swarming over the bully, fists and feet pummeling him. It was over in seconds, but a bruised and bloodied Hughes was a while getting up, his spirits quashed and his bullying days over.

In the mess hall, Joseph was introduced to dishes he'd never eaten. Creamed or chipped beef on toast was both filling and tasty. It was served at breakfast. Joseph liked it but was disgusted with its marine name, SOS. SOS was a mildly disparaging reference to food in comparison to, say, diced weiners in tomato sauce which were crudely likened to the reproductive organ of the male genitalia cooked in blood. Even more indelicately labeled were cold-cut sausages likened to the male equine appendage.

Joseph never had eaten spareribs and sauerkraut and swore if he ever had the power, he'd do away with the sour cabbage. The slumgullion wasn't bad if any tidbits of meat remained on the platter when it reached him. On Fridays, it was fried barracuda steaks, always too salty. Swiss steak was good, but served only once a week. Dessert was usually Jello or puddings, like tapioca, another anomaly to his French Louisiana palate. Sundays and holidays, there was ice cream and cake. Fresh milk was on the tables every other day, but seldom green salads, which didn't bother Joseph, since he didn't like "rabbit food" anyhow.

There was nothing like good martial music to stir the spirits and pride of the recruits and enliven their steps. Days would start with all the base units and recruit platoons in formation for morning colors. At eight o'clock, all would be brought to attention. The band would strike up "The Star Spangled Banner," and a three-man color guard would snappily hoist the flag up the high pole. Joseph envied the color guard. They reminded him of the postcard he had sent home from New Orleans.

After colors, the band would continue to play snappy John Phillip Sousa martial tunes. The recruits would literally prance to the beat with chests pushed out enough to pop buttons.

There was more weapons instruction with the Colt semiautomatic .45 pistol, the Browning automatic rifle, and hand grenades. The BAR was the enforcer of the infantry squad, capable of firing automatic bursts or single shots.

The platoon heaved dummy grenades and stabbed straw targets with bayonets. With the horrors of the World War still fresh, there were hours of instruction on the identification of poison gases and how to protect oneself from it. In detection tests, they cautiously sniffed from sample bottles of mustard and phosgene. Inside a small shed with the door barred, tear gas grenades were dropped at their feet. Recruits not quick enough to remove gas masks from their pouches and clap them over their faces emerged panic stricken, gagging and coughing.

One evening after chow while the platoon was relaxing and writing letters home, an angry Cameron burst into the squad bay. "On your feet," he bellowed. "Grab your buckets and fall out." Over the dunes he drove them at double time all the way to the beach a quarter of a mile away. As they panted for air, he instructed them on the exercise.

They were to gouge out a bucket of wet sand from the water's edge where it was heaviest, hoist the bucket on a shoulder and double-time back to the barracks. The buckets would be emptied on the deck in the middle of the squad bay, and then they'd double-time back to the beach for another bucketful. "What the hell's going on?" some would ask out of range of Cameron's sensitive hearing. No one knew.

On the third trip, half the platoon had dropped to the ground. Joseph gritted his teeth and managed to deliver his third bucket into the chest-high pile on the floor. After a short break, Cameron ordered them to refill the buckets and lug the sand back to the beach. Less than a third of the platoon remained to complete the task. When the last of the sand had been removed, Cameron gave the order to sweep down and swab the deck.

"If you shit heads had done it right this morning, you wouldn't have had to go to all this trouble." It turned out that the officer of the day on his inspection had been displeased with the appearance of the barracks, and Cameron had been chewed out.

There had been a follow-up physical examination at the base dispensary. To his surprise, Joseph had put on three pounds. Like the doctor in New Orleans had said, boot camp had put meat on his bones. Joseph had all but forgotten Doc Percy's cement fillings until seated in the dentist's chair. A navy lieutenant commander in a white smock approached. Joseph knew his rank from the uniform jacket hanging on a rack in the corner. It had two broad gold bands and a narrow one on each sleeve like the chart in the barracks that identified the rank insignia of navy and marine officers.

"Open wide," ordered Commander Sir in a bored tone.

One look into Joseph's mouth turned his face into an angry scowl. "Another one of these wise guys," he snarled. "Well, by the time I drill out all that crap, you'll regret you tried to fool us. Believe me, it's going to hurt like hell."

He wasn't kidding. Without novocaine, he commenced drilling. Joseph's only consolation was that the drills were electric and ground smoother than that with Doc Percy's foot treadle. Still, Commander Sir fairly made cement dust fly from his mouth. Joseph endured the one-hour torture sessions for three days. At times he wanted to cry out, but he refused to flinch. By the third day, he no longer closed his eyes and began staring into the dentist's. At one point, he detected an uneasy look in the other's eyes. Finally, the ordeal was done. The commander backed off, apparently pleased with his handiwork.

"You were a good patient, Private," he said. "Your teeth are in good shape. Now take care of them."

The boot camp routine had been too hectic for Joseph to experience any of the loneliness he had felt soon after leaving home—until one day when the platoon was scrubbing their clothes and he was hit with a pang of longing for his mother. His clothes always had a clean, sweet smell from her laundering. On Monday,

Clarissa would rinse out the big, black, cast-iron kettle in the backyard and fill it with water pumped from the well. With wood she kept in a stack for the kitchen stove, she'd build a fire under the kettle. As the water heated, she would shave slivers from a bar of Octagon soap, and when the water had come to a boil, in would go the laundry. Occasionally, she would stir the wash with a long wooden paddle, fish out a garment known to have been soiled, and inspect it.

Into a washtub of clean water would go the clothes for rinsing and then hung on a clothesline to flap in the breeze until dry. Clothes that needed ironing went into a bath of starch before being hung out. Then, alternating a pair of flatirons heating on the stovetop, she would expertly press out the wrinkles so that the finished garments would nearly stand up from their stiffness.

It wasn't until the fourth year of Joseph's enlistment that Mama got her first washing machine. That was when Ornas bought a house in town that had indoor plumbing and electricity.

There were few light moments while being shaped into the mold of a marine, but old Queenie provided a few laughs. Queenie was a mottled gray mongrel bitch who hung around the mess hall garbage shack. Her drooping teats gave rise to the speculation that she probably had a litter in the trash dump near the beach. Recruits emerging from the mess hall always had a scrap of food for the dog, but she hung close to an old drill sergeant who wore false dentures. Once when Queenie started barking during his roll call, he drew out his false teeth and, using his hands, clicked the external choppers into biting motions while advancing toward her. Tail between legs, she gave a yelp and made for the boondocks.

Once, Queenie got in the way of another drill sergeant, who was putting his platoon through its paces. After shouting out a long string of commands preliminary to a complicated maneuver, he glanced at the dog who was about to get trampled. Without missing a beat in the cadence, he lowered his voice, "Queenie get out the bod damned way," then shouted, . . . "Harch!" Queenie expertly dodged milling feet as the platoon stamped from a column of fours and emerged as two straight, horizontal ranks. She was used to that game.

After week three, Sergeant Staley gave the order to pack seabags and prepare to move to the rifle range the following morning. The range was inland from La Jolla several miles up the coast. They made the trip in ancient, World War I trucks that looked more suitable for hauling beer kegs than troops. The camp was nestled under a eucalyptus grove and had long, wooden barracks painted green. The atmosphere was relaxed and informal, like a recreation camp. A new set of NCOs took over, friendly and easygoing. They were all expert marksmen and members of the base rifle team, which competed nationally in NRA meets.

Behind Ray Ban sunglasses, the shades of choice among shooters, their eyes squinted from years of peering through peep sights. They taught the platoon the shooting positions, how to estimate wind speed and direction, line up the targets in their sights and squeeze the trigger. Gently, they would say, "Like squeezing a woman's tit." Joseph had no idea how gently this was.

But he had a good enough imagination and qualified as a marksman, not a great achievement, but better than a nonqualifier. All marines were required to qualify with small arms once a year, and in subsequent years, Joseph improved to expert, the highest ranking, with both the rifle and pistol. At La Jolla, they also qualified with the pistol and the BAR.

Saturday afternoons and Sundays were free. One Saturday while the platoon was "crapped out" on their bunks after noon chow, Corporal Arneson stomped in. "Fall out," he shouted. "Without arms."

He marched them out of camp and across Highway 101 toward the cliffs overlooking the blue Pacific. Treading a steep, narrow trail, he led them single file 200 feet down. They slid on backsides, grabbing at bushes, rocks, and even cactus to slow their descent, eventually reaching the broad beach with scratched hands and torn khakis. The beach was deserted.

Following Arneson's moves, they stripped down to their skivvy drawers and waded into the cold surf. Such an escapade could never again happen, what with the cliffs now occupied by affluent homes and the beaches filled with people. After a dip, Arneson showed off his chest slides. He would take off running at full speed along the beach where the sand was smooth and slick, launch his body forward and slide on his chest fifteen or twenty feet. A few foolhardy recruits tried it, resulting in bruised and reddened pectorals. Arneson's act was hard to follow.

After the swim, they struggled back up the cliff and fell in formation.

"Did anyone go down to the beach today?" Arneson quizzed.

"No sir," the boots chorused.

"Did anyone go swimming today?" he pursued.

"No, sir," they shouted.

"Right face, for'd harch," Arneson commanded. An unforgetable afternoon had ended.

The next day, they lined up in alphabetical order for their first payday. A second lieutenant sat at a table covered with a green Marine Corps blanket, a stack of bills before him. Joseph scooped up the ten and two fives counted out by the lieutenant. Wasn't the pay supposed to be twenty-one dollars a month? he wondered. The answer came later. The navy deducted twenty cents a month for medical insurance. Only once every five months would they receive the remaining dollar.

On the Saturday after qualification firing, they were granted their first liberty. Spruced up in their new greens, they boarded a Greyhound bus on the highway for San Diego. In the city, most of the men headed for bars and brothels.

Joseph and Private Dortch walked to Lane Field, an ancient green wooden monster of a ball park at the foot of Broadway where the Padres of the Pacific Coast League played. Dortch's hometown team, the Seattle Rainiers, were playing that day. They basked under a warm spring sun, drinking beer from paper cups and munching hot dogs. The conversation of Padres fans seated around them was about a kid named Ted Williams, who had just left the team to play for Boston in the big leagues.

Joseph was in heaven. Baseball had always been his passion. In Lake Tarsa, he was the Charlie Brown of the neighborhood. It was a ritual every spring. With the first bloom of wildflowers, he would muster a small gang of kids to set up a diamond. Selecting a vacant lot was no problem: there were plenty. With shovels, they would skin the weeds off to form an infield, knock down crawdad mounds, and scoop off cow pies. If they found enough chicken wire, they would erect a backstop. If no chicken wire, old gunnysacks stitched together served the purpose. Unlike Charlie Brown, Joseph was the catcher. Adam, the older of the Broulliard brothers, was left-handed and, therefore, an obvious pitcher.

Lane Field was a world away from the Lake Tarsa's baseball diamonds, though the Padres weren't exactly the class of their league. Publicists and sports writers referred to the Coast League as being "a step from the majors," attributed to the fact that all of the eight members were farms for the major league teams. Their rosters were sprinkled with young players sent out for more seasoning and over-the-hill veterans enjoying their last hurrahs. These, in particular, caught Joseph's eye, for he remembered their names from the fine print of the box scores he and Erv Miller had scrutinized under the dimness of the street lamp in Lake Tarsa.

After the game, they boarded a streetcar and rode out to San Diego's world-famous Balboa Park Zoo. Then to a movie theater to watch a Victor McLaughlin picture and, finally, to a restaurant for steaks. It was the first time Joseph had ever eaten an entire piece of meat of the size of that T-bone. At the YMCA on Broadway, they waited for the bus. Their comrades staggered back mostly disheveled and in various stages of inebriation, exchanging stories. Supposedly, marines on their first shore leave had a duty to get stewed, screwed, and tattooed.

Joseph and Dortch had failed the test miserably. The others listened disbelieving as the two owned up to having gone to the zoo. "You mean to say you didn't get laid?" they chortled. Private Murphy had completed the hat trick. He exposed an ugly tattoo on one bicep, sore and festering from the needle punctures.

Old Mississip', a lanky redneck from the delta country, was among the inebriates. He kept offering a pint bottle of corn whiskey about half-full, but the mood for any of the fiery stuff had passed them all. "Gotta finish it," he drawled. "Can't take it back." With a grimace, he took a final chug and promptly puked in the gutter.

Four
Home on Leave—1939

The completion of boot camp was an anticlimax. The platoon boarded the ancient trucks for the ride back to the recruit depot. They piled seabags in the street and stood by. A first sergeant came up with their service record books and their orders. Privates Martin and Vance were headed for sea school just across the street. After three weeks of nautical schooling, they would be assigned duty aboard ship. The others were envious. Sea duty meant travel to distant lands.

A disappointed Joseph studied his assignment sheet. He and Hank Michalsky were to report to the 2nd Battalion, 10th Marines. Artillery. They shouldered their seabags, slung rifles, and walked 200 yards to the 10th Marine barracks. It was just one down from the barracks where they'd spent their first days. Neither would've ever guessed the second deck would be their home for the next two years.

In the Fox Battery office, they handed their records to a grizzled old first sergeant who sucked deeply from a long ivory cigarette holder with a Chesterfield stuck on the end. He studied the pair, jotted something down, and sent the office clerk to find Sergeant Bulkowsky, who would be their section chief. Bulkowsky was on his third "cruise," a veteran with twelve years service, three of them in China.

Soft-spoken and deliberate, Bulkowsky assigned them bunks and steel wall lockers in the second section and briefed them on the routine. He escorted them to the supply room to draw packs and field equipment. "Seven eighty-two gear," it was called in the quartermaster's lexicon.

There was a tin helmet of World-War-One vintage, a haversack, and knapsack with mess kit. Hooked to the back of the haversack was a collapsible entrenching shovel. There was a rubberized poncho, cartridge belt, and a canteen and cup that nestled into a pouch hooked to the belt.

They also got web pistol belts with leather holsters for .45-caliber pistols. Artillery men packed "hog legs" while manning their field pieces but retained their rifles for drills and ceremonies.

The next day, Bulkowsky marched his eight-man section to the gun shed. The newcomers were introduced to the stubby .75-millimeter pack howitzer and the old French .75-millimeter gun of World War fame. The *soixante quinze*. Both pieces were modernized with pneumatic tires for highway towing. The howitzer was intended as an Army mountain gun, which could be disassembled and carried on the backs of mules.

The Marine Corps adopted them because they could be taken apart and put ashore from small boats. The standing joke was that the Marine Corps substituted manpower for mules. The two newcomers would remain in artillery and fight the upcoming war with howitzers. Michalsky had a good head for numbers and was later assigned to the fire direction center. They became close friends and remained so for the next four years.

The old first sergeant welcomed recruits. They filled his mess detail for the month without complaint, unlike the regulars who were likely to protest or found to be medically disqualified while being treated for the clap. Soon Joseph found himself in the galley as a pot walloper, wearing a rubber apron. Slopped up pots and utensils big enough to cook for a battalion tumbled into a stainless steel vat to be scrubbed in hot soapy water after each meal. It was the lowliest job in the mess hall.

After a week, he graduated to messman, serving two ten-man tables, racing to and from the kitchen to replenish empty food platters. When the food ran out, he faced the wrath and griping of his table clients. "'If you weren't so damned slow, we'd a got more ham before it gave out,'' they'd bitch.

One day as he was carting off a wire basket of heavy china coffee mugs, he slipped on a wet spot and landed on his backside. The mugs went flying upwards, then, obeying Isaac Newton's law, rained down, bouncing off his head and face.

For a few moments, he remained on the floor in a daze. Broken crockery lay all about. "Sign here," he heard. The mess sergeant was standing above him, extending a receipt book and pencil. His signature would authorize the forfeiture of the extra five dollars a month paid messmen. The officer of the day approached. "You might at least give the man time to get up." Unfazed, the mess sergeant garnered the signature and disappeared into his cubbyhole office in the galley. Joseph didn't blame the mess sergeant, only his timing. If you broke or lost government property, you were expected to pay for it.

Joseph was further embarrassed when he turned out for his first inspection after his thirty-day stint in the mess hall. Messmen arose an hour early and toiled until darkness, cleaning up after the evening meal. They were excused from inspection, drill, and other normal routines. As a result, he had neglected his equipment and personal appearance. His shoes weren't shined, his uniform not pressed, and his rifle had a lackluster appearance. He needed a haircut.

Lieutenant Fields, the battery executive officer, scrutinized him as he brought his rifle up to the port arms position and snapped the bolt open for inspection.

"Been on mess duty, haven't you?" he questioned in a mocking tone.

"Yes, sir, since the day after I joined," Joseph stammered.

"Gunny, get this man squared away," the lieutenant barked to Gunnery Sergeant Bell, who was following along busily jotting down notes.

Joseph was embarrassed and angry with himself. He vowed he would never again be reprimanded for his military appearance. From that day on, he would put all his efforts into making himself the sharpest marine in the outfit. He was embittered at that old gray-haired bastard who had assigned him to mess duty before he could unpack his seabag and get his feet on the ground. Dammit, he'd show him.

Without waiting to be "squared away by Gunny Bell," he beat it to the barber shop for his first haircut since the skinning he had gotten in boot camp.

At the pressing table in the barracks, he toiled with a heavy electric iron, putting creases in the right places on his uniforms and ironing out wrinkles from his shirts.

He spent evenings polishing his shoes until they had the gloss of patent leather. The leather bill and chin strap of his frame cap got the same treatment. He polished the leather sling of his rifle and burnished the brass claws that adjusted its tension. He rubbed linseed oil into the stock until the oak grain achieved a rich luster. Before inspection, he would apply a light coat of oil to the metal surfaces, not enough to come off on the hands of the inspecting officer.

Like a fanatic housewife, his zealousness began to annoy a few of the less motivated around him who resented being outdone by a recruit. There were attempts to ridicule him. "What're you trying to do, make sergeant in your first cruise?" To their jealous taunts, he would respond with the usual barracks retort. "Up yours."

Hank Michalsky became an ally. They'd sit side by side on their footlockers relishing the spit and polish routine. On the brass buttons of their dress blue uniforms—which they had finally been issued—they applied Brasso, then brushed off the dried polish until the buttons glittered like gold. They put a gloss on their white leather belts with polish and steel wool. The heavy brass buckles on the belts were buffed until they reflected the sunlight like mirrors.

On the next inspection, Fields approached, an imposing figure in his green cavalry officer jodhpurs, shiny cordovan boots, and matching Sam Browne belt. His ivory-handled sword dangled at his side in its silvery scabbard. Joseph relished the moment.

The lieutenant crisply swiped the rifle out of his hands, whipped it around like a drum major's baton, and peered into the barrel. He scrutinized the stock then snapped, "No shoe polish on stocks."

"It's linseed oil, sir," Joseph answered. "Keeps the wood from cracking."

Fields glared approvingly at him and moved on. He was an outstanding and respected officer. By war's end, he would be a general.

On Friday afternoons, the base troops turned out for parades. They always attracted a small crowd of civilian spectators who sat in stands behind the flagpole. Sometimes film crews from Hollywood came for shots. Marines parading in dress blues was standard fare in B movies with titles like "March On Marines."

The uniforms for parades varied week to week from dress blues to service greens and to khakis with canvas leggings, field packs, and steel helmets. No matter what the uniform, all were uncomfortable on troops frozen at attention for long periods. The choke collars on the blues were closed with metal hooks that bit into the flesh of the neck. Any attempt to wiggle a white-gloved finger under the collar to relieve the soreness while in ranks would be glaringly obvious and an invitation to a reprimand from an NCO or officer.

The steel helmet worn with the combat uniform had an uncomfortable leather headband, always good for a headache. The ritual of a formal parade, with the troops held at attention for long periods, was excruciating. It was a welcomed relief when the adjutant would finally sing out, "Pass in review." The band would swing out with "Semper Fidelis." Legs numbed from prolonged standing would suddenly be revived, and a thousand left feet would stamp out simultaneously to join the beat.

The approach to the reviewing stand would be heralded with muffled orders from sergeants to get in step and straighten up the ranks. Units with ragged ranks would suffer the glare of the commanding general. If he turned aside to his chief of staff, it was a sure sign some unfortunate battalion commander would be getting a rebuke.

Back in the barracks, there would be boisterous commentary about the parade as troops shed their shackles. Colorful sports shirts and civilian jackets would soon replace uniforms in preparation for a weekend of liberty. In French Louisiana, the happy phrase, *laissez les bon tons rouler,* would have been in order. Dago, as the salts referred to San Diego, was not the preferred liberty town on weekends. Los Angeles was. Marines felt more welcome in L.A.

A few of the troops kept jalopies on the base. A car owner would suddenly be surrounded with five or six new-found buddies who would pile in. The beaches up the coast were popular destinations. In L.A. the opportunities for having fun were unlimited.

East Coast Marines liked to disparage their brethren in San Diego by calling them Hollywood Marines. The pejorative was not entirely misplaced. The Marine Corps had a reserve artillery battalion in Hollywood commanded by W. S. Van Dyke, the legendary movie director. They drilled without weapons until the war clouds began gathering.

Headquarters in Washington decided the 10th Marines weren't going to fight a war with the old French guns, the pack howitzers being more practical for amphibious landings. So a battery of four French guns would be turned over to the Hollywood reserves.

Fox Battery, commanded by Captain Shell, was to deliver the guns. Shell, a VMI graduate with a trick football knee that would buckle at inopportune times, made extensive preparations and briefed the men *ad infinitum.*

No detail was left to chance. To avoid traffic on the 120-mile journey, the truck convoy of men and guns followed the back roads into L.A. The French guns were towed by new three-quarter-ton trucks which the 10th Marines had been issued as "prime movers" for their artillery pieces. There was a stopover for chow at a city park in Fullerton, where the field kitchen had gone in advance to prepare the meal. From there the convoy rolled on to Chavez Ravine and the armory where the Hollywood battalion held their drills.

This was some twenty years before the Dodgers had forsaken Brooklyn for L.A. and built a stadium in the ravine. Major Van Dyke had organized a formal ceremony, with the press in attendance, for the transfer of the guns to his battalion. His executive officer was reserve Captain Franklin D. Roosevelt, Jr. Afterward, an elated Van Dyke announced there would a reception that evening at his Brentwood home for the men of Fox Battery. The anticipation of the troops was overwhelming. Visions of nubile starlets, champagne, and caviar danced in their heads. But they were about to be Shell-shocked.

Captain Shell declined the invitation on the grounds that he wanted his men rested and alert for the return trip the following morning. Amid much grumbling, the men wandered around the armory, plotting schemes to get out on the town. Before leaving for the Van Dyke party with his officers, Shell had posted Gunny Bell at the door. No one was to be let out.

Diversions were created. Someone let the air out of a tire on one of the guns parked in the armory. The problem was reported to Bell who went to have a look. A half-dozen men quickly vanished through the door into the balmy Los Angeles evening air.

Private First Class Anderson, a truck driver, reported that his vehicle had a problem and likely wouldn't start the next morning. As Bell investigated, more men disappeared through the door. It became apparent, however, that Bell wasn't that much of a dupe.

He knew what was going on and figured what he didn't see didn't matter.

But the skipper's fears about the condition of his men, particularly the truck drivers, had been justified. As daylight broke, small bands of artillery men were still straggling in. A foursome was dropped off from a car by squealing women. It was mid-morning before the last of the stragglers staggered in. Hangovers were in epidemic proportions.

"Hell," Joseph said to no one in particular, "we couldn't have been in worse shape going to Van Dyke's party."

Captain Shell grimly watched the scene with a resigned expression, but never delivered the expected chewing out. Finally, he turned to the gunnery sergeant and said, "Mount up."

The casual peacetime life began to change from the day the Gothic headlines in the *San Diego Union* shouted the news that Adolf Hitler had invaded Poland. For years the Japanese army had been rampaging through China, but no one seemed concerned. Now there was talk of fighting them.

Newcomers arrived to beef up combat units of the Fleet Marine Force. Allowances of training ammunition were increased, and firing exercises on the Kearney mesa took on more realism. The Marine Corps expanded to 30,000 men. Joseph got his first promotion to private first class. No sooner did he have his new chevrons sewed on when he made corporal. He felt wealthy with his forty-two dollars a month, double his private's pay.

But while the mobilization of the nation's military was slowly under way, life on the Marine Corps base continued at a leisurely pace. The base fielded respectable athletic teams that competed in football and baseball with state colleges in California. Corporal Conklin, who occupied a bunk next to Joseph's, was an infielder on the baseball team. In a game with UCLA, Conklin slid into second base attempting to steal. His spike snagged a corner of the bag and snapped his ankle into a grotesque contortion. The second baseman, a black player, tagged out Conklin for the third out. He stood momentarily astride the injured man, then flung his glove into short center and trotted into the UCLA dugout. His name was Jackie Robinson.

Robinson's nonchalance had the appearance of unconcern for Joseph's injured friend and a lack of sportsmanship. But in reality,

Robinson could have done nothing to comfort Conklin. Besides, the racial slurs he had suffered all through the game from marines in the stands could not have left him in a charitable mood. He responded by hitting the ball to all fields and driving in several runs for the Bruins.

Joseph himself went out for the battalion baseball team in intramural competition and was positioned at center field. One day they played a team from base troops with a hard-throwing pitcher. If there had been a radar gun at that time, his fast ball would have been clocked at close to one hundred miles an hour. In his first at-bat, Joseph connected for a solid line drive to right field. His next time up, the pitcher glared at him, then fired the first pitch right at his head. It came so fast, Joseph could only freeze in place. The ball whistled over his cap and popped into the catcher's mitt like a cannonball. Batting helmets hadn't been invented. That very moment, Joseph decided he had better uses for his head. He'd had enough of baseball. Despite the pleas of lieutenant and coach, Joe Stewart, Joseph turned in his baseball uniform after the game.

Once a month Fox Battery pulled guard duty, providing security for the base. One morning, as corporal of the guard on the four-to-eight watch, he was assigned to the colors detail for the raising of the flag. Three flags were kept in a plywood cabinet in the guard house. One was the garrison flag, which was flown routinely. There was a larger flag, which was flown on holidays, and the smallest of the three, the storm flag, was used on inclement days.

Joseph selected the garrison flag, which was neatly folded into a triangular bundle with only the field of stars showing. He clasped it to his chest with both arms. At a quarter of eight, two members of his detail fell in at his sides. They marched smartly to the flagpole on the parade ground, fastened the corners of the flag to the snaps on the halyard, making sure the stars were right side up, and waited at attention for the band to form. Momentarily, Joseph thought of the flag-raising on the postcard he'd sent home from New Orleans.

Base units were drawn up in formation up and down the parade ground. Butterflies danced in Joseph's nervous stomach as the band director raised his baton at exactly eight o'clock and the band began the "Star Spangled Banner." Activity ceased all over the base, including vehicles, whose occupants dismounted and saluted.

Joseph's man on the left had the honor of pulling on the halyard to hoist the flag. The other would control the second loop on the halyard, letting it slide through his hands to keep it from fouling. As the band struck up the national anthem, Joseph gave a nod to his man on the left. The first few pulls on the halyard were to be done slowly to allow the flag to unfold from its triangular bundle. When half of it was unfurled, it would be briskly raised to the top of the pole.

To Joseph's surprise, his man jerked mightily on the halyard as though he had a record marlin on the end of the line and not ten pounds of bunting. The flag shot out of Joseph's grasp still in a tight bundle and was well on its way up the hundred-foot pole. From the corner of his mouth, Joseph ordered the man to jerk the cord a couple of times in hopes of unfolding the flag. He did, but with the same vengeance he had used in starting the flag.

The cord snapped, and the flag began to descend, unfolding like a parachute as it fluttered to the ground. The band completed the last note of the national anthem with Old Glory draped over it. The bandsmen laid down their instruments and kept the flag off the ground. The officer of the day was on hand for the ceremony. He ordered another flag raised on a back-up pole over the headquarters building.

As Joseph and his men retrieved the errant flag from the band and refolded it, he was sure his corporal's chevrons were history. The O.D. approached and inspected the halyard where it had parted. The cord was rotted. "It should've been changed a year ago," he growled. The other problem, Joseph explained, was that the color detail that had folded the flag the evening before had overdone it. It was much too compact. Joseph's corporal stripes were saved.

* * *

A year had gone by, and Joseph was eligible for a thirty-day furlough. After collecting a month's pay in advance, he had more than enough for bus fare to Lake Tarsa and back. But his battery mates said this was a waste of money. Put on that blue uniform and use your thumb, they counseled.

Following that advice, he packed a small bag and took the streetcar to the end of the line in east San Diego. It was about noontime before he snagged his first ride to the mountain town of Jacumba. Another hop took him to El Centro and following his third ride, he was already in Yuma, Arizona.

It was late afternoon, and he had decided beforehand not to try hitchhiking at night. He found a cheap hotel and checked in. Upon awakening the new morning, he looked out the window and saw that it was raining. Downstairs in the restaurant, a sign caught his eye: "Free Breakfast Any Time it Rains." It didn't rain very often in the Sonoran desert.

He ate a complimentary breakfast of hotcakes and bacon. So far, his travel had cost him only the hamburger he'd had for supper. By noon, the rain had ceased, but there was very little traffic moving east.

Joseph had almost decided to take a bus, when he met and joined up with a sailor hitching his way to Texas. Late in the afternoon, a little green coupe stopped, and the driver, a man of about thirty, who might have been a salesman, opened the door. They drove towards the darkening eastern sky. After a while, the driver fished out a flask from under the seat, chugged a drink and passed it around. Joseph declined. The man was driving with only his index finger on the wheel. *Showing off,* Joseph thought, *like a dude.*

As they motored on into the night, the headlights picked up a dark form on the roadside. Dude had already driven past before he realized it was a woman. He slammed on the brakes, reversed, and told Joseph to open the door. A wild-looking female in a long, dark dress and straight black hair reaching to her shoulders hesitated, then crawled in. There were now four in the front seat. She wedged herself in, half on the sailor's lap and half on Joseph's.

She wore no makeup, and her pale face was accentuated by the darkness of her hair and dress. Dude shifted through a range of gears and soon had the coupe buzzing along. Out came the flask, but she refused with just a shake of her head. Dude's conversation was effusive, but the girl spoke not a word. After a while, the dude reached out a hand to her thighs. She lashed out at him like a wildcat and the wheel spun out of his hand.

They'd been doing about fifty miles an hour. The car swerved right, left, and then off the pavement. The wheels spun crazily in the sand. Straight ahead was a concrete culvert over a dry wash. The coupe smacked into it head-on and jumped off the ground a couple of feet with the impact. The doors were flung open. Joseph and the girl tumbled out. No sooner had she regained her feet, she was off running up the highway like a wounded animal.

The others gingerly felt their bruises and minor cuts. Dude eased out of the seat and tested his legs. It was a miracle no one had been seriously hurt. A car approached, slowed down to survey the scene, and began to regain speed. Then the driver spotted the girl on the roadside ahead and slammed on his brakes. The tires squealed to a halt, the fleeing girl got in and soon the red taillights of the car vanished into the night.

A full moon arose, illuminating the desert. Coyotes howled. They were in the proverbial middle of nowhere. Dude's radiator was hissing. In pain he was holding his left arm with his right. After a while, a pickup truck with two guys stopped to offer help.

Joseph and his sailor friend hopped in. Dude stayed with his car, saying there was a garage in the next town and to have a tow truck sent. The guys in the pickup listened to the story of the mystery girl and of Dude's advances leading to the accident. "There's a women's mental hospital not far from here," the driver ventured. "They're always running away. Bet that was one of 'em."

Five
Louisiana Revisited—1940

The guys in the pickup were going all the way to El Paso. One of them knew of a shortcut. It was a mountainous route over a rough, boulder-strewn road. At times they dipped into Mexico. Although it was late spring, they were in a high elevation and the night was freezing cold.

After an all-night ride, they finally made it to El Paso. Joseph had had enough of hitchhiking. He remembered hearing his buddies in San Diego talking about travel bureaus. After several inquiries, he found one. It was a private agency through which drivers going on long trips would agree to take passengers for modest fees. By noontime, Joseph was on his way to Dallas in a warm, comfortable sedan. Three other passengers were in the backseat. They were well-dressed Mexicans, an elderly man, and two women. They conversed in Spanish all the way. By nightfall, it was raining hard. The driver dropped Joseph off at the Greyhound bus station in Dallas. After a change of buses in Houston, he was back in Dennings. At the post office, he got a ride to Lake Tarsa with the mail carrier.

Nothing much had changed in the past year. Ornas and Clarissa still lived in the little frame house at the edge of town with a privy in the backyard. The house had no electricity or indoor plumbing, still Joseph had enjoyed living there in his adolescent years. On each side of the house were fig trees that bore sweet purple fruit in July and August. There were five acres behind the house, one of which was a garden. The rich gumbo soil yielded an abundance of vegetables, most of which were put up in Mason jars by Clarissa, along with the figs and peaches from a small orchard.

The other acreage was pasture land where Joseph's horses grazed. He had had three, not all at once. Two had been loaners from his grandfather, the first a former cutting horse named Prince. Joseph's first tack was an old army cavalry saddle and a bridle with a snapper bit, the kind used on plow horses and mules. Prince had a knack for running away with Joseph in the saddle. He would be riding far out in the countryside with the two Broulliard boys, when Prince would decide he'd had enough for the day. From a leisurely canter, he would suddenly bolt for home at full speed, and no amount of sawing on the bit could stop him until he became winded.

Once as he was racing at full speed with Joseph grimly hanging on, they came to a side road. Prince put the brakes on, stopped on a dime, wheeled, and took off in the other direction. Not anticipating the sudden turn, Joseph was pitched over Prince's head in the original direction and landed fifteen feet away on his own head. He thought he saw every star in the universe, but by the grace of God, he got up uninjured.

Adam Broulliard had an idea after he had caught up with the runaway Prince and led him back. "He's taking the bit in his teeth so you can't rein him in. You need a curb bit. That'll stop him."

Adam happened to have a spare bit in the barn at his house. Joseph readily agreed to try the suggestion. When he next offered the bridle to Prince, the big bay eyed him suspiciously as the strange bit with a U-shape in the center was forced into his mouth. Joseph rode him back to the same road where he'd last run away and spurred him into a gallop. With that encouragement, Prince was off and running for home. When at full speed, Joseph pulled back on the reins. The horse felt the U of the bit digging into the roof of his mouth, put on the brakes, and slid down to his haunches. It was the end of Prince's runaways.

Grandpa Max had sold Prince, but offered Joseph a replacement. It was a young chestnut stallion by the name of Garfton who had become an incorrigible rogue, thanks to the abuse of his previous owners. His favorite trick was to start bucking as soon as his rider had one foot in the stirrup and was halfway in the saddle. Dismounting was equally hazardous. He had a habit of sidling up close to trees or fence posts so as to scrape his rider's legs. Garfton was also a biting horse. He liked to catch Joseph unawares and take nips in his back even when the ingrate was being led to the oats in his feeding trough.

Garfton soon went back to Grandpa, who quickly sold him. Ornas and Joseph then bought a docile little gray mare who had none of the bad habits of the other two horses. He named her Belle. Along with his new horse, Joseph got a new mail order saddle and bridle from Montgomery Ward. He was intoxicated by the sweet smell of the new russet-leather Western saddle with embossed designs.

Lake Tarsa was still in the throes of the Depression. Once it had been a prosperous little town with a sawmill and rice mill. Both had shut down, leaving only a cotton gin, which operated but a couple of months of the year. In the town's heyday there was a green, three-story frame lodge among the oaks on the lakefront, frequented in the winters by sportsmen who came to shoot ducks and geese. Joseph had watched boats returning from the marshes to the south with their cockpits loaded to the gunwales with waterfowl. The lodge burned to the ground, as did a pleasure pier next to it that featured a high wooden tobogan chute over the water. The remaining attraction was the lakeside park. The Fourth of July was the big event of the year. Visitors from all around the region came for the celebration.

Rice farming in the rural environs remained the area's primary economy.

The town was situated on the first of a chain of shallow lakes formed by the Manatau River as it flowed sluggishly on its way to the Gulf. Except for the waterway, the town was off the beaten path. No major highway or railroad came through. Large deepwater tugs pushed their barges on a course in the center of the river channel and rarely ventured into the shallow water to tie up on the wharf.

Politics was the main diversion from the town's economic doldrums. Huey P. Long, first as governor, then U.S. senator, occasionally stumped the town at election time to tout his corrupt local candidates. His ward bosses would roast a cow, hungry voters being more inclined to listen to a political harangue with their hunger satisfied.

On a makeshift platform under a mossy old oak tree Long, in a white seersucker suit with sweat stains at the armpits, would belly up to the microphone and rant about the corporations and rich people who were stealing bread from the mouths of the poor. A shock of curly brown hair would tumble across his perspiring forehead and his voice would become hoarse as he worked himself to a frenzy. His delivery combined the fire and brimstone of a north Louisiana Baptist preacher with the pent-up anger of an Adolph Hitler. Huey Long was an innovator and the first politician to employ a sound truck. Having made the rounds of the unpaved streets of the town announcing the arrival of the "Kingfish," the sound truck now boomed his speech far and wide.

"Every Man a King," was Long's credo and his, "Share the Wealth" plan, a manifesto for the redistribution of wealth in America. His mixture of populism and demagoguery played well with dirt farmers and unemployed rednecks. They'd stroke the stubble of unshaven chins—razor blades being a luxury in that time of want—and chuckle with approval as the "Kingfish" lampooned his enemies. Even after he left the governor's office for a seat in the U.S. Senate, Long maintained an iron grip on Louisiana politics. Over the years, he had woven a machine that reached into and controlled practically every local governing board in Louisiana. You knew when you were entering a parish where the elected officials were not in the Long camp. The white concrete ribbon of pavement would abruptly give way to a gravel roadway in need of maintenance. On the banks of rivers in anti-Long territory, ferryboats still conveyed vehicles across instead of bridges.

Lake Tarsa was not a Huey Long town, due to its predominately Catholic population. The "Kingfish" had his major strength in the piney hill parishes of Protestant north Louisiana.

To his credit, Long did much for the state. He built needed roads and bridges, hospitals, and schools. He initiated free textbooks in the public schools and even launched a program to educate illiterate adults. What angered people was the way he went about it, raising taxes in a period of depression and ruthlessly crushing opponents in the style of a dictator. In Washington, he harassed President Franklin Roosevelt and ridiculed FDR's ineffective work relief programs while building a national constituency that made him a serious threat to unseat the President in the next election.

Long turned his attention to the state university in Baton Rouge. He built up the new campus of Louisiana State University on the banks of the Mississippi River and increased enrollment. The Tiger football team and the school band became his playthings. He had the band enlarged to over 200 members and offered his hand coaching the football team, much to the annoyance of the coach and players. He wanted a new stadium but faced opposition from the state legislature which had other building priorities.

Undaunted, he came up with the idea of a stadium that would enclose the empty space beneath the stands and make it into a much needed student dormitory.

To fill the stands, Long promoted football along with his political agenda. On one Saturday, the Ringling Brothers and Barnum and Bailey Circus was due in Baton Rouge for a performance that conflicted with an LSU game with Southern Methodist University. Obviously, the circus would cut into the game's attendance. Long got on the phone with circus owner, John Ringling, in Texas from where the circus would arrive in Louisiana. He implored Ringling to reschedule the performance at a later date. Imperiously, Ringling's response was that the schedule of the circus was set long before and would never be altered.

Long, who practiced law successfully before entering politics, had dug up an arcane state law that compelled livestock to be periodically dipped in creosote for parasites.

"Did you ever dip a tiger?" he asked. Before the nonplussed circus owner could reply, Long asked again, "Or how about an elephant?"

It didn't take Ringling long to decide that the circus would perform in New Orleans that Saturday.

On another occasion, LSU was having a successful season with a chance to play in the Rose Bowl. Ahead was an important game against Vanderbilt in Nashville. Long wanted all the support his team needed and proposed taking the band and all 2,500 members of the ROTC cadet corps. He called the traffic manager of the Illinois Central Railroad, which controlled most of the route to Nashville, and asked for a rate quote. The best he could do was nineteen dollars per person, the railroad agent said. "Too much," Long replied. "Can you make it six dollars?"

The agent had not stifled his laughter at the six dollar offer when Long reached the president of the Illinois Central in Chicago and repeated his request for a cheap rate. At the same time, he casually mentioned that the railroad's bridges in Louisiana were greatly undervalued on the tax rolls and would probably have to be reassessed. Next day, Long had his answer ... six dollars a person. Some students couldn't even afford the six dollar ticket, so they lined up as Long handed each of them seven dollars, the extra dollar going for subsistence in Nashville. The LSU contingent, between 4,000 and 5,000 students, traveled to the game in six special trains of fourteen cars each.

LSU's band was not only big, it was flashy, colorful and entertaining. Long hired New Orleans musician Castro Carazo to as band director. Carazo was a creative band leader. Often, the "Kingfish" himself would seize the baton and strut at the head of "his" band through the streets of cities where LSU was playing. His meddling reached into the football team then coached by Biff Jones, a no-nonsense army captain who had coached at West Point. Dissatisfied with the Tigers' performance at one game Long burst into the locker room at halftime to offer advice and give the team a pep talk. Jones would tolerate none of that and ordered Long from the locker room. "Either you go or I go," was Jones's ultimatum. It was the "Kingfish" who exited the room but Jones was not far behind. At season's end he resigned in frustration.

On a sultry September evening in 1935, the turbulent career of the "Kingfish" was ended by an assassin's bullet from the gun of Dr. Carl Weiss, a talented young physician, in the marbled lobby of the skyscraper capitol building. Weiss was himself cut down in a fusillade of bullets from Long's bodyguards. His father-in-law, a district judge in southwest Louisiana who was anti-Long, had been gerrymandered into a hostile district where he was certain to lose his office in the forthcoming election. The shooting was an act of vengeance. Adding a twist to the tragedy, typical of Southern Gothic novels, was the rumor, said to have been spread by Long, that the judge "had Negro blood."[1]

Joseph soon became bored with his home visit. His best friends were still in school, and the dullness of the town made him long for the bright lights of San Diego. He went to a basketball game at his old school. The outdoor court with a dirt surface was the same except that lights had been strung for night games. In his last two

---

[1] The author recalled to memory most of the incidents involving Huey Long which were widely reported in state and national newspapers and by word of mouth. However his recollections were refreshed by a reading of *Huey Long*, a biography by T. Harry Williams, Alford Knopf, 1970.

years, he had played on the team. His skills at ball-handling and shooting were marginal, but he was tenacious on defense, often drawing the praise of Coach Charlie Groth.

He thought briefly of putting on his dress blues and making a visit to his former classrooms, but the thought of showing off scared him. They might ask him to give a talk, and his self-assurance wasn't up to it. Instead, he decided to hitchhike to Baton Rouge in his blues and visit his aunt and cousins.

In the barracks, there were unending tales, mostly apocryphal, of marines being picked up by gorgeous babes unable to resist the uniform. On the highway in Lafayette, the fantasy became reality. Four college girls in a sporty canary-yellow, convertible sedan offered him a ride to Baton Rouge.

Sitting between the two girls in the front seat, Joseph found himself in a surrealistic dream world, intoxicated by the wafting scents of perfume and face powder and of blond windblown manes. The driver's skirt crept higher above her knees each time she pumped the clutch and worked the gear shift. Their girlish laughter had a teasing quality. They seemed to be practicing their seductiveness on their captive hitchhiker, albeit an unresponsive guinea pig.

Joseph felt an obligation to uphold the marines' fanciful hallmark as lovers and make some kind of a move, but the thought left him paralyzed in fear and uncertainty. When the girls deposited him in downtown Baton Rouge an hour and a half later, he let out a sigh of relief. He'd never confess to this hitchhiking story in the barracks.

* * *

Back in San Diego, Joseph resumed his military routine. He had joined the Corps to travel, but it appeared he'd get no farther than California. Finally he did make it to the high seas. Once a year his artillery battalion would go to San Clemente Island, sixty miles off the coast, for firing exercises. The navy had a small facility there. They made the journey on a seagoing tug towing a barge laden with their guns and equipment. It was an ignominious way to travel the high seas when one had cruisers and battleships in mind.

They set up a tent camp on level ground in the middle of the island and lived there for six weeks. It was named Camp Nimitz, after the rear admiral destined to leave his name in the history books. San Clemente was the southernmost of California's Channel Islands, the best known in the group being Catalina. It was a barren rock of fifty-six square miles, arid and devoid of trees. Cactus plants were the main vegetation. Its Alcatraz-like isolation made it a deadly boring place, especially between activities.

The navy ran a boat to the mainland on weekends, but only officers and married NCOs were granted leaves. Swimming and baseball were the main diversions of the troops in their off-duty hours. From a rocky outcropping forty feet above the churning water on Pyramid Cove, they dove daringly in games of chicken, aiming their bodies at openings between boulders and beds of kelp below.

Joseph was fascinated by the depth and transparency of the water on the rocky shoreline, so unlike the café-au-lait waters of the shallow Louisiana Gulf coast. They pried abalones off the rocks and steamed them on beds of rocks heated with driftwood. The cooked meat was about as chewable as the rubber composition soles on their boondockers.

Joseph was the trail shifter on his gun crew. When the gunner was unable to traverse the required lateral shift with his hand wheel, Joseph would move the howitzer to one side or the other with a handspike inserted into the trail.

They fired rounds of shrapnel percussion and H.E. (high explosive). On detonation, the shrapnel projectile would scatter lead balls the size of a thumbnail. The H.E. shell simply disintegrated into shards of steel. Shrapnel, which took its name from the British general who invented it, would be discontinued when the war started, although the name became synonymous with all high explosive shell fragments.

Occasionally, officers on the observation post amused themselves by targeting herds of wild goats grazing in the impact area. The goats, introduced at the turn of the century, were responsible for the barren landscape of the island, chewing away at the vegetation. There were thousands of them scattered about the island. Foxes were also numerous. Their barking and yipping helped keep Joseph awake on lonely nights when he pulled guard duty on the ammunition dump.

* * *

After six weeks of living under canvas, the barracks in San Diego seemed like a luxury hotel. Joseph was flush with money he squirreled away during the island sojourn. He had avoided the all-night poker games that had left some of his mates as broke as the day they had sailed for the island. He bought a small radio. With permission from the first sergeant, he set it up on a little table near his bunk. The stipulation was that it had to be removed for inspections. He strung a wire antenna outside on a window screen. Evenings after chow, a small crowd would cluster around the radio listening to Fred Waring's "Chesterfield Hour."

Radio was in its heyday. It blared out big band orchestra music from the likes of Benny Goodman, Glenn Miller, Tommy Dorsey, and Sammy Kaye. Sunday nights featured comedians Fred Allen, Jack Benny, Fibber McGee and Molly, and Burns and Allen. Last would come the staccato voice of Walter Winchell railing about the activities of the German-American Bund in New York while conferring hero status to J. Edgar Hoover and his F.B.I. There was the hoarse voice of Republican isolationist Wendell Wilkie, in his campaign against Franklin D. Roosevelt, shouting "Amurica for Amuricans." And FDR, in melodramatic tones, denouncing Benito Mussolini's declaration of war against France: "The hand that held the dagger has driven it into the back of its neighbor."

With the United States drawing ever closer to war, Kate Smith's powerful rendition of "God Bless America" awakened the latent patriotism in the hearts of millions of listeners. Tom Harmon, Joe Dimaggio, Lou Gehrig, Joe Louis, and Ted Williams were sports heroes. The magic of their exploits would come alive through the voices of Red Barber, Bill Stern, and Don Dunphy.

One day just after morning chow, there was a commotion in the adjoining barracks occupied by a battalion of the 6th Regiment.

A company commander had come bounding up the staircase on the way to his office. As he reached the top landing, a rifle was poked into his stomach. A sergeant holding the rifle pulled the trigger and disemboweled his C.O.

The sergeant's brother, a renowned criminal lawyer from Florida, defended him in the trial before a state criminal court in San Diego. Pleading temporary insanity, he not only escaped the death penalty, but received a light sentence. His defense was that the captain had been out to get him when they served in the same outfit in China several years before. Upon returning to San Diego, he was assigned under the same captain and again subjected to his skipper's threats.

Ed Sparkman was another of Joseph's close buddies. He had an imposing physique and played end on the base football team. He weighed 190 pounds and had such broad shoulders that in a game in Los Angeles, a sports writer for the *Examiner* referred to him as "a giant end."

In a game one night in San Diego's Balboa Stadium, the team was going through their warm-ups, without helmets as they did then. Sparkman was running for a pass and collided with a teammate, catching the other's head smack in the face. He was knocked out for several minutes and had to miss the game. When he returned to the barracks late that evening, his face was so swollen and discolored with black and blue that he was barely recognizable. Sparky and Joseph made a lot of liberties together. They parted company the following year and did not meet again for three years. That meeting came on Guadalcanal.

One evening, Joseph and Hank Michalsky were walking past a nightclub in downtown San Diego, when they were forced off the sidewalk by a guy with four young women, a pair on each side, their arms interlocked. As the two marines gave way, they recognized movie star Errol Flynn. He had docked his yacht in San Diego on one of his well-publicized cruises. Hank had been a Golden Gloves boxer in Chicago and would become pugnacious after a couple of beers. He wanted to go after Flynn, who quickly ducked into a nightclub with his harem.

On another occasion when Joseph and Hank were in town, they passed a gray-haired senior citizen walking slowly. "I hope I never get that old," Michalsky remarked. He never would. A mortar shell exploded in the fire direction center of the 10th Marines during the fighting on Saipan, killing Hank and severely wounding his commanding officer, Colonel G. R. E. Shell.

Another of Joseph's pals was Bobby Adkins, a short, blond kid from Oregon. They made liberties together in Los Angeles. Adkins and another lad named Whalen, from Colorado, were restless from the dull garrison life. They volunteered for China duty, meaning they would have to extend their enlistments two years. They tried to talk Joseph into going, but he had long decided four years was all he was going to spend in the Corps.

Adkins and Whalen were in Shanghai when in November 1941 the United States decided to withdraw the Fourth Marines to the Philippines in anticipation of war with Japan. The regiment was placed under command of Gen. Douglas MacArthur in the defense of Corregidor and the Bataan Peninsula. Adkins and Whalen were taken prisoners.

Many years later, Joseph heard a gruesome story concerning the fate of Adkins. A former prisoner in the Philippines, Master Sergeant Al Mount, told him Adkins had been in a prison camp on the island of Palawan.

As U.S. forces began the liberation of the Philippines in 1944, the Japanese on Palawan herded their prisoners into trenches, doused them with gasoline and burned them alive. Adkins was one of them. Whalen had been in a different camp and survived.

* * *

Before the invention of the Higgins boat, which had a drop ramp at the bow, the Marine Corps experimented with ways to land heavy equipment and vehicles from the navy's motor launches. Someone came up with a set of lightweight iron beams that could be bolted to the bow of the boat and, with heavy planks, form a ramp strong enough to land light vehicles.

The navy and army were about to conduct a joint amphibious maneuver off the California coast. The marines were called on to demonstrate the landing apparatus, and the assignment went to Sergeant Bulkowsky and his gun section. At Long Beach, Joseph finally set his feet on the deck of not one but two battleships. At first, the detail boarded the USS *Oklahoma*. Then it was discovered that *Oklahoma* had a problem with its launches, so they shifted to the 32,000-ton *Tennessee*.

After several days of cruising on the battleship, Joseph decided sea duty wasn't all that glamorous. The ship was like a small city with 1,500 sailors and officers going about their duties in cramped spaces. There were no bunks to relax in. At night, the crew slung canvas hammocks in spaces that were used for eating during the day. After the evening meal, the mess tables and benches were hoisted and secured overhead.

At night, men walking under the hammocks while going to and from the head would have to bend over to avoid bumping their heads on the slumbering forms above. A bumped rump would trigger angry oaths from the awakened man. "Keep your stupid head down, Mac," they would mutter. Bulkowsky's men were put to work deep down in the bowels where ammunition and supplies were stored. Narrow passageways and a low overhead rail for moving fourteen-inch shells were a constant threat to crack careless skulls.

The battleships steamed in various formations, while simulating battle situations. One night, as the darkened ships steamed in a single line, Joseph experienced an eerie sensation while standing on the fantail. The ghostly hulk of the ship behind *Tennessee* appeared much closer than it actually was. Its massive prow moved up and down in slow motion, shoving phosphorescent waves aside as it plowed through the swells.

Within the year, half those ships would be at the bottom of Pearl Harbor or severely damaged. The battleship was already a dinosaur since Billy Mitchell had proved they could be sunk by aerial bombs.

In Monterey Bay, they rendezvoused with the army transports. *Tennessee* lowered a motor launch with the landing apparatus aboard. Bulkowsky's crew climbed down a ladder and boarded. The launch sidled up to a transport ship, and a light army truck was lowered into the boat. They circled endlessly waiting for the signal to land. It was discovered that the vehicle they were carrying was a PX truck loaded with Hershey bars. As the driver slumbered at the wheel, they raided the truck. The three candy bars Joseph had eaten, combined with the rolling and pitching of the boat and the smell of diesel fumes soon had him leaning over the side feeding the fish.

Finally they were waved in. The launch grounded in the surf some thirty feet from shore. Quickly Bulkowsky's crew worked to install the ramp. Heavy surf pounded them with cold water as they worked. As Joseph was helping lift one of the beams, his high school class ring was scraped off his finger. He saw its glint as it disappeared in the swirling foam. He clawed frantically into the sand at his feet but came up empty. After Doc Heinan had cut the band off his swollen finger, he had carried it in his pocket. In San Diego, he had it repaired and had begun wearing it again. They did get the truck off the boat safely, but Bulkowsky and his men knew there had to be a better way.

In late 1940, the 10th Marines added a third gun battalion. Joseph was transferred to H Battery, promoted to sergeant, and given his own gun section. The barracks overflowed with new men, including reservists from the Hollywood battalion, so Joseph's battery was assigned to a new tent camp across the parade ground. Before long, the regiment was moved to Camp Elliott on the Kearney Mesa, where new wooden barracks had been built.

The camp bustled with activity as the 2nd Marine Division began serious wartime training. The spit and polish routine of the peacetime Corps had given way to the reality of its existence—fighting. New units were added, like tanks and paratroopers.

During their firing exercises, Joseph's outfit would watch the navy's dive bombers from nearby Miramar. The planes would plummet straight down, release their bombs, and pull out within yards of the ground. One day they were watching parachute jumps when they witnessed the beginnings of one of the most extraordinary feats in aviation history. A man hanging by his feet upside down with his chute caught in the tail of a DC-2 was being dragged in circles 300 feet above the ground.

Second Lieutenant Walter Osipoff had been supervising a jump by twelve of his men. As canvas cylinders containing ammunition and rifles were being pushed out the door, one of them caught the release cord to Osipoff's chute, pulling him out of the plane and prematurely opening his chute. The chute was snagged by the tail wheel of the DC-2. The force pulled the harness the length of Osipoff's body until he was hanging by his ankles and held only by the cords of the chute.

The crew aboard the plane was unable to reach him and pull him aboard. The plane circled for some time, then took off for North Island, passing over San Diego with Osipoff dangling helplessly. People watching on the ground murmured prayers. The pilot circled over the air station where he had taken off.

Marines at Camp Elliott soon began hearing accounts of the mishap on the radio, and the following day's newspapers told of an incredible air rescue. On the ground, Navy Lieutenant Bill Lowrey quickly had sized up the situation and decided to attempt a rescue in his two-seat, open cockpit observation plane. His chief mechanic, John McCants, jumped into the rear cockpit. Someone threw him a hunting knife to cut the shroud lines. The DC-2 pilot headed out over the water where the wind was calmer with the observation plane in pursuit. Lowrey maneuvered his plane under the transport, so close that at one point, his propeller nicked the tail of the other plane. Slowly he worked his biplane under Osipoff until he had the lieutenant draped across the fuselage in front of McCants in the rear cockpit.

Because he was holding Osipoff with both arms and Osipoff had a death grip around his own shoulders, McCants was unable to cut the parachute lines. Again, Lowrey maneuvered his plane closer to the tail of the transport and, with the precision of a surgeon, severed the lines with his propeller. With Osipoff draped over the fuselage and part of the parachute wrapped around the rudder, Lowrey managed to land safely. Lowrey and McCants were each awarded the Distinguished Flying Cross.

In 1945, Warrant Officer George Green was having a drink in the officers' club at Camp Lejeune, North Carolina. Green had been an artillery observer with the infantry company on the front line next to Joseph's in the battle on Iwo Jima's airfield number 2. Green struck up a conversation with a field grade officer sitting at the bar next to him, Major Walter Osipoff. After several months in the hospital, and recovered from his ordeal, he went back to parachute jumping.

At Camp Elliott, the parade ground discipline of the men gradually became secondary as the 2nd Division concentrated on battle readiness. One day a corporal in Joseph's battalion, name of Cotton, had just been relieved from his watch on the main gate.

Across the street was a strip of small, wood-frame shops, the kind that sprang up overnight near new military bases. There was a laundry and dry cleaner, a couple of bars, and a short order restaurant.

With his .45 still strapped to his side, Cotton made for the first bar and a cold beer. The juke box was playing "San Antonio Rose." Cotton downed his beer and ordered another. The jukebox continued blaring "San Antonio Rose." Cotton dismounted from his bar stool and announced, "If I hear that damn song one more time, I'm going to put a bullet in that jukebox."

Another marine arose from a booth and went to the jukebox. He inserted a quarter and selected "San Antonio Rose." Making good on his threat, Corporal Cotton strode to the jukebox, drew his pistol, and fired a bullet through the glass, shattering the record and silencing it forever. The next day, former Corporal Cotton was peeling spuds in the mess hall.

The Second Battalion next door was being brought up to full strength. Something was brewing. The rumor was they were being deployed overseas.

To his surprise, Joseph was transferred back to Fox Battery and his old friends. They were packing their gear and camp supplies in wooden crates. The howitzers were given a fresh coat of green paint and the moving parts slathered with heavy grease. When ready, the guns were bundled in stout canvas covers.

Civilian clothes and unneeded personal gear were packed and stored in a supply shed. Joseph gave his radio to a friend in H Battery. Down the street in the buff-colored barracks, the Sixth Marine Regiment was making its own preparations. Major John Bushrod Wilson's artillery battalion, with Dog, Easy, and Fox Batteries, was attached to the infantry regiment.

No one had an inkling of what lay ahead, but to Joseph, it was the most exciting time of his enlistment. The suspense was intoxicating.

Six
Iceland and Beyond—1941

On May 31, 1941, the 6th Marines, reinforced, boarded three navy attack transports, the *Fuller, Heywood,* and *Biddle,* and three fast destroyer transports. Fox Battery trooped aboard the *Heywood.* Without fanfare, the convoy slipped out of San Diego Bay and turned south. At least they weren't going back to San Clemente Island. No one had the slightest inkling where they were headed, but the course they were taking, due south along the Baja California coast, made it apparent it would be the Panama Canal.

Not even the officers knew the destination. Speculation centered on Martinique in the Caribbean. The French island was under the pro-Nazi Vichy government and could pose a threat to U.S. interests in the Caribbean region. Riding at anchor at Fort-de-France were three French warships, including the aircraft carrier *Bearn*. Ironically, the *Bearn* was loaded with 106 U.S.-made fighter planes intended for the defense of France. But France had thrown in the towel and was under Nazi occupation. American overtures to Admiral Georges Robert to surrender Martinique to the United States were stubbornly refused. A regiment of marines might induce him to reconsider. Another possibility for the deployment of the marines was the Azores, where a Nazi presence would have had a crippling effect on the Mediterranean.

After three days' sailing, the convoy arrived off Panama City. At nightfall, all hands were sent below into the uncomfortably hot troop compartments while the ships made their transits through the canal. Supposedly, any secret agents hanging around would see only empty troop ships going through. Not until they had anchored at Colon the next day were a few men allowed on deck. There would be no liberty.

Once again at sea, the ships headed on a northeasterly course. So much for Martinique, which lay to the south. As the troops lounged on deck in the tropical sun, special details began stamping out identification tags. Crooked lettering on oval stainless steel tags spelled out each man's name, serial number, blood type, and religious preference. It was the first reminder of the seriousness of the expedition. Tropical rain squalls brought swarms of naked men to open decks to take advantage of the only fresh water showers available.

On June 16, the ships entered the harbor of Charleston, S.C., and tied up. Had the reinforced regiment simply been redeployed to the east coast? The answer lay inside the crates of supplies on the dock waiting to be lifted into the cargo holds. The cargo net around one of those crates tore loose from its hook in midair, and it came crashing down on the dock, narrowly missing the work detail below. The crate split apart and scattered fur caps, sheepskin coats and rubber arctic boots about. Obviously, the expedition was headed for a northern destination, one very far north.

As the loading progressed, the troops were granted liberty. Scores headed for Folly Beach. In the sultry evenings, marines crowded into joints and road houses to guzzle cold beer and listen to juke box music. One memorable evening, they huddled around a radio hearing the staccato voice of the ringside announcer describe the pulsating action of the Joe Louis-Billy Con world heavyweight championship fight in New York. Local newspapers chronicled Joe Dimaggio's hot hitting streak that was destined to reach fifty-six consecutive games.

After a week, the troop transports cast off the gritty docks and made for the open sea. The convoy turned north and followed the Canadian coast to Newfoundland. At cold, foggy Placentia Bay they dropped anchor to await escort ships.

When once again in open waters, the ghostly outlines of two battleships, *New York* and *Arkansas,* appeared through the mist. They were a comforting sight. Farther out on the picket line of the convoy were the cruisers *Nashville* and *Brooklyn,* along with four destroyers. Navy PBY patrol planes scoured the seas from aloft. President Franklin D. Roosevelt had made sure the marines were well protected from Adolf Hitler's U-boats in the North Atlantic.

While supposedly maintaining neutrality in the European conflict, in secrecy, Roosevelt was already waging a shooting war in the Atlantic allowing U.S. destroyers to protect convoys carrying war materials to Great Britain and Russia. Had a troopship taken a torpedo with loss of lives, Roosevelt would have faced the wrath of an isolationist Congress and a disillusioned public. In winning reelection to a third term in 1940, Roosevelt pledged to keep the United States out of the war.

As it was, one U.S. senator, Republican Burton K. Wheeler of Montana, a bitter opponent to any U.S. involvement, got wind of the expedition and revealed it on the floor of the Senate. The news was received by the ships' radios and printed out for distribution to troops and crew. Hitler fired back with a threat to destroy the American force, but it was all bluster. He needed first to finish off Russia before making any attempt against the United States or the British home isles.

On the *Heywood,* Sergeant Rodden, the section chief of Fox Battery's .50-caliber antiaircraft machine gun crew, recognized the *Nashville,* his old ship. He had pulled a cruise on the *Nashville* several years earlier when it had gone to France to pick up a load of gold bullion, a payment of France's debt from World War I.

For a couple of days, the convoy was enveloped in a dense fog. The ships crept along at two knots, maintaining contact with flashing signal lights and foghorns. Once clear of the mainland, the fog was swept away by gale winds from the arctic regions and the ships pitched and yawed on mountainous cobalt waves. Woolen overcoats were dug out of seabags. They had been the first item of clothing packed at Camp Elliot and therefore at the bottom.

The *Biddle* steamed through an area littered with the wreckage of the British battleship *Hood,* sent to the bottom by the German battleship *Bismarck* a month earlier.

In Charleston, the regiment had grown to a brigade with the addition of a marine antiaircraft defense battalion and a company of light tanks. Major General John Marston had joined to take command. Even he did not know the destination of the expeditionary force until he unsealed his secret orders when the ships left Placentia Bay.

He was directed to proceed to Iceland with his Marines and relieve the 25,000 British troops occupying the island. The Brits were veterans of disastrous campaigns in France and Norway. British Prime Minister Winston Churchill needed his troops for the defense of their homeland, but Iceland was too important to be abandoned. The island nation, part of which lay within the Arctic Circle, was astride the main shipping routes from North America to Europe. It was invaluable as a naval base and weather station, though within reach of German bombers in Norway.

Marston's orders from the War Department stated that the marines were to organize a defense of the island. Within three months, they would be relieved by an army occupation force.

On July 7, Iceland's jagged mountaintops crept into view over the horizon. As the transports entered the tiny harbor of Reykjavik, troops hanging over the sides saw green valleys bathed in bright sunshine, not the barren wintry scene they had envisioned. It was the season of the midnight sun. The air smelled of fish.

An Icelandic coastal steamer crowded with vacationing natives, blond and rosy-cheeked, was pulling away from the dock. The marines waved. In return they received stony stares. It would be that way for the seven months of their stay. In spite of Hitler's ruthless conquests in Europe, including the Scandinavian countries, most Icelanders admired the Germans and were resentful of the Allied occupation force. Years before the war, German engineers had shown them how to pipe hot water from the island's many thermal springs into the city. The Germans had also built a few roads.

A contingent of Canadians serving with the British troops invited more animosity from the natives by practicing machine-gun fire on their sheep.

Its howitzers and vehicles unloaded, Fox Battery proceeded to the heights above the town to Camp Harrogate, their new home. It was a neat collection of rounded, corrugated metal Nissen huts built by the British and named after the Yorkshire town. As a gesture of gratitude, the Brits had vacated their huts and moved into tent camps. Fox Battery settled into a semblance of their routine at Camp Elliott, although now in a war zone.

Robert Hyatt, a first lieutenant from Indiana, commanded the battery. His round, rosy face and blond features suggested a sunny disposition, belying a mercurial temper. The flush in his face would rise like a thermometer when things went wrong. He was dedicated to looking after his troops, but the NCOs thought he was a bit too friendly with the men. His familiarity invited a laxness in discipline. Lieutenant Appleton, the executive officer, stayed in the background and quietly went about maintaining order and smoothing over matters following Hyatt's frequent eruptions.

The howitzers were emplaced in sandbagged pits and sighted in the direction of the harbor three miles distant. German reconnaissance planes made routine flights over the island, and air raid sirens would wail from the British command center. The artillery men would rush out to the gun pits, rip the canvas covers off the howitzers, and "stand by." For what purpose was a mystery. No one had ever shot down a German plane with a howitzer. However, there was always the possibility of an enemy landing by gliders or parachutes. Seven hundred miles across the North Sea in Norway were three German divisions.

In the evenings, small groups of men would promenade about the neighborhoods looking for flaxen-haired maidens. But the very sight of forest green marine uniforms was enough to send the *stulkas* scurrying into their houses. The Icelandic government had enacted a morals policy known as *astand*. It forbade girls eighteen and under from socializing with troops. Those that did were ostracized. Yet, within weeks, there were several pregnancies attributed to marines. Conversely, several cases of gonorrhea were reported by the brigade medical officer.

British cockneys referred to the natives as "fish-eating baastuds," conveniently ignoring their own appetite for fish and chips and the fact that Britain was buying all of Iceland's export catch.

In mid-August, the British commander, Major General H. O. Curtis, alerted the various Allied commands that a "very distinguished" visitor was expected and issued plans for a parade. The visitor was the British Prime Minister, en route home from Argentia Bay, where he and Roosevelt had signed the historic Atlantic Charter, a blueprint for the defeat of Hitler.

Winston Churchill, natty in a navy blue seafaring uniform, debarked from his warship on a pleasant, sun-splashed day. After a courtesy visit to the ancient Icelandic Alpingishus, the world's oldest parliament, he was driven to the outskirts of Reykjavik, where thousands of troops were arrayed on a treeless plain. There were British regulars and Dominion troops from all corners of the empire, along with small contingents of Norwegians and Dutch who had fled the continent. Along with the marines were detachments of the U.S. Army and Air Corps who headed the advance of their occupation force.

Leaning on a walking cane, Churchill slowly trooped the lines, occasionally halting to chat with the men. He paused before Joseph and studied him briefly. A nod of his head before moving past was interpreted by Joseph as an expression of approval. The great man appeared pale and stooped, yet wore a determined bulldog countenance. A veteran marine sergeant down the line politely corrected the Prime Minister when addressed as an "old soldier."

"Sir, I'm an old marine, not a soldier."

"Well, an old sea soldier; isn't that a good term?" Churchill rejoined, quite accurately.

"Yes, sir," responded the sergeant.

The troops paraded along a concrete road, perhaps the only surfaced road in the entire country. The skirling bagpipes of the Tyneside Scottish regiment echoed across the field, mingling with the brassy sounds of the "Marine Corps Hymn" played by the brigade band.

Upon returning home, Churchill confessed that the strains of the marine war song had played hauntingly in his mind through the remainder of his journey.

Iceland is a treeless, volcanic island roughly the size of Kentucky. With its spiny coastline, it resembles a balled-up porcupine. The northern coastline lies at a tangent to the Arctic Circle. Only the coastal areas are habitable. But for its geysers, whitewater streams and falls, the interior resembles a moonscape with its craggy mountains, lava beds, and heaps of boulders. To the marines, it was both eerily beautiful and depressingly bleak.

In the fall, the weather was mostly dry and clear. Working alongside their British counterparts, the marines turned to, building huts for the Army troops who were beginning to trickle in. Accustomed to uninterrupted work days, according to the Puritan ethic, the Americans at first scoffed at the tea breaks of the Tommies.

Midmornings, the lorries of the NAAFI, an acronym for the Navy, Army, Air Force Institute canteen, would park on the work sites and dispense hot tea and cookies, which were called biscuits. They would return in midafternoon. Soon the marines were adapting to the British custom and enjoying it.

British noncoms had beer and rations of spirits in their messes, which they shared generously with their marine counterparts. In return, they got American cigarettes, along with tins of corned beef, Spam, and tongue of oxen, delicacies to them but detested by the marines.

While fighting in Norway, General Curtis's troops adopted a distinctive shoulder patch with a polar bear on an ice floe. In a gesture of mutual cooperation, he suggested to Marston that his marines also wear the patch "because of their efficiency and conduct." Headquarters in Washington approved, and soon the marines were sporting the polar bear on the shoulders of their green uniforms.

By Thanksgiving, the cold drizzles turned to snow. Freakish storms resulted when the arctic air descended and collided with the warm waters of the gulf stream flowing off the west coast. The snowfalls tended to be of the warm weather variety with large wet flakes. Heavy drifts of snow would suddenly thaw and the ground would turn into a soupy slush. The huts, which slept up to twenty men, were heated with potbellied coal-burning stoves, one at each end. Parkas, fur hats of the type worn by Russian cossacks, ski mittens, and rubber boots with felt insoles were issued. They proved to be adequate for the conditions.

In November, Fox battery vacated Harrogate and was redeployed thirty miles up the coast to Sauerbaer, a towering headland overlooking the entrance to Hvalfjordur. They occupied huts next to a British coastal defense battery. At the far end of the deep fiord was the naval base.

From the heights, marines watched crippled ships entering the fiord below. Victims of Nazi submarine torpedoes, they'd make their way painfully to the naval base. Some listed awkwardly, others revealed gaping holes in their hulls, and there were a couple with their bows shot away. For all their wounds, they were the lucky ones. Others in their convoy lay at the bottom of the North Atlantic.

Joseph and three other NCOs went to the American military hospital in Reykjavik to visit Sergeant Rodden, who had had surgery to remove a cyst from between the cheeks of his buttocks. In the ward, they came by the bed of a young sailor from Lafayette, Louisiana. He had been on the forecastle of the U.S. destroyer *Kearney* when it took a German torpedo in the bow. The impact drove the steel deck upwards, crushing both his legs. He motioned with one hand towards the foot of his bed. The blanket was flattened. He was a double amputee. His war was over before it had been declared. Seven of his buddies had died and dozens seriously injured. Pearl Harbor was still a month away.

Wintry gales of major hurricane force were common. They were particularly fierce on the exposed heights of the Sauerbaer headland. Blasts would often exceed one-hundred miles an hour, then suddenly die down, creating a weird sensation inside the rounded huts, as though a vacuum was sucking the air out. Within seconds, the howling outside would resume. The huts would shake and shiver like they were about to be airborne. Fortunately they had been sandbagged and sodded on all sides leaving no exposed areas for the winds to exploit. Outside activities ceased during the storms, which might last a day or two.

Getting to and from the mess hall and latrine would have been impossible if not for the improvised handholds of field telephone wire strung on barbed wire stakes augured into the tundra. If the ground was icy, it would be nearly impossible to stay on one's feet even with the lifeline. By midwinter, daylight had been reduced to barely two hours. The nights were interminably long. Some nights the black hole of sky would be illuminated by the light shows of nature, the colorful displays of the aurora borealis. Training or any outside activities were greatly reduced. Discipline grew lax as the boredom wore on.

The camp had no hot water for showering, so the troops took "spit baths" from pans of water heated over the stove. One day Joseph and Hank Michalsky walked to a stream on the mountainside near camp. From its crystal water, Sergeant Frank Deline had snagged several trout, using a hook fashioned from a safety pin. Only its swift descent from the mountain kept it from freezing over. On a dare, they removed their clothes with the intention of wading in, lathering up, and rinsing off before their goose pimples froze. They got as far as stage one, splashed water under the armpits, and crawled back on the rocky bank, their shivering bodies already turning blue. Mercifully, back in the hut, Sergeant Caganich had a roaring fire going in the stove, otherwise they might have gotten hypothermia.

The artillery battalion commander, Lieutenant Colonel John Bushrod Wilson, visited Sauerbaer once and was a dinner guest in the officers' mess, which was but a small partition at one end of the troop mess hall.

Hyatt broke out a treasured bottle of scotch, and then surprised the colonel with a serving of roast duck rather than the expected entrée of canned bully beef.

Savoring the meal after a second helping, the colonel idly inquired about the source of the duck. Hyatt responded with a mischievous wink of an eye. "We went on a little duck hunt yesterday, Colonel."

"They're eider ducks, aren't they?" Wilson demanded. "Hyatt, you know damned well eiders are protected by the Icelandic government and we're not supposed to shoot them. There'll be hell to pay if this gets out," he fumed, glancing back at a cook hovering in the doorway of the galley, who had been expecting a compliment rather than an ass-chewing.

Eider feathers were valued for their soft down. It was gathered by the natives around the nesting areas and used in quilts and as insulation for winter clothing.

The duck dinner was but one of several questionable escapades of Fox Battery sanctioned by Hyatt. While at Camp Harrogate near the city, lightly guarded army supply dumps were fair game for the battery's prowling vehicles. As the army build-up progressed, units of the marine brigade were pressed into service as stevedores. They worked in shifts around the clock, unloading ships. It was demeaning duty for the proud brigade that had been singled out as the only body of U.S. troops deemed combat-ready for instant expeditionary duty overseas.

Moreover, the army sent Major General Charles Bonesteel to assume command of U.S. troops. In Washington, the marine commandant protested but to no avail. Being under command of the navy's brass was one thing, but having an army boss was considered a worse fate. In reprisal for being made into a labor battalion, resentful marines pilfered wantonly from those bountiful cargo holds, repositories of new winter clothing, beer, cigarettes, and chocolate bars.

First Sergeant Robbe went after bigger game, most notably a would-be cargo of fresh beef. From a work detail on the dock, he had learned of a ship about to unload sides of beef. That night, using the battery's two-and-a-half-ton truck, he clandestinely joined a line of army trucks waiting to be dispatched beneath one of the ship's booms lifting out cargo.

The dispatcher ordered him to the number-two hold. Having heard from his informant that the meat was coming out of number three, he ignored the dispatcher and drove there. In the darkness, the irate dispatcher had not detected that the truck was a marine vehicle, a green International Harvester, unlike the army's olive drab GM trucks. But when he saw the truck heading for the wrong hold, he pursued it.

"Are you deaf?" he shouted to Robbe, who all the time was keeping his head lowered to conceal his identity. "Get the hell over to number two."

Problem was they were offloading hundred-pound sacks of sugar from number two, and Robbe was left with no choice but to accept a load. Going to the army dump to unload the sugar as directed by the dispatcher could have unmasked the deception and probably invited a court martial. So he headed for Camp Harrogate, routed out a work detail, and had the contraband stashed beneath the canvas tarpaulin in the ammunition dump.

Several weeks later, the battalion's executive officer was making an inspection when he headed for the ammunition dump in a ravine a couple of hundred yards away. On lifting up a corner of the tarp, he uncovered a cache of sugar. Some of the sacks had broken open, and dissolved sugar was running over the crates of .75-millimeter shells. Poor Lieutenant Hyatt was nearly incoherent trying to explain the presence of all that sweetening. Some other outfit, he finally stammered, must have used his ammo dump by mistake. The incident had a sobering effect and spelled the end of Fox Battery's predatory habits.

The brigade's vehicles, built for improved roads in the United States, were no match for the rough Icelandic roads. Sharp lava rocks shredded tires. Potholes jolted trucks until their parts were jarred loose. Replacement parts were nonexistent. General Marston's pleas to Washington for spare parts went unanswered. Why waste equipment on the marines when the army will relieve them in a few months went the reasoning. The "raggedy-assed" marines continued to do without.

Marston's radio messages to Washington had to be relayed through the embassy in London and were often garbled in the encoding and decoding. The Army cluttered the system with nonessential welfare messages, such as one requesting the War Department to notify a soldier's mom that the shoes she'd sent were the right fit.

On a rare off day, Joseph and Hank Michalsky went into town looking for a restaurant. Walking by the Hekla Hotel, an eponym for the island's most famous volcano, they spotted the dining room through the lace curtain in the window. Upon entering, they were politely shown to a table, although the waiters pointed at them and jabbered in Icelandic about America *"sargeis."* They had served officers before, but not enlisted men.

The menu was in Icelandic, so they ordered the day's special, whatever that might be. Plates of stewed meat with boiled potatoes were set before them. The meat was tender and quite good, a bit on the sweet side but tasting like Swiss steak. What kind of beef was it? they asked over demitasses of coffee. "Pony steak," the waiter answered. So, all those furry little horses they had seen in pens were Icelandic livestock.

One day, Joseph took a truck and working party for a load of gravel to fill the mud holes around camp. The rock quarry was in a remote cove. Nearby was a work camp of Faroe Islanders, conscripted by the British as a labor force. Their homeland was a cluster of Danish islands in the North Sea, south of Iceland. The Faroese were quaintly dressed in black knickers and jackets with large shiny buckles on their square-toed shoes. The ensemble was remindful of characters from the fairy tales of Hans Christian Anderson.

The Faroese had a whale hauled up on a ramp at the water's edge. They jabbered excitedly in a mixed Nordic dialect. Two of them were flensing slabs of blubber from the carcass and handing them to a line of men with outstretched arms. They solemnly carried the meat into the camp kitchen. As one of them was passing Joseph's work detail, he dug his face into a slab and gouged out a bite, like a thief eating a stolen watermelon without utensils. His bloodied face had a rapt expression as he chewed on the raw blubber. Joseph had read about Eskimos eating raw fish, but hadn't expected to see it here.

The British had a prisoner-of-war stockade near Reykjavik holding a hundred or so captured German submariners. Joseph and

Michalsky were invited in for a beer one afternoon by the senior British noncom. From behind barbed wire, the sullen prisoners stared at the marines, the first Americans they had seen.

It was time to feed the prisoners, and a British cook placed a basket of freshly baked loaves of bread on a table in front of the NCO in charge. He had a stack of paper labels of the British union jack and the motto, "Britain Delivers the Goods." He moistened the labels and plastered one on the bottom of each loaf. "This is to let the baastuds know their submarines aren't winning the war," he guffawed.

One blustery December night, Fox Battery was unloading a merchant marine ship from the States. A man who had gone into the ship's galley for a cup of coffee came out with an unbelievable story. The ship's radio had received news that Pearl Harbor had been bombed.

The Axis powers had declared war on the United States. It was five months to the day since they had arrived in Reykjavik. Before the work shift had ended, the wind had become a severe storm. It was too dangerous to return to camp. Up on the hill, trucks were being blown off the road. Instead, they were taken to an army camp nearby, where they were fed hot soup, issued sleeping bags, and bedded down in a new Quonset hut. Attitudes about the army were noticeably more positive.

As the storm raged outside, Joseph slept fitfully, his mind racing to fathom the reality that his country was at war. In three months, Joseph's enlistment would expire, along with that of Michalsky. Each day First Sergeant Robbe called the two into his office, trying to talk them into reenlisting. Joseph had saved a little money and harbored an idea of returning to Louisiana and going to college. He had declined extending his enlistment to go to China with Adkins and Whalen and wasn't about to succumb to the first sergeant's entreaties. Joseph and Hank packed their seabags and awaited the first available navy ship headed Stateside.

So it was with relish that Robbe summoned them when news of the outbreak of war was made official. "Okay, men," he said with a fiendish grin, "you have a choice of reenlisting or continuing your service at the convenience of the government." Convenience of the government meant they would remain in the Marine Corps until the war ended or Hell froze over, whichever came first. The two opted for the "convenience."

The NCO mess was like a wake. A somber group discussed what little they had learned about the disaster at Pearl. Most of them had served on battleships that now rested at the bottom of Pearl Harbor. All had buddies on the Pacific islands under Japanese attack. Joseph recalled his short tour of duty on *Tennessee* and *Oklahoma*. Both were reported hit. It was unbelievable that the proud Pacific fleet was all but wiped out.

At first, there was denial, as with the loss of a loved one. Then anger. Sergeant Swede Nielson fulminated about the Corps' decision to arm Wake Island with five-inch coastal guns instead of six-inchers. A career NCO, he had been on Wake with a defense battalion several months before. As it would turn out, an inch in caliber would not make a whit of difference in the defense of Wake.

News of Pearl Harbor rekindled hope that the men of the brigade would be heading to the Pacific, where they were needed, instead of staying on their godforsaken island doing the army's dirty work. Back in the States, volunteers were flooding recruiting offices. The marines in Iceland were bitter and frustrated.

One day in early February, Robbe stomped into the sergeant's hut and hollered, "Go get your men ready and start packing. We're going home." His words were greeted with jubilation.

A week later Fox Battery was on the *Biddle* headed for New York. Of interesting note is that the convoy returning home was escorted only by a light cruiser and a few destroyers. Going to Iceland, there had been two battleships, two cruisers, a flock of destroyers, and PBYs in the sky. The conclusion could be drawn that President Roosevelt had taken all precautions to protect American lives in the months before the outbreak of hostilities while sanctioning his shooting war in the North Atlantic. But now that war had been declared, the safety of the homeward bound marines was of no major concern.

In the late winter, the seas were at their worst, with gigantic green waves tossing the transports around like toy boats. Not even seasickness or the thought of enemy U-boats could dampen the spirits of the troops. After an uneventful voyage of several days, the skyline of New York appeared on the horizon, and soon they were passing the Statue of Liberty on the way to the dock in the Brooklyn Navy Yard.

As the *Biddle* was proceeding to a berth, the troops were presented with an awesome sight. The *Normandie,* a former French luxury ocean liner, was lying on its port side hard against the dock. Barely a month ago, it had caught fire and capsized while being refitted into a troop ship. The marines had seen pictures of the ship on the cover of *Life* magazines that arrived in Iceland two weeks after the disaster.

Men from the states east of the Mississippi had leave papers and orders to report back to Camp Elliott. Those west of the Mississippi would return in a troop train and then get their leaves.

New York was in a somber mood. A movie of the marines' heroic fight on Wake Island was playing in a Times Square theater. It had been hastily produced, full of inaccuracies, a propaganda film at best. The commanding officer at Wake, Major James Devereaux, was supposed to have radioed back to Pearl Harbor, "Send us more Japs" when asked what help he needed. It was vintage Hollywood. A more heroic and accurate message had been sent by Navy Commander W. S. Cunningham when Japanese troops had overrun the island: "Enemy on island issue in doubt."

The Icelandic marines with their polar bear shoulder patches were the nearest thing to conquering heroes. They weren't allowed to pay for drinks in bars. Admiring New Yorkers in Manhattan thrust complimentary theater tickets at them. For four dollars a day, a cab driver put his hack at the disposal of Joseph and two of his buddies. He took them to all the sights, shows, restaurants and bars during their three days in the city. Having made up for the seven months of privation with food, drink, and entertainment, Joseph finally boarded a train at Grand Central Station for New Orleans.

In retrospect, the marine deployment to Iceland had a limited strategic value. Only a few British troops had been withdrawn. The German threat had diminished as the Nazis became overextended on the Russian front and in North Africa. The expedition had tied up some of the corps' best trained men and officers needed for upcoming operations in the South Pacific. But the rapid deployment of the brigade had proven that the Marine Corps was ready "to fight our country's battles," in the words of their hymn. The brigade had been the first combat unit of the United States to serve in the European Theater.

However, the confining life in Nissen huts and the monotonous work days of unloading ships had a corrosive effect on morale and discipline. Although exaggerated, the brigade had been saddled with a reputation of being an unruly outfit.

As the brigade was disbanded and its units returned to the control of the Second Marine Division at Camp Elliott, some commanders made it known that Iceland marines were not welcome in their outfits. Despite the stigma, the veterans of Iceland would distinguish themselves in South Pacific battles and many would die bravely. Others, as in Joseph's case, would leave the division to become the core of cadres forming and training new combat regiments as the Corps accelerated its wartime expansion.

Seven

The Third Marine Division—1942–1943

The war had roused America from its Rip Van Winkle slumber. While industries were humming, Lake Tarsa was still in its Great Depression torpor, though there were signs of an awakening. Many of the younger men had either volunteered or been drafted. Gone was the shovel brigade of Roosevelt's relief program when WPA workers had put in a town sewer system, all dug by hand. Much has been made of FDR's recovery programs, but it was the war that lifted the country by the bootstraps. Slowly, money was beginning to circulate again. Rice farmers were benefiting from federal crop subsidies, creating a trickle-down effect. The East Texas oil boom had spread into southwest Louisiana. People were buying more groceries and household necessities.

Ornas had gone into business, opening a saloon on a corner of Main Street. There was already a bar across the street that had been in business ever since the repeal of Prohibition in 1933, but there was room for another. No matter how rough the times, people found money to spend on beer and liquor. It was the opiate that made them forget their troubles, at least for a few hours. The bar was not the first time Ornas had dabbled in alcohol, though his first legal one.

For a short while during the Prohibition years, in Joseph's childhood, Ornas had been a bootlegger. He had long been making beer for his own consumption and that of a few select friends. Before that he made his own wine using dried prunes. Once, when they were living on a farm, he emptied the marinated remains of the prunes into the hog trough. The pigs went on a binge and soon were rolling on the ground and squealing in delight. A couple of shoats tried to mount disinterested females.

Ornas was better at making beer. In a spare bedroom, he kept a ten-gallon crock fermenting with malt, sugar, and yeast. During cold weather, he burned a kerosene lamp near the crock to stimulate the process. When his floating tester reached the desired gravity mark on the scale, he would siphon the brew into dark bottles and cap them. Joseph would help. Every so often an overactivated bottle would explode, awakening everyone in the night and showering the room with suds and broken glass.

When the beer was aged to his liking, Ornas would buy a block of ice and invite his friends for a few cold ones. Someone would bring a chunk of cheddar and crackers to go along. The party over, the guests would always leave a four-bit piece or a dollar on the table in appreciation.

From there, Ornas graduated to the hard stuff. He found a bootlegger who operated a still in the swamps at the head of the Mamatau River. He started buying small quantities of moonshine, a quart or two at a time to share with friends. When one wanted some to go, he would decant it out into smaller flasks and charge for it. From buying quarts from his moonshiner, he graduated to two- and five-gallon jugs.

The word got around—eventually to the wrong places—and soon he was doing a modest business selling pints and half-pints of booze from the house. The income supplemented the meager paycheck he made on his part-time job grading roads and ditches for the parish. On scorching summer days, he would put in long hours on a road grader towed by a tractor. Turning wheels and cranks on the rig, he would angle his blade to fit the contour of the ditch or roadside and roll the turf and mud aside. It was grueling work and made his bootleg liquor sideline all the more attractive.

As time went by, Joseph, on his way home from school, had noticed a strange, green sedan parked a block or so up the road from his house. Two men were sitting in the car, always with newspapers held up to their faces. One day Joseph got home to find his mother agitated and distraught. The revenuers had busted Ornas's operation, and he was on his way to jail in Dennings. Clarissa herself had been caught heaving a jug over the fence into a weed patch but was not arrested.

A lawyer bonded out Ornas, and he came home a disgraced man. For weeks he sat around moping while awaiting his trial. The house was like a morgue. The judge was lenient, sparing him from doing time, but he had to borrow money to pay the fine, placing an added burden on a struggling family. He resumed his grinding days on the road grader determined to put the bootlegging episode out of his life.

When the opportunity arose, he opened his own little bar. At first, he had only a few friends as customers. They would spend afternoons playing euchre and dominos and guzzling an occasional beer. But he had a good location on the corner, and before long, he added pool tables and was drawing people away from the bar across the street. This would lead to feuding in the war years when liquor was rationed. Richard and Badeau, proprietors cross the street, had a lock on the distributors by having been in business much longer. Ornas was at a disadvantage, getting only a few bottles of spirits to sell each week. In the end, it was beer that carried him through.

With tubs of ice under the bar, he prided himself in serving the coldest long necks of Jax and Dixie in town. Saturday nights, the place would be bulging with farmers and oil field roustabouts whetting their whistles. A slot machine on one end of the bar, courtesy of the state's franchised gambling honchos, made a few dollars. But Ornas thought he should be getting more than the meager ten percent of the gross from the machine. So he took matters into his own hand.

Actually it was a piece of wire that he took. He had found a way to slide the wire inside the chute where the coins dropped when someone made a lucky hit and up into the pregnant belly of the machine where the nickels accumulated. Early in the morning before any tipplers arrived, Ornas would have jiggled his wire and induced a dollar or more to drop from his cash cow. The way he figured it, it wasn't dishonest. The machines were unfairly rigged so that the only winners were the big shots who ran the state's gambling operations.

Puzzled mechanics would scratch their heads on their weekly visits to service the machine and empty the take. They would complain that Ornas's slot was paying out too much and tighten up the machines more, making the payoffs stingier. This would serve as a warning to put aside the wire for a while.

Clarissa pitched in and helped clean up the place, sweeping out the cigarette butts and mud from farmers' boots and mopping the spit off the floor. Most disagreeable was the cleaning job on the toilet in the back room. Men with bloated bladders were careless with their aim, spraying urine all over the place. Clarissa would rebel. "You can hire a nigger to do this, I'm not doing it any more," she would protest. Eventually Ornas would coax her back.

Then there were those drunks who preferred to urinate outside in a narrow space between the bar and the adjacent building. Eventually the odor brought complaints from other businesses nearby and a warning from the town council. A sympathetic friend told Ornas he knew a way to put a stop to the outdoor toilet habits. He spread a web of copper wires on the ground in the target area and attached one end to a twelve-volt battery. The result was shocking to say the least, and soon cries of agony were heard coming from the alleyway as miscreants emerged with flies open and urine soaking their trousers. The outdoor bathroom ceased to be.

Among the several characters who inhabited the bar regularly was an old house mover named Coon. He lived alone outside town, and one of the many stories that circulated about him was that he had an overabundance of genitalia. One snoopy voyeur had even asked a prostitute on Happy Hill if it were true. *"Mais, oui,"* she responded, her eyes widening.

On Fridays, old Coon would buy a catfish from Price's market, at the foot of the wharf. With the fish wrapped in a newspaper and tucked under an armpit, he'd head for the saloon, stationing himself at one end of the bar with a foot planted on the rail. There he'd remain the whole day, downing straight shots of Four Roses and telling stories to anyone who'd listen. As the day wore on, the fish, still in a viselike grip under his armpit, would begin to smell, and Coon's audience would dwindle. One day, Ornas sensed another smell even more odoriferous than the fish. Old Coon had passed up a call of nature, and his baggy pants had become even droopier at the seat. It was one of the few times Ornas ever had to evict anyone. Pisces was one matter, but feces was another. Either old Coon went or he'd have to close up.

Joseph whiled away his leave days visiting the old familiar places in town.

Comeaux's restaurant still made appetizing hamburgers. The decrepit movie theater was still in business, but Joseph wasn't in the mood to watch old B movies while fending off rats foraging among the peanut shells on the floor. The theater brought to mind vaudeville acts that had entertained once a month. One in particular had left an indelible impression on Joseph's young mind. A magician had hypnotized a beautiful girl on the stage and then had her wheeled on a gurney up the street and into Theogene's drug store. They placed her in the window, where Halloween decorations and Christmas scenes were displayed. There she stayed through the night and the following day up to the next performance.

Joseph and several guys maintained a vigil the whole night, gazing raptly on the girl who slept soundly, her bosom slowly rising and falling under the white sheet. Not even a raging thunderstorm that came up in the night elicited a single movement of her eyelids. She was the most beautiful girl Joseph had ever seen, and he was enchanted. Twenty-four hours later, she was wheeled back onstage for the evening performance and awakened by the magician. She walked off the stage on wobbly legs and was taken to the Wave Café for a meal. Joseph and E.J. followed and, from a distance, watched through a window as she devoured a heaping plate of fried oysters.

Soon after opening his bar, Ornas and Clarissa bought a bungalow in town across from the Catholic church. It had indoor plumbing and electricity. They bought a refrigerator with the motor on top and a radio. A washing machine was soon to follow. Clarissa kept up with "Stella Dallas" and "Portia Faces Life" while doing the ironing. An electric iron had replaced the two old flatirons she'd alternate from the stovetop. (As one lost its heat she'd switch with the hotter one on the stove.) In the warm months of the year, the glowing wood stove would turn the kitchen into a sauna. Beads of perspiration would drip from her forehead and evaporate with a sizzle as they fell on the hot iron. Now there was a humming Westinghouse fan in one corner of the kitchen that gently stirred the sticky Louisiana air. For the first time in her life, Clarissa was enjoying some of the luxuries of a modern housewife.

Although coffee now came packaged and ready to use, she still roasted her own green coffee beans once a week. The aromatic flavor of coffee would waft from her skillet out the window and into the street. The blackened beans would then go into a hand grinder on the wall and be reduced to grounds for the extra-strength Cajun coffee, served upon arising in the morning and after the noon meal.

Like the prodigal son, Joseph made the most of the bountiful table Clarissa set day after day of his stay. She'd ring the necks of plump Rhode Island reds and make them into rich, spicy gumbos, followed by nectarous bread puddings.

Platters of fried catfish fillets, fresh shrimp and oysters from the bayous to the south were set before him. His sister Mae and her growing family often joined the table in the feasts. Like the Canada goose that obeys the primal instinct to take wing and fly south, Joseph felt a tugging toward California, where his buddies were assembling into new combat units for the war in the Pacific. The news was all bad. The Japanese had overrun the South and Central Pacific. The Philippines were lost, with only Douglas MacArthur having been saved. The China marines had been evacuated a step ahead of the Japanese attack and put in defensive positions on the beaches of Corregidor. It would be many years before Joseph would learn of the horrible fate that befell Bobby Adkins as a prisoner of the Japs after surviving the Bataan Death March.

A couple of Joseph's old school buddies had been on weekend leave in Lake Tarsa from the army at Fort Hood in Texas. They had a car, and he bummed a ride to Houston, from where he'd take the train. His leave-taking was a somber occasion. This time, he was going to fight, and the odds did not look favorable. His heart was as heavy as when he'd left home four years earlier.

On the train west, he picked up a discarded *Time* magazine and studied its cover. It was a map of the Pacific Ocean with the yellow rays of the Rising Sun stretching across the areas controlled by Japan. Superimposed on the map was a sketched outline of the United States, dwarfed by the magnitude of the Japanese-held territory. How many years would it take to regain all those islands and how many lives? Joseph pondered.

Camp Elliott was buzzing like never before. Columns of dust rose from tramping feet on the mesa. Machine gun practice fire rattled in the canyons, and artillery fire boomed in the distance. The Iceland brigade had been absorbed by the Second Marine Division.

Joseph got the first rocker under his sergeant chevrons. He was now a staff sergeant. Smugly, he recalled the chiding he'd gotten in the days after boot camp for his spit and polish zealousness.

"What're you trying to do, make sergeant in your first cruise," his detractors had nagged. Here he was a staff sergeant and, technically, still on his first cruise, albeit at the convenience of the government.

One day a notice appeared on the bulletin board in the barracks: A cadre of men was being transferred to New River, North Carolina, to form the Third Marine Division. Joseph found his name on the list. Hank Michalsky was staying on.

That evening, they drank a few beers in the slop chute and reminisced about the old days. It would be their last time together. Two years later, Hank was dead, killed on Saipan when a mortar shell exploded in the fire direction center of his artillery battalion. Mike had always said he never wanted to be an old man.

Joseph and a couple hundred specially picked men, mainly noncommissioned officers, boarded a troop train for the cross-country trip. All they knew about New River, later to become Camp Lejeune, was that it had recently been acquired and, with 110,000 acres, was now the largest of the marine bases. Miles of white sandy beaches on the Atlantic afforded excellent landings to practice amphibious operations, which would be so crucial against Japanese-held islands in the Pacific.

One of the quirks of the U.S. military regulations was that navy and marine personnel traveled Pullman class, while army troops roughed it in crowded coaches. Joseph was assigned a compartment that he shared with Sergeant Hooks, who was a mess sergeant.

The troops ate in dining cars with linen napkins, tablecloths, and silverware, served by stewards in white jackets. From time to time, the marine train would slowly pass a crowded Army troop train pulled off on a siding. The soldiers would be lined up and down the length of their train with mess kits in hand to receive meals in the kitchen box car. By the time they had been served, eaten, and washed their mess kits, it was time to line up for the next meal. On the marine train one evening, the entrée was roast turkey. But before the second sitting had been served, the turkey ran out and the cooks broke out canned ham to finish the meal. Captain Robert Howser, the troop commander, was having none of it. It was a time when defense contractors were cutting corners and making fortunes off the military.

"You re being paid to feed these men turkey dinners and not canned ham," Howser fumed at the chief conductor. The conductor complained that there wouldn't be any more turkey available until the train reached Texarkana, a good three hours away. Then it would take two hours to cook the birds.

"So be it," Howser said. At that, the conductor telegraphed ahead, and late in the evening, the turkeys were on board.

Another two hours had gone by when Howser pounded on the door of Joseph's compartment.

"Chow's ready. Get all those men from the second sitting into the dining car," he ordered. "I want every bit of that turkey dinner eaten."

Joseph routed out the men, who by now were sleepier than hungry, and herded them into the diner. When it appeared that not all the turkey would be eaten, he made another foray into the darkened cars, awakened more men and ordered them into the diner. By midnight the feeding was complete and only turkey carcasses remained. Howser and the Marine Corps had not made any points with the railroad, but they did get its respect.

After a journey of six days, the train came to rest alongside a platform on a siding in the middle of nowhere. There was nothing but towering pine trees all around. This was New River. The humidity, which was nonexistent at Camp Elliott, added to the discomfort of the midday June sun. A convoy of trucks rolled up. The men loaded seabags, climbed aboard, and were driven to camp. Pale green plywood huts were laid out among the pines. The artillery camp was the farthest one out.

Joseph was now the acting gunnery sergeant of Battery E, 2nd Battalion, 12th Marines, another .75-millimeter pack howitzer battery. The officers and men to fill out the division were coming from East Coast bases. Most of the troops were fresh out of boot camp at Parris Island, South Carolina. The officers were mainly graduates of the Basic School in Philadelphia, with a few "90-day wonders" from Quantico's officer candidate school thrown in.

Reserve First Lieutenant Clement B. Newbold, a Philadelphia socialite and member of the 1936 U.S. Olympic sculling crew, assumed command of the battery. A tall, lanky, middle-aged individual, he earnestly sought Joseph's expertise in artillery and handling troops in general. Newbold was typical of many Ivy League alumni in the East who gave up cushy corporate positions to volunteer in the marines.

No aspect of the military escaped his keen desire to learn, and he constantly probed Joseph's mind about handling disciplinary problems. Given his attentiveness and the earnestness of his recruits, there were few problems.

This was the period of World War II when the United States was not wanting in manpower as much as in materials and ordnance. The artillery battalion had no howitzers, only the prismatic sights. While awaiting delivery of the howitzers, the sights were fastened to sawhorses, and gunners became familiarized with the micrometer scales graduated in millimeters and which measured angles of range, elevation, and deflection.

Newbold was a stickler for physical conditioning, and he took the battery on frequent hikes through the pine forests. Joseph, in particular, needed the conditioning after fattening up on his mother's Cajun cooking and then idling around at Camp Elliott waiting for the next development.

All during the summer, the one respite from the oppressive heat was the daily afternoon thundershower, which temporarily cooled off the pine forests. Once there was an outbreak of food poisoning from a mess hall that incapacitated some 1,600 men, but not Joseph.

Some evenings after drills and work had ended, Joseph and a few other NCOs would buy a case of beer from the sergeant's club and take it into a clearing in the forest. Hooks, the mess sergeant who had shared the compartment on the train with Joseph, would bring a GI can full of ice with the help of a couple of his messmen. He'd throw in some cold cuts and bread, and they would party into the night until the mosquitoes drove them indoors. Ed Sparkman, the old football-playing buddy from the San Diego days who had arrived at New River earlier with the Third Regiment, would join them.

On weekends, Joseph, Sparkman, and Danny Fellows, another Iceland veteran, would go to the bus station in the town of Jacksonville and queue up to board a coach to anywhere. They wanted to get as far away from New River as possible yet near enough to make it back to camp on Sunday night. Wilson, a railroad town in the tobacco belt, proved to be good getaway. They'd check into the town's hotel, turn on the big ceiling fan in the room, order a bucket of ice to go with the scotch they'd bought at the ABC store, and kick back. With appetites sharpened by the whisky, they'd make for a Greek restaurant in town that served up thick steaks and heaps of French fries. One Sunday, they missed the last bus to Jacksonville and had to hire a taxi to take them the eighty miles.

In August, Sparky's artillery battalion, which supported the Third Regiment, boarded a troop train for the West Coast. Although they didn't know it at the time, the reinforced regiment was headed for American Samoa. The First Marine Division had landed on Guadalcanal in the British Solomon Islands, and the Third Regiment would become a reserve force for the campaign.

Major Alpha Bowser had taken temporary command of the nascent Second Battalion. A quiet-spoken, dignified officer, he was destined to win his general's stars later in his career.

One day he called Joseph into his office and told him he was being recommended for marine gunner, a warrant officer rank. Joseph wasn't enthusiastic and politely declined. He had seen a few warrant officers in San Diego and didn't feel he had the years of experience to be one. He didn't think he would ever be comfortable around officers. A month or so later, Joseph was promoted to gunnery sergeant. It was one stripe shy of master sergeant, the top enlisted grade. Still, being a "gunny" was a most coveted and prestigious rank.

At last the howitzers arrived. The ordnance depot's olive drab paint was sanded off and replaced with Marine Corps green. Joseph and his assistants schooled the new men on the guns until they were ready for their first firing exercise. It turned out to be their only live firing in New River. The battalion had been ordered to the West Coast on a troop train.

At Camp Dunlap in the Imperial Valley near Niland, California, the Marine Corps had acquired a vast chunk of empty desert ideal for artillery firing. With the Chocolate Mountains in the background, there was unlimited range for gunnery practice of all calibers. Bulldozers leveled sand dunes and scraped away tumbleweeds and creosote bushes for the battalion to set up a tent camp. It was midwinter. The men burned under the hot desert sun during the days and shivered in the cold nights. A characteristic of the desert is that despite the unrelenting heat of the day, the sandy surface reflects the sun's rays skyward and retains little heat, resulting in cold nights.

Joseph didn't know it at the time, but the most important event of his life was about to happen. He met Cara. Horace Cline, a fellow sergeant in the outfit, had been dating a schoolteacher in Brawley, and they had planned a cookout in the desert one evening with a couple of the teacher's friends. Joseph went along, and under the starry desert night with the aroma of steaks grilling over a glowing bed of mesquite coals, he met the woman of his life.

Cara was a young graduate of San Francisco State College on her first job, teaching the children of migrant Mexican farm laborers. Joseph had always been shy around women, but with Cara, he felt at ease. He was smitten by her dark eyes, soft brown hair, and a warm smile that revealed two even rows of white teeth. Apparently they both liked what they saw in each other, and they dated a couple of times afterward.

When Joseph's battalion packed up for the South Seas, they promised to write each other. Faithfully, during Joseph's twenty-seven months in the Pacific, they kept a steady stream of letters going. Joseph finally had a steady girlfriend. Cara's letters boosted his morale and gave him inner strength and resolve—something to fight for, he liked to think.

With his friends overseas, he would eagerly talk about "his girl" and show them snapshots she would send. Tom Brokaw, in his best selling *The Greatest Generation,* did not exaggerate in his telling of the role American women played in winning the war with their letters of love and devotion that bolstered the spirits and morale of their sweethearts. In the foxholes of the Pacific, scooped out of sand, coral, and mud, marines lived for the next reassuring letter from the home front, primarily the words of love from girlfriends and wives. Men who failed to receive expected letters became morose and dispirited.

On February 22, 1943, Joseph's outfit sailed out of San Diego aboard the USS *Lurline,* a former Matson Line cruise ship bound for New Zealand. At the international date line, Joseph endured the initiation by the ship's crew and became a shellback. After three boring weeks crossing the Pacific, the *Lurline* entered the picturesque harbor of Auckland. It was surrounded by green hills and neat streets of the city, which funneled towards the waterfront.

A New Zealand military band played the "Star Spangled Banner" followed by the "Beer Barrel Polka." With the Japanese knocking on the doorsteps of northern Australia, the natives were breathing easier with the arrival of the Yanks. A few private cars put-putted about, propelled by gas from charcoal burners mounted on the rear bumpers. Gasoline was a precious commodity. The unloading completed, the battalion was trucked to a camp near the village of Warkworth, some fifty miles away. The camp was a collection of wooden, two-man "turkey hutches," cramped but secure from the elements.

Warkworth, as with most of rural New Zealand, was in sheep country. All around, great herds of sheep were constantly driven from one pasture to another. One herder with a couple of border collies would control thousands of sheep with only an occasional shrill whistle signal to his dogs.

In making pasturage for the sheep, early settlers had denuded the land of forests. Where mature trees once stood, there were holes in the ground left when the stumps had rotted away. They were a constant source of sprained ankles and twisted knees during night training exercises. Almost as treacherous were the thickets of thorny gorse five or six feet in height. They were the primary vegetation on the hillsides, unsuitable even for hungry sheep and another hazard for the "snooping and pooping" exercises of the marines.

At the chow tables, the staple was mutton. The flavor of mutton permeated the grills and cooking pots so that no matter what variation the cooks attempted, there was always the persistent taste of sheep.

New Zealand's young men were off fighting with the Anzacs in North Africa, and the lonely girls flirted openly with the marines. While the 12th Regiment was holding a major exercise near the town of Whangerei, a contingent of Maori troops returned for home leaves. The Maori were Polynesians and the native inhabitants of New Zealand. Angered by the marines' intrusion on their women—intrusions that had been encouraged—gangs of Maori soldiers roamed the streets looking for marines to beat up. The situation got out of hand when the marines brought in their own reinforcements. Military police intervened, and the marines were herded back to their bivouacs. Liberty was curtailed for the rest of the maneuvers.

Following a landing exercise at Martin's Bay, a Hawaiian-style luau had been arranged for the troops of Easy Battery by the officers. The mess sergeant bought a dressed pig from a farmer, found some banana leaves, and set out for the beach with a detail of cooks. An ideal spot for the cooking pit was chosen where the sand was still wet from the previous tide. They built a fire of driftwood in the pit, wrapped the pig in the banana leaves, and placed it on the coals. After refilling the pit with wet sand they retired to a crate of New Zealand beer they'd brought along.

At noon the next day, the troops arrived in trucks hungry for roast pig. They found the mess sergeant and his men feverishly poking sticks in the sand. A high tide in the night had washed away all traces of the luau pit. Captain Benny Barnes, the battery commander, was growing angrier, and hungrier, by the minute. At last, someone hit pay dirt, and the pig was exhumed, perfectly cooked. Barnes broke out into one of his rare smiles.

It was during that maneuver in the boondocks of Whangerei that a radio message came in ordering Joseph to report to division headquarters the following morning to take the examination for warrant officer. He had forgotten about Major Bowser's recommendation at New River, and again protested that he did not want to be considered for the warrant rank. But a stern order from the battalion commander, Lieutenant Colonel Donald Weller, ended his objection.

Here he was, fifty miles from division headquarters at Camp Orfords in Manuera, wearing dirty utilities and badly in need of a shower and shave. If he was going to compete with other candidates, he wouldn't stand a chance.

"You will have a jeep with driver," he was told. "Go back to the base camp at Warkworth and have the rear echelon detail there heat up some water for a shower and shave. Get your greens on and proceed to division. Be there by 8:00 A.M. tomorrow."

By the time he and his driver had started, it was growing dark. It began to rain, and the jeep's electric wiper wasn't working. Luckily they were on a decent road and made fairly good time. Two hours later they reached camp, soaked in the open jeep by the driving rain. Joseph got the camp detail to fire up the boiler, and while they were doing that, he gave his greens a going over with an electric iron in his hut and shined his shoes. It was about 4:00 A.M. when, all cleaned up and shaven, they hit the road again for Manuera outside of Aukland. The rain had stopped.

Being unfamiliar with the area, they had to ask directions to division headquarters several times, and it was approaching 8:00 A.M., when he was to report for the examination. They passed a plant emitting a pungent cloud of white smoke. It made fertilizer from animal blood and bones. The odor gave Joseph a nauseous feeling on top of his queasy stomach. They got to the adjutant's office a few minutes early.

"Your outfit's in the field, isn't it?" the adjutant, a major, queried.

"Yes, sir," Joseph answered.

"We just notified you yesterday afternoon. How'd you make it here?"

"Drove all night, sir," Joseph said.

"Damn," the major said. "You look pretty sharp, except you probably could use some sleep."

After his misgivings about the promotion, Joseph was now determined to give it his best shot.

There were eight or ten other candidates, mostly grizzled NCOs. Joseph was the youngest of the group. He noted with satisfaction that the others, who had come straight from billets far more favorable than his pup tent in the boondocks, were not as sharp as he was. The candidates were interviewed by a colonel and then given a written examination. It was not much more than a literacy test and Joseph completed it in ten minutes. The colonel returned, thanked them for their interest, and dismissed them.

Joseph returned to his jeep and driver. Hell, he thought, now that the ordeal was over, they might was well relax and enjoy a little liberty. They drove to Aukland, checked into a hotel, and went to the dining room for a breakfast of steak and eggs. They slept most of the day, then took in a movie that evening. Afterward, they ate fish and chips and, in a pub, drank pints of dark, room-temperature New Zealand ale.

Joseph knew the battalion was due back soon from the field, so they returned to camp in Warkworth and waited. The next day Colonel Weller called him into his office.

"Congratulations," he said, handing Joseph his typewritten promotion to warrant officer.

His appointment would still need the signature of the secretary of the navy in Washington, but meantime, he could wear the bursting bomb insignia of a marine gunner and exercise his new rank.

He had to move to a hut in officers' country and sadly went back to the one he had shared with First Sergeant Gibbs to pack his things. He got his first salute from Gibbs and a bit of good-natured ribbing. Gibbs was a good old boy from the Tennessee mountains.

Apprehensively, Joseph wondered how the junior grade officers in the battalion would accept him. To his surprise, they were respectful and often deferred to him in conversations. They recognized that his warrant rank represented years of experiences and know-how they still lacked. He paid his dues in the officers' mess and was promptly voted a share of the bar stock: six bottles of Ballantines's Scotch, which he hated.

Officers' uniforms were not available in New Zealand, so he removed the chevrons from his green jacket and pinned on his warrant insignia. The uniform problem was academic, since both officers and enlisted wore combat fatigues, which the marines preferred to call "utilities," except when on liberty. Soon they would be leaving New Zealand for the combat zone to the north, and wool uniforms would be mothballed for the duration.

On June 30, 1943, Easy Battery was aboard the transport *Crescent City* bound for Guadalcanal. The ground fighting on the 'Canal had ceased in February, when the last of the ragged and starving remnants of the 17th Japanese Army had been evacuated. But the Japanese still controlled air bases to the north and regularly bombed the island. The Third Division would step up its jungle warfare training in preparation for the next assault on the Japanese-held Solomon Islands.

Author at age five on running board of family's Model-T Ford. His mother poses at the wheel but only drove once—broadsiding a cow.

Joseph at Marine Corps Base in San Diego, 1938. The cannons were relics of the Chinese Boxer Rebellion.

Joseph (right) and Scotty McGregor turn out for weekly parade in San Diego.

A Nissen hut in Iceland, July 1941. Troops of the First Marine Brigade (Provisional) lived in the huts for 9 months while guarding the island nation during Franklin D. Roosevelt's undeclared war on Adolf Hitler in the North Atlantic.

Author at right (front row) and NCOs of the 10th Marines prepare for parade honoring visiting Prime Minister Winston Churchill in Iceland, August 1941.

Marine NCOs in Iceland Oct. 1941. Author is in background, center.

Winston Churchill salutes colors while trooping the line of the First Marine Brigade in Iceland, 1941.

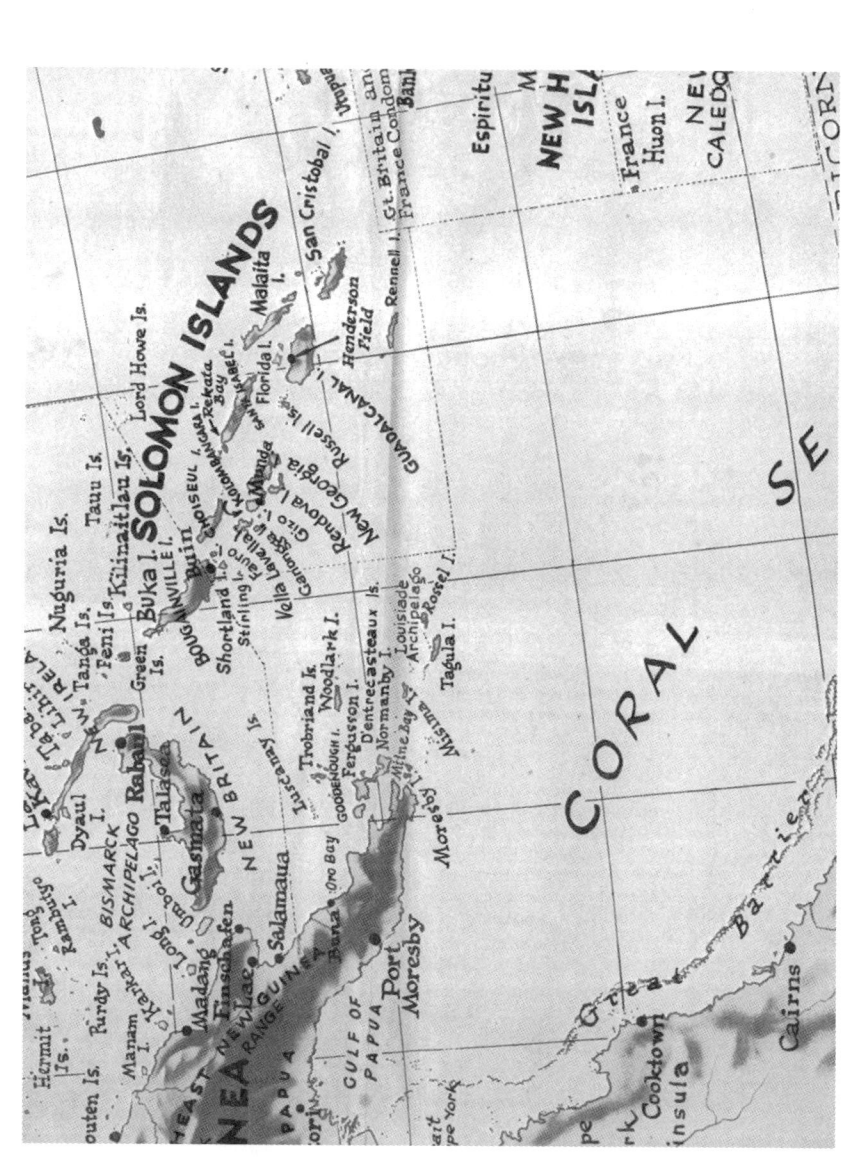

The South Pacific

Infantrymen of the 3rd Marine Division slog through a muddy trail on Bougainville, Solomon Islands in 1943.

Author on Guadalcanal, 1943. Next stop was Guam.

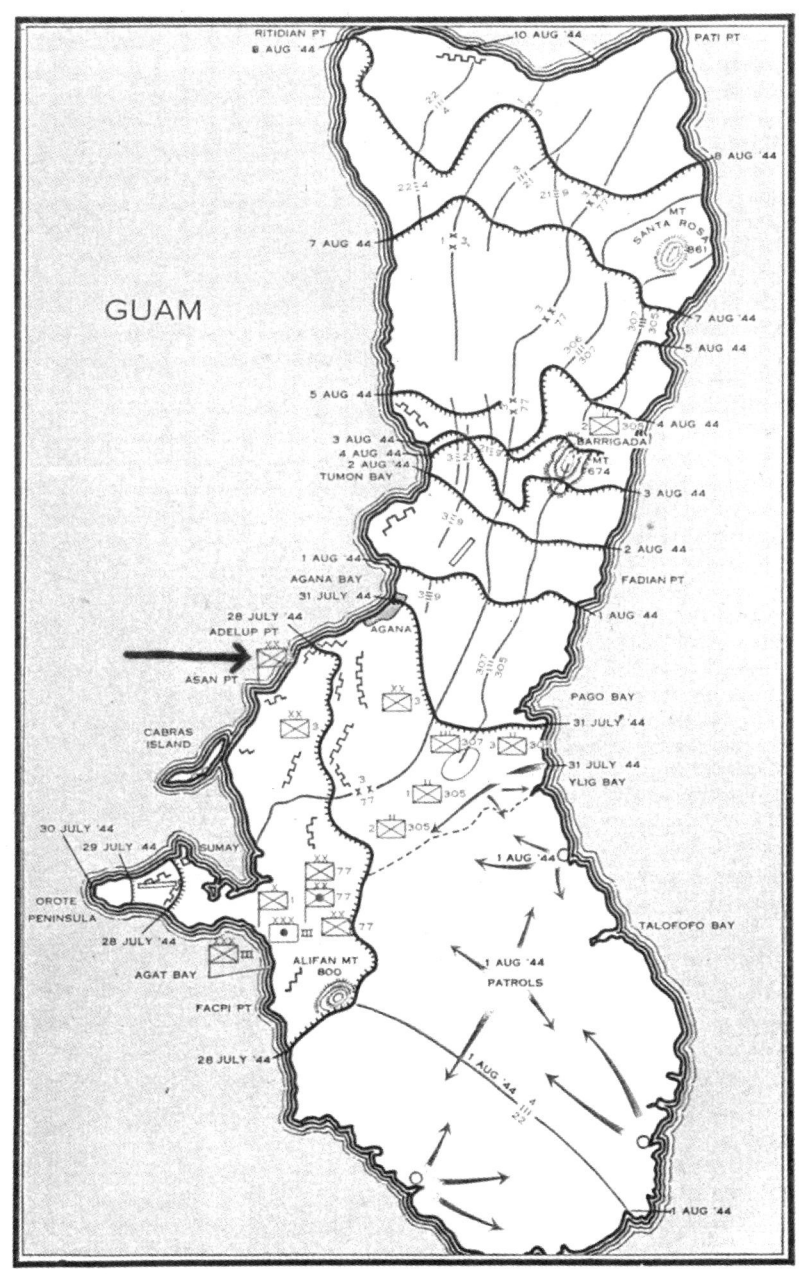

Situational map of Guam, July 1944. Arrow indicates landing beaches of the Third Marine Division.

The beachhead at Asan, Guam, July 1945.

Naval gunfire knocked out this 6-inch gun sighted in on Asan Beachhead, Guam, July 1944.

Assault troops advance across sandy terrace of Iwo Jima February 19, 1945. Mt. Surabachi is in the background.

Marines launch rockets from truck beds on Iwo Jima. The trucks would high-tail it after emptying their racks leaving the front line troops to suffer the Japanese counterfire.

A 75 mm pack howitzer on Iwo Jima. The crew has taken cover from Japanese fire.

Eight
Up the Pacific—1943

The *Crescent City* cruised up the placid Coral Sea and, after three days, dropped anchor off Tetere Beach on the north coast of Guadalcanal. All was tranquil on the island where Major General Archer Vandegrift's First Division had knocked off the Japanese after six months of savage fighting in America's first land offensive of the Pacific war. To the east between Guadalcanal and Savo Island was "the slot," a narrow passage to the graveyard of American cruisers and destroyers sent to the bottom by the cannonballing "Tokyo Express."

On the 'Canal, a gentle surf washed over inviting sandy beaches. Immediately inland were acres upon acres of the Lever Brothers coconut plantation. In rolling foothills beyond the coconut palms, a sea of kunai grass rippled in a sultry breeze before being swallowed by the dark jungle. Far in the interior, a range of mountains reared above a bank of gray-white clouds. Squawking flights of white cockatoos took wing above the jungle canopy.

The 12th Marines (artillery) landed administratively. That was the term used when no shooting was expected, as opposed to an assault landing. Just in case, the troops carried full packs with two days' field rations and live ammunition. There being no dock on the island, the equipment was wrestled from the holds of the ship by sweating working parties, hoisted into landing boats, and brought to dumps on the beach. Having come from the cool clime of the antipodes, the men tired quickly in the humid air.

Easy Battery marched to an open field and dug in. The night skies over Guadalcanal belonged to the Japanese, who sortied from several airfields in Rabaul and the northern Solomons. The target was usually Henderson Field or the phosphorescent wake of any ship that might be cruising in the darkness. Had they known a fresh division of hated marines had come ashore, the Third would surely have gotten its baptism of fire.

Their vehicles and howitzers having come ashore early the following morning, the battery moved through the coconut grove to a city of tents set up by an advance detail. The canvas camp under the canopy of palms would be the division's home base for nearly a year.

In film and print, the South Sea islands were portrayed as idyllic tropical paradises. Here, the brown-skinned beauties in grass skirts were nowhere to be seen. The dark skins of the Solomon Island natives exuded a bluish sheen, like the barrel of a new shotgun, and they bore the features of fierce aboriginals. It was believed that headhunting was still a practice among some tribes in the remote islands.

The newcomers would soon learn that just beyond the graceful coconut palms, sandy beaches, and languid lagoons lay an impenetrable, hostile jungle. Stinging mosquitoes were not only a nuisance but carriers of debilitating malaria and dengue fever. Leeches clung to skin and when pried off—the burning end of a cigarette being the preferred way—left ugly red welts that quickly festered into sores if not treated. Insects of every description crawled over exposed bodies, and the sweat-soaked heavy twill of the marine utilities chafed tender skins.

The equatorial sun bore down relentlessly and blistered exposed faces and limbs. Even the kunai grass was something to avoid. Its sharp blades could slash through exposed skin areas like a razor. The kunai vanished at the edge of the dark, towering wall of rain forest that shut off the sunlight. Thorny vines that reached for sunlight high among giant trees raked at anything that moved on the ground. Only with a machete could a man slash his way through the dense underbrush. At any time, a firm footing could give way to spongy ground where the mud sucked the shoes off one's feet if not tightly laced.

It was difficult to imagine anyone surviving for months in that harsh environment while ducking bullets, shells, and hand grenades from a hidden enemy, but that's what the First Marine Division had done. Not only had they defended themselves again and again against Japanese counterattacks, for a while they did it without any support from the U.S. Navy.

Three days after the unopposed landing on August 7, 1942, the amphibious fleet of Admiral Kelly Turner, with half of the division's equipment and supplies remaining in the holds of the transports, hoisted anchors and fled the area. On the previous night, Japanese Admiral Gunichi Mikawa's fast cruiser squadron had sunk five U.S. and Australian cruisers: *Astoria, Quincy, Chicago,* for the U.S., *Canberra* and *Australia* for the Aussies, and four destroyers. The amphibious transport fleet was not only vulnerable from enemy ships, but Japanese bombers were swarming down from the north. Cautious Rear Admiral Frank Fletcher had withdrawn his precious carrier task force to safer waters.

The marines were left to their own devices, short of ammunition, food, and equipment with the enemy yet to be engaged. Using captured Japanese equipment—their own bulldozers and graders resting in the holds of the fleeing navy transports—marine engineers finished building the airstrip that the Japs had begun. It was named Henderson Field, named after a marine pilot killed in the battle of Midway. A few fighter planes flew in from distant carriers to begin the build-up of the "Cactus Air Force." From captured enemy supply dumps, Vandegrift's troops augmented their meager supply of C-rations with Japanese rice, canned seaweed, and crab meat, occasionally washed down with beer and sake.

The Third Division settled in to a rigorous training routine in preparation for a thrust farther up the Solomons. Guadalcanal's jungle provided a realistic training ground in contrast to New Zealand's sheep country. Nightly visits by "Washing Machine Charlie" were routine, although the feminine "Betty" would have been a more appropriate nickname. It was U.S. military's designation of the two-engine bomber that was the mainstay of the Japanese bombardment force. The planes would arrive singly over the island just as the troops were going to sleep. A siren would wail through the coconut grove, and all hands would tumble into slit trenches alongside their tents. Overhead, the Jap planes would drone incessantly for hours, in a test of nerves, keeping everybody awake before letting loose their bombs. The popping of cartridges in the bomb bays, characteristic of Japanese bombers, meant the missiles were being released.

Then came the whistling noise of the fins—the louder the whistling, the flatter the marines made their bodies—and finally the crump crump of the missiles and the shaking of the earth from the concussions. There would be a collective sigh of relief when it became apparent that the bombs were intended for Henderson Field or supply dumps near Lunga Point and not for the coconut grove.

One night the marines were treated to a spectacular display of fireworks. Unknown to the Japs, a U.S. Air Force squadron of radar-equipped P-38 night fighters had been brought in. "Charlie" was going through his droning routine unaware that he was being tracked in the dark sky by a P-38 "Lightning." As seen from the ground 10,000 feet below, the P-38's .50-caliber tracers appeared as a fiery comet arching into the bomber. Instantly, Charlie was a bright fireball and then a red ember falling lazily into the sea. A hoarse cheer was heard through the coconut grove. After that, the night bombing raids of the Japs were rare. Since marine fighters on Henderson Field controlled the skies by day, Guadalcanal became a relatively safe area.

Storied battlegrounds of the First Division's epic struggle stirred Joseph's curiosity in his wanderings about the island. There were the rivers Ilu, Matanikau, Lunga, and Tenaru, and Merritt Edson's "Bloody Ridge" where the colonel's raiders repelled the last fanatical Japanese attempt to retake Henderson Field. At the Tenaru, the Japs learned the hard way that marines would not be the pushovers they had conquered in China, the Philippines, and Malaya.

Colonel Kiyanao Ichiki was the epitome of Japanese arrogance and contempt for America's fighting men. From Rabaul, his elite regiment had been landed to the east of the First Division and was expected to roll the marine defense perimeter back into the sea. At night, on the heels of a barrage of mortar fire and under ghoulish, green flares, the cocky Japs flung themselves into the marine defenses across a sand spit where the shallow river emptied into the sea.

Colonel Edwin Pollack's battalion was ready. A barrage of artillery and mortar fire rained down on the Japs. Antitank guns firing canister, combined with withering machine gun fire, mowed down the survivors who were crawling over the bodies of their fallen. When the carnage ended, 900 Japanese soldiers lay dead or dying, and Colonel Ichiki had committed hara-kiri. The myth of Japanese invincibility had been forever shattered. The First Marine Division had stopped the Japanese juggernaut in its tracks and set a standard for the conduct of the island war in the Pacific.

Meanwhile, Vice Admiral William F. "Bull" Halsey had taken command of the Navy in the South Pacific and, living up to his nickname, was determined to come to the aid of the marines on Guadalcanal. He sent more planes into Henderson Field and brought in ground reinforcements. Finally, with the situation "well in hand," the tattered remnants of the First Division were withdrawn for a much needed rest in Australia. They suffered from dysentery, malaria, dengue fever, malnutrition, and fungus infections. Some lacked the strength to crawl up cargo nets, and hardened sailors were moved to tears helping emaciated, hollow-eyed marines aboard the ships.

Slowly, the Third Division became acclimated to the jungle and equatorial heat. The infantry regiments waded into the dankness of the rain forests to sharpen their skills in patrolling, maneuvering, and live firing. The artillery men, on the other hand, conducted live firing into the open fields of kunai grass. Dense vegetation made it all but impossible for observers to spot explosions of .75-millimeter shells.

Life in the coconut grove became tolerable. Engineers punched holes in the earth and set up gasoline engines to suck up water for gang showers. Cool showers following days in the broiling sun did much for spirits. Idle time was occupied with rough-and-tumble volleyball games.

A typhoon drenched Guadalcanal, turning the camp into a lagoon. Seabags and equipment floated through the streets of the tent city.

The build-up of planes and troops continued in the Solomons. MacArthur and Nimitz had established their zones of attack: the Army general would continue leapfrogging northwestward across New Guinea in the direction of the Philippines; Nimitz, with Halsey leading the way, would punch straight up the Pacific. Landings were made on Vella Lavella, New Georgia, and Rendova, small Japanese-held islands to the north of Guadalcanal. At the north end of the Solomon chain was Bougainville, the largest of the archipelago. It was occupied by 40,000 Japs, supported by three airfields. The task of seizing a beachhead on Bougainville, only 270 miles from the powerful Japanese base of Rabaul was assigned to the Third Division.

Intensive planning began for the invasion, set for November 1, 1943. As ordnance officer and assistant battery executive officer, Joseph's responsibilities mainly involved the care and feeding of the howitzers.

For the Bougainville operation, he was assigned the duty of loading officer for an LST, a landing ship tank. Even with his experience with navy ships, Joseph had never seen an LST and had no idea what one looked like. His unfamiliarity was understandable, since they were new in the South Pacific theater.

As ordered, he reported to the G-4, the division supply and logistics officer, along with a dozen or so junior grade officers who would supervise the loading of other ships. He was given a diagram of his LST, along with a list of the cargo to be loaded. He also got a manila envelope containing little cardboard templates in the shape of the vehicles and other rolling stock to be loaded. The job was to fit the templates into a representation of the ship's tank deck, leaving room for several tons of ammunition, 200 or so drums of high octane aviation gasoline, crates of TNT and nitro starch to blow up caves and fortifications, and barbwire for the front lines. Studiously, as if solving a jigsaw puzzle, Joseph arranged his vehicles and cargo until every item on his manifest was in place, then he traced the outline of each template on the ship diagram with a pencil.

Now Joseph had to contact the units whose supplies and equipment would be carried on his LST and locate staging dumps on the beaches. It was an arduous job, bouncing in a jeep for miles along the dusty beach road from Tetere to Tassafaronga to confer with unit commanders.

By candlelight, the night before departure, he wrote letters to Cara and his family. He couldn't give any hint that he was going into combat. Then he set about packing his personal gear.

Into his knapsack went toilet articles and a small khaki-colored face towel, two sets of green skivvies, and two pairs of socks. He stuffed a spare set of utilities and K-rations for two days in his haversack. Included in each carton of K-rations were a couple of sheets of rough, brown toilet paper. The field rations made for sluggish bowels, which at some length and with enough abdominal pushing, produced a stool of dry turds. It was a joke with the troops that after a BM a whisk broom would have been more practical for the intended purpose than the toilet tissue.

Joseph rolled a blanket into his shelter half, bent it into a U-shape and strapped it to his pack. He now had a heavy marching order. He cleaned and oiled his .45 pistol and loaded three clips of ammunition. One he inserted in the weapon and the other two in the pouch of his cartridge belt. He oiled the blade of his K-bar knife and replaced it in its leather sheath. Wearily, he stretched out on his canvas folding cot with no mattress and dropped off to sleep. Before daybreak, he was awakened by the corporal of the guard. The vast encampment had not yet stirred, and the men were enjoying their last peaceful night of rest. Joseph loaded his gear on a jeep and headed for Lunga Point and a rendezvous with his LST.

The rising sun glittered off the waters of Iron Bottom Bay, silhouetting the distant island of Tulagi and a flotilla of ships riding at anchor in Sea Lark Channel. An odd-looking ship was heading for the beach. It was shaped like an oil tanker with the bridge and cabin perched on its after-end. It was his LST, with its bow doors open like a clam shell, exposing a cavernous tank deck inside the maw. It came aground thirty feet from the beach, abreast the rusting hulk of the beached Jap troopship *Kinryu Maru*. A steel ramp lowered by cables splashed into the surf. A seaman inside motioned, and Joseph came aboard.

The longest day of his military career had begun. He walked through the tank deck where his cargo would be loaded. The real thing had only a vague resemblance to the diagram he had worked with. Military planning seldom meets expectations, and this one didn't disappoint. Murphy's Law kicked in from the start. Vehicles that were to be loaded first were late in arriving. Truck loads of 155-millimeter projectiles went to the wrong ship. Vehicles broke down on the ramp, blocking the loading operation. A dump with two tons of barbwire for the 21st Marines couldn't be located.

By midafternoon, the situation began to improve and Joseph breathed easier as the tank deck began to fill with its combat load. All the while, the ship's skipper, a nervous lieutenant, kept badgering Joseph on the progress of loading and fretting about the arrival of the next tide, which would float them off the beach. Joseph surveyed his cargo. The vehicles were in neat rows, side by side. To protect against rough seas, steel cables were wrapped around bumpers and tightly fastened to grommets on the deck beneath. Against the bulkheads on the port and starboard sides along the length of the ship were rows of 55-gallon drums of aviation gasoline stacked two high. Planking was laid atop the drums upon which several tons of 155-millimeter projectiles and an undetermined number of cases of TNT and nitro starch were stacked. Nets were draped and tied around the loose cargo to hold it in place. Only the barbed wire was missing.

Joseph sent a sergeant with a jeep searching for the wire, but he returned with a negative report. Now the nervous captain had one eye on his watch and the other on the ramp slowly being flooded by the rising tide. Joseph was still hopeful a truck would show up with the wire, but just as it began to get dark, the captain ordered the ramp raised and the bow doors shut. With the screws of the LST reversed and churning up mud and sand, the LST slowly wriggled free, backed into the channel, and dropped anchor.

In the officers' wardroom Joseph ravished a tough piece of beef and a bowl of watery freezer ice cream, then found a bunk and wearily dropped off into a deep slumber.

A couple of hours later, he was roused from his sleep and confronted by a burly figure wearing the gold leaves of a major. He recognized Major Fissell, the executive officer of the infantry battalion whose barbed wire had been left behind. He wasn't buying Joseph's explanation that the wire had obviously not been placed in the right dump and couldn't be found.

"Mister," the major intoned in a threatening voice, "if that wire isn't on Bougainville when we need it, your ass is in for a court martial."

"If the wire had been placed where it was supposed to be, it would be on board," Joseph argued. "And if the captain will go back ashore, we'll get it on board if you'll tell us where it is," Joseph added, knowing the captain wasn't about to return to the beach.

In a huff, the major strode back to the Jacob's ladder on the top deck and climbed down into his waiting boat.

Hell, Joseph thought before dropping back to sleep, if we're lucky enough not to get blown out of the water by a torpedo before we get to Bougainville, a court martial won't be all that hard to take.

Joseph's LST did escape the torpedoes, but the *McKean*, a destroyer escort carrying troops wasn't so lucky. In the predawn hours at Empress Augusta Bay, a torpedo launched by a Jap plane hit the *McKean*. Sergeant Danny Fellows, an Iceland veteran and pal of Joseph's was aboard the ship. "I stood there on the rail with the ship sinking and thought, damn, this is it," Fellows told Joseph the next day.

Foremost in Danny's mind were the sharks. The waters around the Solomons were teeming with them. But jump he did and luckily was pulled aboard another ship, along with most of the men from the ill-fated *McKean,* which quickly sank. Thirty-eight men were missing. No telling how many were victims of sharks.

Bougainville, about twice the size of Guadalcanal, was but 210 miles east of Rabaul, placing the Japanese stronghold within easy range of fighter planes. Likewise, Bougainville was just as vulnerable from Japanese fighters. With a fighter strip in place, the U.S. forces could neutralize Rabaul and continue to attack the Japs up the Central Pacific. However, seizing Bougainville and building an airstrip was not going to be easy. Impenetrable jungles, mangrove swamps, torrential rains, and an active volcano had to be dealt with, not to mention some 40,000 Japs. The good news was that most of them were on the opposite side of the island, separated by mountains and jungle with poor trails to cross over.

On November 1, 1943, the Ninth and Third Regiments, each accompanied by a raider battalion, landed abreast on Cape Torokina. The Third encountered the stiffest opposition and took heavy losses before subduing some 300 Japs in pill boxes on the beach.

Joseph's LST was directed to land and unload on the tiny island of Puruata, just off the tip of Torokina. The main landing beaches were already congested, but Puruata itself was a chaos of supplies and equipment, stacked haphazardly among bomb craters. There were spools of barbwire piled into a small mountain, and Joseph wondered if some of it belonged to Major Fissell's battalion and had been hijacked by another ship. The vehicles came off first and were parked willy-nilly among the piles of rations and ammunition. They would have to be boated to the main island in vehicle landing crafts. Not my problem, Joseph thought. Jap planes had pounded the island hours before, and the shore party commander was in a frenzy. Joseph's skipper was no less nervous. He wanted his ship off the beach before the next raid. He stomped around impatiently, trying to hurry the unloading. Joseph quietly urged his men to hurry the task, but they were near exhaustion from the tropical heat.

About two hours had gone by, and only the gasoline drums remained aboard. The antsy skipper had lost his nerve. "I'm pulling out now," he shouted to Joseph and the beach master. "I'll have my crew push the drums off the bow, and your men can get them when they drift ashore." With that, he ordered Joseph's men off and began retracting.

Some fifty yards out, the drums began splashing off the bow. But the current was moving offshore and carrying the drums out to sea. After a while, the drums were only specks bobbing up and down and moving toward Rabaul and the setting sun.

Later in the afternoon, a Jap cruiser force had been detected leaving Rabaul and moving toward Empress Augusta Bay. Facing a fanatic enemy in the jungle while being pasted with 5- and 6-inch naval shells from the sea was not a pleasant prospect for the Third Division. Like the cavalry riding in at the last moment came Rear Admiral Arleigh "30-knot" Burke and his own cruiser and destroyer force. When the thundering naval battle far out at sea had ended, Burke's ships had sunk a Jap cruiser and four destroyers. The beachhead was safe from the sea, and the marines proceeded to consolidate their tenuous perimeter.

Joseph herded his men aboard a landing boat hauling cargo to the main island. It was a trip of barely five minutes. The beach at Torokina was a tangle of decapitated palms and banyans and plowed up with shell holes. Dead Japanese soldiers were yet to be buried. Past the beach, they slogged through a fetid swamp and found the artillery battalion emplaced in a clearing on dry ground some 300 yards inland. The howitzers were already blazing away at unseen targets. Joseph resumed his duties with the battery. Unknown to him at the time, a reinforced company patrol of the 21st Marines had been ambushed along the Numa-Numa trail a mile or so inland, and Major Fissell had been killed.

With the darkness came the bombers from Rabaul and Kieta on the opposite side of the island. The searchlights of a defense battalion pierced the skies with probing fingers of light beams. A bomber caught in the glaring light, resembled a moth, except that a moth flies into the light, whereas the planes twisted evasively to escape it. A battery of 90-millimeter antiaircraft guns roared into action, their shells exploding in fireballs thousands of feet high. The bombs came crashing down adding to the din, and the soft earth quivered like Jello.

The howitzers had ceased firing so as to not give away the artillery positions with muzzle flashes and everyone was flattened in slit trenches. Recalling Ernie Pyle's memorable words, Joseph was certain there were no atheists in the foxholes of Easy Battery that night. The first light of morning revealed numerous bomb craters. A platoon of pioneers bivouacked nearby had several men killed, but the battery had survived its first battle unscathed.

That first week, the bombers came nightly. Luckily, their aim was bad, apparently from having to seek higher altitudes to avoid the antiaircraft fire. In one raid, a 500-pound bomb landed on Dog Battery, immediately adjacent, killing Gunnery Sergeant Statlander, a contemporary and friend of Joseph's when he was a gunnery sergeant himself. The battalion medical officer wandered about the stricken area in the darkness calling out Statlander's name. It turned out the poor doctor had lost it and would soon be evacuated as a neurosis case.

On the front lines, the fighting was a series of isolated, but deadly, battles as the Japanese probed and maneuvered trying to find weaknesses to exploit in the perimeter. Two battalions of Nips were landed from four destroyers near the Koromokina River. A vigorous response by the 9th Marines on the left flank, combined with devastating artillery and air attacks, completely broke up the Japanese force, which suffered over 500 men killed.

Elsewhere on the perimeter, marines slowly pushed their way through stinking, black mud and slimy swamps. Daily torrents of rain made trails impassable. Trucks and jeeps carrying rations, ammunition, and water wallowed from side to side and frequently were burrowed up to their axles. The marines were fighting under the worst conditions of any campaign in the war thus far. They slogged on until reaching higher ground and a series of densely forested ridges. Forward observers for the artillery often had to climb trees to direct fire on the Japs.

A couple of weeks into the campaign, a large Japanese force was detected where two forks of the Piva River converged. The 12th marines, augmented by an army artillery battalion from the 37th

Division, delivered the heaviest concentration of any action in the Pacific thus far. Tons of shells fell on the Jap positions, spraying hot steel that shredded trees and churned up the ground. The Japs retreated, leaving hundreds of their dead. It was the last major threat to the beachhead.

We have fought in every clime and place
Where we could take a gun

In the Pacific the pack howitzer was the epitome of that gun.

The 75s, smallest of the artillery in the battle, were affectionately nicknamed "peashooters" by their own crews. They fired a twenty-four-pound shell a little less than three inches in diameter. A high-explosive shell had an effective killing radius of thirty yards. It dug a crater sixty inches in diameter and a yard deep. Fuses could be set at "quick" for bursts at ground level or "delay" to penetrate fortifications. Some rounds had fuses with a time ring graduated in seconds. Settings could be made for the shell to burst several feet above the ground, spraying open trenches and foxholes. A battery of four howitzers sited in a parallel sheaf covered a space one hundred and twenty yards wide. It could "walk" its barrage by increments of fifty or more yards backward and forward.

What they lacked in size was made up by their rapid rate of fire, twenty-two rounds per minute. They could launch their projectiles to a maximum range of nine thousand yards or, by elevating their snubby muzzles, arch shells into steep trajectories to reach defiladed positions as close as one-thousand yards. There were four to a battery, twelve to a battalion. With techniques developed by the army at the artillery school in Fort Sill, Oklahoma, a battalion could instantly mass the fire of its three batteries on a single target. Likewise, the artillery regiment could concentrate the fire of its four battalions, forty-eight guns, with extreme accuracy.

On Bougainville, maximum use was made of artillery support for the infantry. Of the many hundreds of Japanese killed in the campaign, it was estimated that at least half died from artillery fire. The Japanese, on the other hand, never bunched their artillery batteries. Their guns were scattered and fired independently, probably to reduce the chances of being wiped out.

One night the Japs attacked the 21st Marine sector, and Joseph's battalion rained a torrent of high explosive shells on the attackers. As Easy Battery's gunners were firing at the maximum rate, the section chief on the number-four piece reported over the intercom to the executive officer that his gun was behaving strangely. Joseph ran to the gun position and learned from the section chief that the barrel and lower sleigh were not returning to the forward position after recoiling. The gun had been reloaded, but Joseph called it out of action to avoid the possibility of serious damage. As it was not advisable to unload a hot projectile, Joseph went to work on the loaded gun.

He reasoned that the hydraulic oil in the mechanism had overheated and expanded from continuous firing. The remedy was to drain some of the oil by "bleeding" to relieve the pressure. Using a special wrench while the section chief held a flashlight, Joseph began loosening the plug, just enough to allow a trickle of oil to escape. At that moment, with his head perilously close to the muzzle, the gun fired. The man pulling the lanyard wore a set of headphones and had been dozing off. When he heard the executive officer shout "fire" to the other guns, he instinctively jerked the lanyard, forgetting that his gun had been declared out of action.

Joseph felt the hot muzzle flash inches from his head and the explosion deafened his ears. Partially unscrewed, the recoil plug blew out, spraying Joseph in the face with hot oil. Coming to and spitting recoil oil, he approached the man still holding the lanyard on the smoking gun, grabbed his wire and ripped off his headphone, all but taking his ears with it and wishing he had.

"Now, maybe you can hear better, idiot," he screamed at the sulking crewman. The ringing in his Joseph's right ear had begun, and he would learn to live with it the rest of his life. Tinnitus, doctors called it.

The naval construction battalion, those industrious Seabees, soon had an airstrip in commission, built of compacted coral and overlaid with interlocking strips of steel planking called Marston matting. One day Joseph walked to the new strip to watch the fighters take off.

Several pilots were sitting in the shade of a canvas fly tied to coconut trees, and Joseph recognized one of them. Private Nystrom, a Minnesota lad from his old 7th Platoon in boot camp, was now

Lieutenant Nystrom of Major "Pappy" Boyington's Black Sheep Squadron. They chatted about old times until Nystrom was called to the flight line. Joseph watched admiringly as Nystrom eased his thick body into the cockpit of a Corsair, gave a thumbs up signal and cranked shut his plexiglass cockpit canopy. His fighter joined a line of planes waiting to take off and soon he was roaring off for the skies over Rabaul.

Life in the artillery positions settled into one boring day after another. Field galleys had been set up, and the troops returned to their Guadalcanal fare: powdered eggs, dehydrated potatoes, Spam, and canned beef. At most meals, the beverage was hot coffee or reconstituted juice made from powdered citrus and served at Bougainville temperature. Appropriately, it was called battery acid. Always stationed at the end of the chow line was the battery's navy corpsman with a bottle of atabrine pills. The pills effectively warded off malaria carried by the anopheles mosquito, but they turned skins the color of jaundice, and the men hated taking them.

The division bakery was set up, and fresh bread was available. Thanksgiving came, and Bull Halsey's navy saw to it that the marines got a holiday meal of turkey. It was an example of the lengths caring commanders would go to shore up morale. Every unit got its ration of frozen, but rapidly thawing birds. Jeeps and trucks sloshed their way to the front lines, bringing hot containers of roast turkey, mashed potatoes and gravy, fresh rolls and pies. Some front-line troops on outposts nowhere near cooking ranges roasted their birds over campfires or boiled them in empty food tins.

Perhaps it was a coincidence, but there was a bountiful mail bag that day. There were three overdue letters from Cara and one from Lake Tarsa. Joseph found a shady spot under a banyan to digest his holiday meal and enjoy his mail. Cara had left her classroom job at Brawley for a better teaching job in Oceanside.

The men were swabbing the bores of the howitzers and tidying up around the gun pits one day, when came the sound of a Ford tractor in the sky. There suddenly appeared, skirting the treetops, an old bi-wing, single-engine Japanese scout plane, so low that the surprised expressions on the faces of the pilot and tail gunner in their open cockpits could be plainly seen. They were the only live Japs Joseph saw on Bougainville.

Midway over the battery position, the gunner in his rear open cockpit swiveled his machine gun and cut loose. Bullets splattered all around, and men dove for cover and fumbled for rifles. Joseph managed to jerk off a couple of rounds from his .45, but the intruder was already out of range and disappearing beyond the canopy of trees.

"Anybody hit?" Joseph called out. No answer. Then Corporal Salvaggio piped in. "The bastard hit my ax handle and split it."

Axes were vital tools around the guns, used to pound stakes for tents and camouflage nets and to cut down shrubs in the line of fire. To Joseph's chagrin the battery exec and his gunnery sergeant had allowed, and even tacitly encouraged, gun loaders to pound balky projectiles home with the end of an ax handle. Jams would occur when gummy deposits of gunpowder obstructed a clean entry of rounds into the chamber. The correct procedure was to push the projectile and brass powder casing back out with a bore staff from the muzzle end and then swab the chamber and barrel clean. A brass, bell-shaped device screwed to the end of a staff would fit around the fuse like a cup and on the shoulders of the projectile. A push on the staff by one or two men would force the shell safely out the breach. But young lieutenants dreaded the taunts of the S-3 (operations officer) over the field telephone in the battalion fire direction center who didn't want to hear about their gun problems.

At the battery a typical scenario would go:

"Sergeant Moreman on number three, sir. We've got a jam."

Executive officer: "Hurry it up,"

Bap, bap, bap would go the ax handle.

"Number three clear, sir."

"Fire when ready."

Predictably, the practice ended when a loader's ax handle struck the primer of a partially loaded shell casing. The brass casing, containing four charges of gunpowder, detonated externally, taking off all the fingers of the man's hand.

Joseph had noticed men follow a trail into the jungle and emerge carrying their canteen cups upright. He followed the trail until he came to a Lister bag, a rubber water container, hanging from a tree. Lifting the lid he peered inside at a sour-smelling brew of fermented raisins and sugar. Bug juice, the troops called it, and from the smell, it must have produced a good alcohol buzz. Relishing the role of a revenuer, he drained the bag, cut it loose from the tree, and had it cleaned and returned to its intended purpose.

In his shelter half under trees, Joseph slept on a single blanket on the ground with a poncho under it. One end of the pup tent was left open for ventilation, and he slept with his head out until the rain came. One night he kept hearing a rustling noise in the tree branches above and was on the verge of drawing a bead on what was undoubtedly a Jap in the tree. On closer observation, it turned out to be a small animal that closely resembled an Australian koala bear. Probably a banana bear, some "expert" ventured the next day.

The troops were lining up for chow early one morning, when the ground suddenly began shaking violently and the trees swayed as in a typhoon. Mount Bagano, an active volcano in the interior, was erupting. Joseph was knocked to the ground. Feeling foolish, he got up only to get knocked down a second time, so he stayed on the ground until the tremors had stopped. Visible in the distance, Begand was blowing out clouds of white steam. Joseph had experienced tremors in California, but nothing of this magnitude.

When they finished the airstrip, the Seabees began building a road three miles long from the beach through jungle and swamps to the front line supply dumps. With millions of cubic yards of coral, they built a smooth road bed with a crown five feet high that would have been the envy of any Stateside department of transportation project. The Jungle Highway they named it. The Japs were observing the project from their treetop OPs and siting their guns on stretches of the road that passed through exposed areas. As soon as the six-bys and jeeps began using the new road, they opened fire. By observing the clouds of dust they could judge closely the approach of vehicles into open areas where their guns were zeroed in. Likewise, drivers knew what they were in for, so it became a cat-and-mouse game. They'd wait for their cloud of dust to settle then push the pedal to the metal and try to outrun the incoming shells.

Joseph was at the wheel of a jeep returning from a conference at the battalion CP with three lieutenants as passengers. He slowed down as they approached a curve in an open stretch of the road where the Japs did most of their shelling, then picked up speed to make a run for it. At the same time, an oncoming six-by-six truck was barreling at full speed and using most of the road. A round landed just behind the truck, and it spurred him on directly into the path of Joseph's jeep.

Caught in the what-if dilemma of meeting an oncoming car head-on or leaving the road, Joseph, at the last instant, veered sharply right. His wheels spun in the loose coral at the edge of the embankment, and the jeep hurtled through the air, flinging lieutenants in all directions. Hanging onto the steering wheel, Joseph saw the jeep roll over him. He was nearer to death than he had been from the Japanese bombs. As the jeep was coming to rest sideways on the driver's side, he planted a hand on the ground and felt his elbow give.

But for a few bruises, none of the three lieutenants was seriously hurt. Joseph didn't know it, but his arm was broken at the elbow. Back at the battery position, the corpsman gave him a couple of APCs, and he spent a sleepless night in pain. The next morning, the battalion medical officer gave him an injection of morphine and placed the arm in a sling. Ignoring Joseph's objections, the doctor ordered him evacuated to the mobile hospital at Guadalcanal. "You're no good around here with one arm," he said.

Amid stretchers in orderly rows that rested men in blood-soaked bandages, Joseph waited to board a DC-3 cargo plane. An officious navy junior grade lieutenant walked about with a clipboard, making notes and giving orders. Many years later, Joseph would read about a presidential candidate who, as a young naval officer named Richard Nixon, had been in charge of evacuating wounded men from Bougainville. He had been too drugged from morphine to remember clearly, but Joseph always believed it was Nixon who directed the loading of the plane. Feeling out of place with a sling that was unbloodied and an injury not directly from a Japanese shell, he took a seat on a canvas bench against the buklhead and awaited the first plane ride of his life.

Nine
Crossroads of the Pacific—1943–1944

The Douglas DC-3 bounced and dipped over the Marston matting, left the ground near the end of the runway, and cleared the coconut trees on the beach. It climbed laboriously while turning southward and, in a few minutes, reached its cruising altitude. Joseph studied the blank faces of the walking wounded in the seats opposite his. Those in the litters strapped to the fuselage two-deep stared at the ceiling. Two corpsmen wandered about, checking straps on the litters and adjusting IV bottles. They were young kids, these grunts, and Joseph suddenly was engulfed in a wave of compassion. A few seemed to be barely hanging on. He said a silent prayer. He wanted to talk to his neighbor who also carried an arm in a sling but would have had to shout above the roar of the engines, so he gave up the idea. Still drugged from the morphine the doc had given him, he dozed off and on.

When he awakened, he half-turned to the window on his left to view an unforgettable aerial postcard. They were flying low over small islands in the Vella Lavella and Kolombangara group in the central Solomons. Emerald jungles were clasped by bands of platinum beaches that greeted the pale green waters of coral lagoons. The green hues blended to turquoise farther out and the turquoise finally melded into the cobalt blue of the deep sea.

He decided the fly boys had it pretty good. Their view of the islands had it all over the ground troopers with their noses mired in muck. When the airman returned from a mission, assuming he did, it was to an ice machine, hot chow, and a shower.

Joseph's daydreaming literally returned to earth as the DC-3 circled Henderson Field once and dropped into the sticky, humid air of Guadalcanal. Navy ambulances loaded the litters for the short drive to the mobile hospital. The wounded would have their filthy utilities cut away and their bodies cleansed with alcohol sponges. Joseph mounted an open truck with the walking wounded.

The field hospital was a rambling, prefabricated structure of plywood and corrugated metal. Joseph was assigned to one of the steel beds neatly made up with clean sheets, white wool blanket, and pale-blue navy bedcover. The ward was airy, with screened-in plywood awnings opened all around. He took a hot shower and sheepishly put on the pajamas laid out on his bed. With only a broken arm, he didn't feel at all like a patient.

However, the navy doctors had other ideas. Judging from their questions and entries in their logs, he might have been an amputee. They placed his arm in a cast and gave him a couple of sleeping pills. He didn't need them. Gunner Revels, late of the Third Regiment, had the bed next to his. He claimed headaches from having been too close to the friendly fire of an artillery battery while on patrol in enemy territory. His patrol had taken cover near a dead tree, which turned out to be an artillery checkpoint. His story was repeated each time a new doctor came on duty. Joseph had heard it so often he could help fill in details Revels omitted. The doctors, fresh from the States and dealing with their first combat casualties, were riveted.

One day, who should come padding by in a hospital gown, but Captain Clem Newbold, Joseph's old battery commander in New River and of late the C.O. of Fox Battery. Newbold had a bad case of asthma that acted up with the approach of a doctor or corpsman. His breath would become wheezy and labored. One night he had an attack so severe, he was given a shot. He was definitely ticketed for Stateside evacuation.

Joseph had figured he'd be sent back to Bougainville in a week or so. To his surprise, and disappointment, he was told he would be sent farther back, to Noumea in New Caledonia. They needed the beds in the field hospital.

The trip to New Caledonia was by ship and took two days. An island between Australia and Fiji, it was about the size of New Jersey. A French possession, it was valued for its mineral deposits, primarily nickel. It was also a penal colony. *Liberers,* paroled prisoners exiled for life on the island, roamed the streets like lost souls.

Noumea, the capital and major port, was the headquarters of the navy in the South Pacific as well as a major supply depot for the army and air force. At the crossroads of the South Pacific, ships and planes supporting the war converged on the island. MOB 8, the navy's mobile hospital, was a rambling wooden structure on the outskirts of town. Orange poincianas blossomed on the grounds above flaming hibiscus bushes. There was a veranda on two sides, where patients played chess and cards or just lazed the time away. Joseph was assigned to an individual room. Early each morning, everyone had to be in his room for "sick call."

Still not feeling like a patient, Joseph sat on a stool in his room waiting for the doctor. A prim, blond nurse with a strikingly fair complexion came in. She wore the insignia of a lieutenant junior grade on the collar of her starched white uniform.

"You're supposed to be in bed," she snapped.

"I was, but I got dressed and went to breakfast," Joseph answered.

She stuck a thermometer in his mouth, felt his pulse, and took his blood pressure. Joseph gazed blankly straight ahead, waiting for the completion of his "sick call." When he turned to her, he was caught in a pair of blue eyes staring intently at him. She was pretty in a way, but devoid of any form of expression. He squirmed and thought, *Damn, is there something really wrong with me?* She blushed, as did Joseph, but she spoke not a word, just kept on staring. Uneasy and annoyed, Joseph wanted to say something to break the awkwardness, but couldn't think of anything to say. Finally, she departed, leaving Joseph to wonder if he looked like some kind of freak. Or perhaps she had a problem. Each morning the routine was the same: The thermometer, pulse count, blood pressure, and cold stare.

Joseph knew her real name but preferred to think of her as "Nurse Blanche," a fitting appellation for her delicate blond features. There probably weren't a half dozen words exchanged between the two in all her visits.

Lieutenant Hensel occupied the room next door. A former tent mate on Guadalcanal, Hensel had a severe case of kidney stones that flared up while he was on detached duty as a naval gunfire spotter in a diversionary attack in the Russell Islands. Atabrine was the suspected cause.

The poor guy would groan in agony as doctors coaxed the stones to exit via his urethra. "I know what it's like for a woman to give birth," he would comment after a session. When Joseph mentioned Nurse Blanche, Hensel just shrugged. "Oh, her," was his only comment.

After a while, Joseph was allowed to leave the hospital for several hours each day. He bummed a ride to the army supply depot and bought some new khakis. He and Gunner Revels, who was awaiting evacuation to the States, toured the souvenir shops looking for gifts. Most of the shops were run by Tonkinese merchants from French Indochina. The choices were limited, but he found a mother-of-pearl bracelet and a teakwood jewel box for Cara.

The navy had an officer's bar in town, said, believably, to be the longest in the Pacific. At all hours of the day or night, it was packed with officers going to and from combat areas. It was one continuous happy hour. For a dime, one got a small highball glass of crushed ice with a shot of rum, whiskey, or gin and a splash of Coke or Seven Up. Joseph drank rum and Coke. After a couple of weeks, the doctors had cut off his cast and given him a six-pound weight on the end of a cord to carry around by his left hand. It was to keep his arm straight and prevent atrophy. With a foot on the rail and the dumb weight hanging from his hand, Joseph was the butt of friendly jokes. Imbibers, standing three-deep, told stories about the war and their adventures in little known islands.

Aviators laughed about faking engine troubles and making emergency landings in remote islands where the women were not bad to look at. Had Joseph been so inclined—and he forever regretted that he was not—he could have filled a notebook with yarns that would have made up his own tales of the South Pacific. One evening, Joseph was introduced to a visiting dignitary standing next to him: Jim Crowley, halfback of the immortal Four Horsemen of Notre Dame. Paunchy and in his mid-forties, Crowley was a delightful and congenial personality. Joseph was reminded of the memorable lead Grantland Rice had written of the Notre Dame-Army game of 1924:

"Outlined against a blue-gray October sky, the Four Horsemen rode again . . . " The old horseman was touring the Pacific with a group of famous athletes, including Jack Dempsey, entertaining troops and doing their bit for morale.

In a courtyard behind the bar, a French chef grilled ground beef patties and served them on French rolls. *Hamburgeurs,* he would call out. Joseph and Newbold were lured by the aroma of the cooking meat. It wasn't bad, especially after all the Spam and canned beef they had consumed, but the rolls were like shoe leather. They chewed and chewed until their mouths were sore, finally discarding the bread and eating only the meat. They decided the French had a lot to learn about making good American-style "hamburgeurs."

After a month in MOB 8, the doctors relieved Joseph of his dumb weight and released him to a transient camp to await reassignment. He was heartened at the prospects of returning to his old battery, which was now back on the 'Canal. But things moved at a snail's pace in the rear area, and Joseph had to wait for an appearance before a survey board, which would decide his fate.

He palled around with two young doctors fresh from the States and took hikes with them in the countryside. One excursion took them by a small Catholic church set in a grove of coconut and breadfruit trees. Atop its whitewashed clay walls sat a small Norman bell tower, which clanged like a cow bell at the approach of Sunday service. They chatted with some of the smiling natives in their Sunday best as they filed into the church. They spoke a pidgin English with a French accent, and were much more sociable than the Solomon Islanders.

On another walk, they found a fast-moving, tree-lined stream where women were beating their laundry against the rocks. They proceeded a ways upstream to a deep pool, stripped down and plunged into the cool, clear water. Then they sunbathed on boulders worn smooth by the running water until they were dry enough to dress. Joseph had put the war out of his mind until the doctors turned from discussing their recent internships at Bethesda and resumed questioning him about life in combat areas.

One day as they were returning to camp from the beach, they passed a two-story pastel pink house. Wrapped around the building in at least two loops was a line of army GIs waiting in the broiling sun for their turn in the whorehouse. It was regulated by the army. The doctors made jokes about their army counterparts whose wartime duties were to inspect the women for VD.

Another Frenchman ran a casino from his colonial chateau in the foothills, for officers only. In an expansive upstairs room, probably built as a salon but stripped of furnishings, he had two baize-covered pool tables where high-stakes crap games prevailed. Officers lined up two-deep with fists of ten- and twenty-dollar bills shouting for their combinations on the dice. Booze flowed from a corner bar, and most of the players were feeling no pain.

One night there was a commotion and temporary stoppage of play. A navy commander was reading the riot act to a young ensign and flashing an ID card in his face. "Naval intelligence," he informed the ensign. "See you in my office in the morning at COMSOPAC." The ensign had been preying on the most inebriated players by placing side bets with them and scooping up the money, regardless of the outcome of the roll. Joseph wondered what interest naval intelligence would have in a crap game, until it occurred to him that civilian spies might have been present and military secrets would be easy to come by, given the atmosphere and state of mind of the players.

Finally, Joseph was summoned before the survey board. Four doctors sat at a table, one holding Joseph's medical record. He recognized another as his former battalion surgeon, the one who had been evacuated with neurosis after a bombing raid on Bougainville.

He answered a series of perfunctory questions about his health and attitude and was declared fit to return to duty on the first available transportation. That was aboard a merchant marine ship newly arrived from San Francisco. Joseph was assigned a cabin below decks with a navy chaplain, a Protestant and a jolly fellow in his middle age. There was a handful of other officer passengers. While still at dockside, the temperature in the cabin was warm, but tolerable for the tropics. But once underway, it became unbearably hot. Joseph and the chaplain took cold salt water showers and then hit the sack, hoping to fall asleep before the heat got to them. It didn't work. They went topside, only to be run off by the deck watch and told to remain below.

"Don't you know we're in a war zone?" the deck watch said.

"No kidding," Joseph muttered.

At breakfast the following morning, they complained about the heat to the first mate.

"We're in the tropics, you know" was his reply.

The passengers were drinking coffee in the wardroom the day of arrival at Guadalcanal when the mate walked in.

"Sorry about the heat down below, gentlemen." he said. "It was cold when we left San Francisco, and we had the steam running in the vents. Engine room forgot to turn it off when we got into the tropics."

"Bastards," Joseph said aloud. He had no respect for the civilian seamen who treated passengers as so much cargo. They were drawing fat paychecks, and their ship owners were getting rich off the war.

Easy Battery was in its same camp in the coconut grove. Joseph dropped his Valopac on an empty cot in a tent with Lieutenant Brooks, Friday, and Millsaps. Captain Jim Leffers, the battery commander welcomed him back. He and Leffers had become close friends, and Leffers confided more in Joseph than with the other junior officers. Leffers poured drinks from a bottle of scotch into canteen cups, lit a cigarette, and settled back to hear Joseph's report of life in the rear.

"We won't be here much longer," Leffers said, tilting the aluminum cup to his lips. "They're already making plans in regiment."

The war had moved northward into the Central Pacific. The 2nd and 4th Marine Divisions had concluded the conquests of the Marshall and Gilbert Islands.

The talk was all about Tarawa, the toughest nut to crack. The 2nd Division paid for its capture with a frightful cost of lives. More than 1,000 men died, including 57 officers and 2,300 wounded, in only 76 hours to capture an atoll the size of Central Park.

"Tarawa was a mistake," Marine General Holland "Howling Mad" Smith wrote in hindsight. He had opposed the operation but was overruled by the admirals, who boasted that after the "softening up" bombardment, the marines would walk in unopposed.

"It looks like we're going to Kavieng," Leffers said in a lowered voice. It was not a secret, Joseph having heard of it in Noumea.

Kavieng was a settlement on the northern end of New Ireland, a mere 150 miles from the Japanese air and naval base at Rabaul. The rumors soon became official, and preparations began. An Australian coast watcher who was familiar with New Ireland was brought in to give a briefing on the topography. He was one of several intrepid Aussies who had lived on the islands as government officials or commercial entrepreneurs before the war. Protected by loyal natives, they hid in the hills and radioed reports of Japanese ship and air movements. The island, he droned on in his nasal Aussie twang, was solid coral and fresh water would be hard to come by. It would also be hard to dig in.

A marine colonel from the division G-2 staff followed with a generalized plan of the attack. Landing beaches around the harbor were limited, and one assault unit would have to seize a pier. In a departure from the marine doctrine of amphibious warfare, the artillery regiment would land ahead of the infantry with battalions on four small offshore islands to support the main assault the following day.

It became apparent that the risk factors outweighed the benefits, and the navy brass was loath to repeat the tragedy of Tarawa, which still resonated with shock and outrage on the home front. At the very last, with ship loading already under way, the navy decided to bypass Kavieng and let it wither on the vine. Instead, the next objective would be the Mariana Islands with landings at Saipan, Tinian, and Guam.

Leffers, who had a way with women, had made contact with navy nurses in the field hospital. He got Colonel Donald Weller's ear and convinced the battalion commander that it would boost morale to have some nurses as guests for dinner. He was certain they would accept an invitation.

Negotiations completed, Leffers commandeered a carry-all van from regiment, and with Joseph riding shotgun, they were off to fetch the nurses. They had arrived after Joseph had been evacuated to Noumea and lived in a stockade near the hospital behind a pale of barbed wire ten feet high. Four nurses emerged from the Stalag gate, fetching in crisp seersucker dresses and jaunty overseas caps. They smelled like the perfume counter at I. Magnun's. All along the way, troops on the road whooped and whistled as they got glimpses of the women.

Approaching the rickety wooden bridge across the Balesuma River, the women pretended not to notice a company of naked swimmers frolicking in the water. Joseph blushed.

The officer's mess consisted of a canvas tent fly draped across a ridge pole over a screened enclosure. The ground was bare. For the occasion, a blue cargo chute had been hung overhead, and palm sprouts growing from coconut husks rimmed the enclosure. Flickering candles on the wooden bench tables covered with tablecloths of clean sheets lent a festive ambience.

Leffers was also a talented scrounger, and he had been at his best for the occasion. On a ship, he had exchanged a few Jap souvenirs for steaks. Under his direction, a heart-of-palm salad was whipped up along with fried bread fruit. A Seabee camp came through with a supply of crushed ice for the Del Prado rum and canned fruit juice. The battalion cooks baked a pretty decent cake. The women were soon gushing with happy talk, and the young lieutenants soaking it up. Some had shaved closely and sloshed on handfuls of Aqua Velva lotion. A few had tied wrinkled field scarves (marine neckties) to their equally wrinkled khaki shirts.

Like Cinderella, the nurses had to be back in their confines by ten o'clock, so off they went an hour before, leaving a few broken hearts in their wake. The boys had something to write home about: the first white women they had seen since leaving New Zealand.

* * *

Loading began for the Marianas, with Easy Battery going aboard the *Wharton,* an ancient passenger liner converted into a troopship. She was slow but had ample space for the troops. A promenade deck ran the length of her port and starboard sides. Her wardroom was the size of a hotel ballroom with neat rows of tables covered with white linen. Gleaming silverware settings flanked heavy china dinner plates and coffee cups in decorative saucers. By far, *Wharton* was the most luxurious troopship Joseph had ridden, including the Matson Line's *Lurline* that had carried the 12th Marines to New Zealand.

Joseph and a dozen or so junior officers were quartered in a spacious dormitory-like compartment with portholes that were open, unlike those of the APA's (attack transports) that were always dogged down.

But Joseph suddenly had a personal problem. He had developed hemorrhoids. The first night aboard, he was in such pain that sleep was impossible. He left his bunk and searched out the compartment of Dr. Fred Schlumberger, the battalion medical officer. It was next to the sick bay. Schlumberger was a mild-mannered, middle-aged urologist always of a pleasant disposition. He had left a thriving practice in Los Angeles to serve in the war. Sleepily, he listened to Joseph's complaint, then led him into the dispensary. Joseph crawled on a stainless steel operating table with a bright overhead light.

"My God, you do have a case," Schlumberger said. "They're ripe for surgery. I can take them out right now."

"But won't I miss the landing?" Joseph asked.

"Probably," said the doctor.

"In that case I refuse to have surgery," Joseph replied. "I don't want to miss the landing."

Without a show of impatience, the doctor gave him couple of sleeping pills and sent him back to his compartment.

But sleep did not come, and hour later, Joseph was back at Schlumberger's bedside.

"I need something stronger," he said.

"Go back to your bunk, and I'll be there in a bit," the doctor ordered. He came to Joseph's bunk with a syringe of morphine. "Drop your drawers," he ordered before driving the needle in Joseph's buttock. It was almost noon the next day before Joseph emerged from his drug-induced slumber. The hemorrhoids were no longer swollen. He sought out Dr. Schlumberger and reported his relief. The doctor just shook his head and grinned.

As the convoy got under way, out came the maps and montages of aerial photos. The 3rd Division and the 1st Provisional Marine Brigade would invade and seize Guam, a former U.S. naval base taken by the Japs in 1941. But first, two marine divisions, the 2nd and 4th along with the Army 27th Division, must seize Saipan, the northernmost of the Mariana Islands. The 3rd would be held in floating reserve. Once Saipan was secured, the 3rd would carry out its assault of Guam.

Navy reconnaissance planes had flown in low over the landing beaches between Asan and Adelup Points on Guam where the division would land. Their photos were so detailed when studied through a stereoscopic pair, one Jap had been photographed in the act of moving his bowels.

Leisurely the Guam attack force cruised toward the Marianas and then stood off some 250 miles from Saipan.

Ten
The Marianas Landings—June–July, 1944

June 15, 1944, the 2nd and 4th Marine Divisions began landings on Saipan. They established their beachhead but immediately met with stiff resistance. The ships of the Southern Landing Force, carrying the 3rd Division and the 1st Provisional Brigade, played a waiting game. Two days later, they began steaming on an eastward course away from the Marianas, leaving the puzzled marines to wonder what was going on.

The answer: A U.S. submarine had sighted a Japanese battle fleet in Philippine waters steaming in the direction of the Marianas. There were six carriers, four battleships, and several cruisers and destroyers. The prudent Admiral Raymond Spruance ordered all transport ships in the Saipan operation plus the Southern landing force to safer waters before heading his own carrier force to confront the Japs.

In the resulting Battle of the Philippine Sea, AKA the Great Turkey Shoot, Spruance's aviators shot down 400 Japanese planes and sunk three enemy carriers. The menace to the Saipan landing was eliminated, but the Guam landing was postponed indefinitely, and the Southern force was ordered to a sanctuary in the Marshall Islands.

Life aboard the *Wharton* continued its leisure pace. Mornings were devoted to meetings and inspection of troops and equipment. The rest of the day was mostly free. The ship's loudspeakers softly wafted tunes from *Oklahoma,* the current Broadway stage musical. There were late-night card games among the junior officers, with Hearts the favorite. The ship's boats began ferrying the troops to Eniwetok for physical exercises. The battered island wasn't much to look at with its coconut trees wearing the "Halsey haircut," but the broad beaches of the atoll were alluring. Joseph lay on the sand with his feet in the water.

The blue sea appeared vast and swollen, as if it could engulf the tiny island with one surge. Joseph recalled the old *Life Magazine* cover in which an outline of the United States had appeared so small when superimposed over the vastness of the Pacific. Now he basked in his skivvies at the epicenter of the Pacific war and soon, if all went well in the Marianas, Japan would be within range of the Air Force's B-29s.

Saipan had proven much tougher than expected, but finally was subdued. Hank Michalsky, Joseph's boot camp buddy and San Diego sidekick, had died, the victim of a direct mortar hit on the FDC of the 10th Marines.

Finally, the *Wharton* weighed anchor, and once again the Guam landing force headed for its objective. The carefree mood on the ship abruptly turned grim. The war had been forgotten, but now, reality set in.

At 4:00 A.M. on July 21, 1944, the ship's loudspeakers routed the troops from their sleep. True to its hospitality toward the marines, some of whom would eat their last meal, *Wharton* served up a breakfast of steak and eggs. In semidarkness, Joseph worked his way to the main deck past swarms of crewmen busily preparing to launch landing boats. The bombardment by the fleet was in full fury. Projectiles left fiery traces on their way to targets. As dawn approached, the silhouetted hills of Guam came into view. And with the first rays of the sun, the two landmarks that defined the 3rd Division's landing beaches, Adelup Point and Asan Point, became visible.

Guam is a peanut-shaped island, thirty miles long and eight miles across its middle. The southern half is mountainous and open, with few trees and fields of chest-high sword grass. The northern half is a dense jungle and rain forest. It was defended by eighteen thousand Japanese soldiers and naval personnel. The Japs anticipated the Americans would land on the west side of the island heavily mined and fortified the beautiful inviting beaches of Tumon Bay. But the 3rd Division had selected the Asan beaches farther south, near the town of Agana, which were guarded by coral reefs.

Shortly after 8:30 A.M., the tracks of the amphibian tractors carrying the assault wave morphed from steel paddles propelling their craft through water to caterpillars gripping solidly on the coral reef. They clattered across the 300 yards of coral and delivered the infantry to the beach.

The naval guns lifted their fire from the beaches to the foothills beyond. Assault battalions of three regiments swarmed ashore, the 3rd on the left flank, the 21st in the center, and the 9th on the right. They were met with mortar fire, but casualties were relatively light.

On the *Wharton*, Easy Battery's howitzers emerged from their hold and were swung out on cargo booms to landing craft waiting below. Joseph climbed down the debarkation net with the fourth gun section, whose howitzer was already nestled in the LCVP. The landing craft cast off and joined a group of boats circling away from their mother ships.

All eyes were on the control ship, an LCI (landing craft infantry) easily identified by the array of colorful pennnats it hoisted and lowered as signals to the landing craft. Joseph's boat would have to wait for an available amphibian tractor near the reef. When the rendezvous was made, they would break down the howitzer and lift it piece by piece over the gunwales into the amphibian tractor. Meanwhile, the circling pattern of boats carried them between a heavy cruiser and the shore. The ear-splitting 8-inch rifles of the cruiser were deafening.

Farther in, a destroyer had ventured close to the rocky promontory of Chonito Heights. It was poking its smoking 5-inch guns point blank into caves in the face of the rocky outcropping.

Finally, Joseph's boat was signaled in to an amphibian tractor waiting just off the reef. Plumes of water from mortar rounds were rising all around. Off to the left, another amphibian was hit and burning. The coxswain coolly eased his boat alongside the amphibian, and the two were lashed together. Quickly, the men began dismantling the howitzer and lifting the parts into the amphibian. There was a moment of panic when a mortar round sprayed them with water. "Don't look around, do your job," Joseph shouted. "The longer we hang around, the more likely we are to be hit."

The shells were rendered harmless by exploding underwater. With his knowledge of fuses, Joseph correctly assumed that the Japs were only killing fish. In less than three minutes, the fourth section had transferred its gun and crew and was crossing the reef. The tractor steered past huge shell craters to the battery position a mere fifty yards from the beach. The 12th Regiment set a record by having its guns firing in support of the advancing infantry in less than two hours after the initial assault.

This was made possible by the heroic work of artillery survey teams who followed close behind the infantry. Under fire, they set up transits and measured angles, taped off legs of triangles by the hundreds of yards, staked the exact position of each base piece, and accurately computed compass directions and ranges to registration points. Likewise, communications parties worked under fire, laying telephone lines that tied in every battery with its battalion fire direction center and the FDCs to the regimental command center. There was no haphazard shooting, but a coordinated and accurate delivery of fire that kept the Japs pinned down and helped the infantry consolidate its tenuous beachhead.

The beach became relatively calm, with only an occasional artillery round from the Japs keeping the war from being boring. It was different for the battery's forward observer teams attached to the 21st Marines. Lieutenants Brooks, Grissom, and Millsaps were directing fire from the front lines.

By the second day, the 21st and 9th reached the high ground and consolidated their lines. They could move no farther without losing contact with the 3rd Regiment on the left. It was stymied by a long spur that ran from a hill massif in the interior all the way to the beach. It was called Chonito Heights. With a naked eye, Easy Battery's cannoneers could easily observe the deadly battle raging only 500 yards away.

There would be a preparation of artillery fire, followed by carrier planes strafing and bombing at low level. Through the smoke and dust, the infantry would start up the hill only to be repulsed by the Japs popping out of their holes and rolling grenades on the attackers. The marines would be sent tumbling back to the base of the spur.

Late in the night of July 24, three days after the landing, the forward observers began calling fire almost on their own positions. The Japs had counter-attacked in a wild, drunken banzai charge, exploiting a hole in the lines of the 1st battalion, 21st. The marine artillery blazed all through the night. At one point, the telephone man in the battalion fire direction center began relaying fire commands to Easy Battery in a whisper. He was surrounded by Japs.

They had swarmed all the way to the artillery command post located in a ravine just ahead of the firing batteries. Some had even reached the division hospital. Wounded marines grabbed rifles and left their sick beds to stop the onslaught. By daylight, troops from various units near the beach had surrounded the Japs and were picking them off. Many of the Japs blew themselves up with satchel charges and grenades. In the aftermath, it was estimated that 3,200 enemy had died in the front lines and 300 in the rear areas.

Lieutenant Brooks was dead. He of the blond curly hair and pink dimpled cheeks who sang "Mairzy Doats" in the tent on Guadalcanal. "Buck" Grissom had been wounded and would later receive the Silver Star. In the battalion CP Sergeant Hooks was killed. He was the mess sergeant who had shared a compartment with Joseph on the train to New River and later provided cold cuts and ice for the evening beer parties among the pines.

Captain Leffers summoned Joseph to grab his gear and head for the front to replace Brooks. He already had a map in his dispatch case and a pair of seven-by-fifty binoculars.

He climbed up the hills, panting for breath under the tropical sun, past heaps of dead Japs. He paused at the company command post of Lieutenant Cousins and got a fast briefing on the location of the front line platoons. "We haven't slept one wink since we came ashore," said First Sergeant Nunnaly, without a trace of complaint.

On a ridge line that overlooked the battlefield, Joseph found a two-man pit. A communications team following close behind strung a wire and installed a field telephone. He cranked the phone and chatted with the operations officer in the battalion FDC. "Nothing but dead Japs up here and damned little activity," he reported.

As the tropical midday sun bore down, the stench of decaying bodies was overpowering. Occasionally, a mild breeze would waft the awful smell back toward the marine line. With his binoculars, Joseph scanned the valley and spotted a Jap tank concealed in a draw. He cranked the phone. "Fire mission," he called to the FDC. "From Check Point Charlie right 400, down 200." The searching round was on line but well short. "Up 300." The next round sprayed dirt on the tank. "Fuse delay. Fire for effect. . . . Clobbity bob," Joseph shouted enthusiastically as two volleys from the 75s blanketed the tank with black TNT and dust.

"I think that tank was already knocked out," a lieutenant from the front line platoon said, deflating Joseph's ego.

"Well, let's say it is now damned sure knocked out," he retorted.

Joseph was intrigued by the low-keyed attitude of the grunts in the rifle pits just below the hole. The night before had been a hellish nightmare when the banzai charge swept through, yet they were nonchalant about the whole thing. Gunnery Sergeant "Slug" Marvin saw to it that his men stayed loose. Joseph had known "Slug" in San Diego. A career NCO and former boxer with a face to prove it, he had coached the base boxing team. One of his fighters had even fought and won a main event against a big time professional in the San Diego arena.

"Anybody want some crab meat?" Marvin called out from his hole, captured canned Japanese crab meat being a cherished item. There was a chorus of "Yeah, Sarge," whereupon Marvin stood up and scratched his pubic area. "Well, I got the crabs, come and get it." His humor was infectious and typical of the cockiness that prevailed in the front lines.

Later in the day, the attitude of the platoon turned morose. Marvin had taken a bullet in the stomach, while moving about the foxholes checking on his men. He quipped jokingly with the stretcher bearers as he was being taken to the aid station. "Anybody but "Slug" would be dead," the doctor said, "but I think he'll make it."

It was not to be. Word came back that "Slug" Marvin had died on the hospital ship.

Equally sobering was the sight of a truck being loaded with dead marines, eight or ten of them, their boondockers jostling from lifeless limbs, limbs that had spirited them to crawl and die on that red clay ridge. Everyone was smeared from head to foot with the ochre colored clay. Joseph stood out in his yet unstained utilities like a substitute football player on a muddy field.

Through the day, the marines dug in deeper, tightened the apron of barbwire in front and sighted in machine guns and BARs. Supplies of ammo and hand grenades were distributed. If the Japs came that night, they would get a bigger dose than the night before.

Late in the afternoon, Leffers came up. "Thought you'd like company tonight," he grinned. It was like him to be concerned.

Joseph was not a school-trained forward observer, so his skipper would see to it that he got some help. Before dark, Joseph and Leffers adjusted fire on suspected Jap assembly areas and recorded the coordinates. Joseph tried eating a can of C-ration beef, but became nauseated with the smell of dead bodies. Leffers, ever the resourceful one, had snatched a bottle of sake from a Jap dump on his way up. At dusk, they nipped gingerly on the fiery wine. "I'll take the first watch," Leffers said. But neither slept, waiting for the expected banzai.

Occasionally, they took careful sips from the bottle, not enough to fog their minds. Star shells fired from destroyers offshore cast a pale, eerie light over the battlefield. A sliver of moon appeared above Mount Alutom. Occasionally Japs in the distance screamed, "Morene, you die!" Slowly, the night passed with no banzai.

No one was certain at the time, but the Japs had shot their wad. They had lost the bulk of their men in one fanatical charge. The following morning, Colonel Weller came huffing up the hill for a look. As the battalion commander was surveying the front with his field glasses, a mortar round whistled overhead and exploded yards away. Three bodies went flying for the safety of the pit. Joseph and Weller butted heads with a clang of steel helmets. The colonel looked sheepish. Joseph was embarrassed. He'd never butted heads with a colonel. Then everybody laughed.

Except for the Chonito Heights stalemate in the 3rd Regiment's sector, the battle for Guam was over. The battle plan called for General Shepherd's brigade, which had cleared the Japs from the southern end of the island, to wheel northward, along with the army 77th Division. The 3rd Division would be the pivot on the left flank.

But there could be no advance as long as Chonito remained in Jap hands. General Holland M. "Howling Mad" Smith, corps commander for the Marianas operation, impatiently stormed ashore and headed straight for the 3rd Regiment's command post.

Heatedly, he issued his ultimatum to the harried regimental commander, who had suffered heavy casualties attacking the stubborn hill. "Either you take that hill by sundown or you are relieved." Sundown came and went and Chonito remained in enemy hands. The luckless colonel was reassigned to a staff post.

Smith had a reputation of being reckless and brash in other campaigns. He could not tolerate delaying tactics. His credo was the longer you stayed put in one place, the more casualties you were likely to suffer and the more your troops would lose their aggressiveness and will to fight.

Smith had incurred the wrath of the army brass in the Pacific by dismissing the 27th Division's General Ralph Smith on Saipan. The marine general had grown impatient with the 27th's stalling tactics. A marine general dismissing an army commander was unheard of, and the army brass in Hawaii lost no time in convening a board of inquiry to exonerate their Smith and castigate Holland Smith.

Ultimately, assisted by an encircling movement of the 9th Regiment, the 3rd reached the top of Chonito. The price: 850 casualties.

As the three divisions were poised to move abreast up the island, a typhoon struck full force. The fury of the storm halted all movement. Joseph had been recalled to the battery position. He pitched a shelter half over his foxhole, but it only funneled water into the pit. He saw his leather stationery portfolio floating away—it was a gift from Cara—and grabbed it as it was about to disappear in a torrent of muddy water headed down the hill.

Although there were 23,000 Chamorro natives on Guam, none were seen during the heat of the battle. When the U.S. invasion was imminent, the Japanese rounded them up and forced them into makeshift concentration camps in the interior of the island. They lived in lean-tos under wretched conditions, suffering from malnutrition, tuberculosis, dysentery, and sundry diseases. They were constantly beaten by the Japs and even beheaded if suspected of showing disrespect for Japan and loyalty toward the United States.

With the Japanese resistance broken, following the banzai, the natives began trickling through the U.S. lines. They were a pitiful lot in dirty rags and with open sores. Women carried sick, naked babies.

They told stories of Japanese cruelty and brutality. Women had been forced to work in rice fields while the men labored on roads and airfields. Of particular annoyance to the Japanese was the whereabouts of navy radioman George Tweed, the lone American who had eluded capture when the Japs took the island in December 1941. Tweed had remained hidden in the jungle, given food by the natives and spirited from cave to cave while eluding his pursuers.

Tweed became a symbol of hope for the natives in defiance of Jap authority, although any one suspected of aiding him was beaten or even beheaded.

Among them was Father Jesus Duenas who refused to kowtow to the Japanese. Duenas was a thorn in the side of the Japs and achieved martyrdom in his defiance of their authority. Only nineteen days before the marine landing, a collaborator falsely accused Father Duenas of providing food to Tweed, whereupon he was beheaded by the secret police.

Tweed had avoided capture for three and a half years, until he finally managed to signal a U.S. warship and was rescued days before the invasion. He proved to be a disappointment to naval and marine intelligence officers, who had hoped to learn much about Jap defenses. He knew very little and was promptly shipped back to the States.

One day Joseph chanced to be near the beach, when he noticed a small group of people where a landing boat had just beached. There was Tweed in his new navy chief petty officer's dress uniform making his triumphal return. If he expected a hero's welcome, he was disappointed. The natives had risked their lives harboring Tweed, and most resented the pain and suffering he had caused, especially those whose loved ones had been put to death by the Japs.

The final push up the island began against token resistance. The battle lines retreated inland and weary cannoneers swabbed their gun bores shiny to break the monotony. One day, a lieutenant of engineers was walking along the beach behind the gun position carrying an armload of Jap land mines. The next instant there was a blinding flash and a deafening roar. The lieutenant literally disappeared in the blast. Fragments of his flesh clung to bushes, all that remained of what had been a live human seconds earlier.

Quickly the infantry regiments moved beyond the range of the howitzers. Easy Battery was ordered to displace forward. Joseph took a demolition team to clear trees from the new position. At Finegayan Village, they waited as the 9th Marines was engaged in a spirited fire fight against a Jap road block. With one-pound blocks of nitro starch and detonating cords that were wrapped around trees, they quickly cleared a field of fire. With an aiming circle, Joseph oriented the firing position and staked off each of the four howitzer positions. But now, few targets remained for the artillery.

Organized resistance had faded into scattered groups of Japs hiding out. The island was declared secure, although several thousand armed Japanese remained holed up in caves and jungle hideouts.

Mopping up began with patrols fanning out in a roundup of Japs. Joseph took his turn leading a platoon on a three-day searching patrol. It was raining hard the morning he mustered his platoon, composed of men from all units of the battalion. He inspected their rifles, ammunition, grenades, and rations. Each man carried two canteens of water. The radio man checked out his SCR 300 radio, which Joseph suspected wouldn't work when needed. It didn't.

The route ordered by the battalion intelligence officer took them straight into a liana forest. With machetes and bayonets, they hacked their way through while staying wary of being ambushed by Japs. It was torturous going, and if not for the incessant rain, the men would have soon become exhausted.

By late afternoon, they emerged from the grips of the foliage into a clearing occupied by a small ranch house. Cautiously, they surrounded the house, calling out for anyone to come out. It was deserted. The Chamorro owners apparently had fled to the hills. Nothing appeared disturbed inside. The beds were made up neatly. The kitchen was clean with dishes neatly stacked in a cupboard. In one corner of the living room stood a Victrola console with a set of classical records. Obviously, the owners were well off by the standards of Guam's natives.

"Set up security," Joseph called out to his platoon sergeant. "We'll spend the night here, but I don't want a damned thing in this house disturbed." Even as Joseph was giving his orders, a corporal had already wrung the neck of a chicken he had caught in the yard and was plucking it for cooking.

There was a supply of charcoal near a stone-lined pit in the cooking area adjacent to the kitchen. "Not one more chicken, do you hear?" Joseph shouted.

They ate their rations and settled down for the night. For the first time since he could remember Joseph stretched out on a clean bed, after first removing his muddy boondockers.

The rain ceased during the night, and at daylight, Joseph prepared his men to move out. They were in open country with red clay hills and fields of sword grass. In a shed near another abandoned house, they found a half-dozen dead Japs. Another marine patrol had been there recently. They spent the second night on a hilltop in a grove of Australian pines. After making sure his security outposts were alert, Joseph was soon lulled to sleep by the whispering pines.

On the third day, they reentered the jungle and came upon a Japanese bivouac in a dense growth. Fresh footprints and discarded equipment indicated the campers weren't far away. Joseph decided to occupy the site and set up an ambush on a hunch that the Japs would return during the night. They did, but his trigger happy BAR man fired off a clip without any result, and they were gone.

The patrol was not only destined to come up empty, but nearly met with disaster. On the final day, they came upon a clearing where the clay had been freshly bulldozed. As the men walked slowly into the area, Joseph spotted the horn of a land mine exposed by erosion from the rain. "Halt!" he shouted. "Don't take another step. Go back exactly the way you came." Cautiously withdrawing from the perimeter of the area, they could see that they had nearly walked into a tank trap. They were at Tumon Bay, where the Japs had prepared their best defenses.

A couple of days after returning to camp, Joseph began feeling feverish. His joints ached and diarrhea kept him running to the open air latrine. He had dengue fever. Someone summoned the battalion medical officer, a young red-faced Boston Irishman who had recently joined the battalion. He didn't know one fever from another. Nonchalantly, he gave Joseph a couple of APCs, the navy's standard bromide for all ailments.

The rear echelon had arrived from Guadalcanal with pyramidal tents but no folding cots. So Joseph slept on the ground with only a poncho and blanket beneath. Between trips to the latrine, he writhed in agony and drifted in and out of deliriums. He went from shivering to sweating. While dengue fever had not been known to be fatal, its symptoms gave every indication of being so. The doctor returned, took his temperature, and decided stronger medicine was in order. "Take these, all at once," he said, handing Joseph a handful of quinine tablets and a canteen of water.

The quinine worked. Joseph's fever was broken but the old ringing in his ears from the howitzer incident on Bougainville resumed. He had lost several pounds.

Slowly, the battalion's camp took shape and soon resembled the one on Guadalcanal. With Leffers in charge, a detail of natives built a nipa hut for the officers' club. The bar served skunky beer in rusted cans. Occasionally, there would be a bottle or two of Del Prado rum to mix with Coke. No ice.

With the arrival of the personal gear and equipment from Guadalcanal, Joseph was assigned to inventory the effects of Lieutenant Brooks for shipment to his mother in Vermont. With heavy heart, he made a list of the meager items. He went through a stack of mail from the mother, found her address, and wrote a personal letter. Weeks later, as the battalion was loading for the Iwo Jima operation, he received a reply from the heartbroken mother, expressing her gratitude. In the confusion of the moment, he misplaced her letter, ending any chance of further correspondence.

One evening, Joseph and his three tent mates were startled by loud shouting just outside their tent, followed by the crack of a carbine. They rushed out, and there on the ground with the glare of flashlights in his face was a young Japanese soldier surrounded by guards. He had tried to escape from the division POW stockade. The bullet had ripped into his legs and shattered his shin bone. Why, Joseph wondered aloud, would he want to escape? The prisoners were being well fed and humanely treated by all accounts. In the jungle, he would only starve slowly while being hunted like an animal. The Japanese were an enigmatic enemy.

The year slipped slowly by, and the specter of another operation loomed in everybody's mind. Training intensified. In one firing exercise, a 105-howitzer battery dropped a short round on an infantry unit, killing twelve men. Talk about realism.

New Year's Day, 1945, the troops were in a holiday mood but with nothing to celebrate. Joseph struck up an acquaintance with a young infantry lieutenant from the 21st. Johnson was his name. He had drunk a couple of beers and at intervals would shout out umbriago! It sounded like a Jimmy Durante expression and was adopted as the rallying cry of his platoon. Soon Joseph was calling him Umbriago.

"What say we check out the big party at division," Umbriago suggested. Joseph shrank at the thought of crashing the general's party, but Umbriago was insistent. Joseph changed to fresh khakis and checked his appearance. The two ambled through the coconut grove and crossed the dusty coral road to division headquarters. The officer's hut was a large, screened-in nipa hut with a sturdy plywood deck. Trying to appear nonchalant, the two elbowed their way to the bar past clusters of mostly field grade officers.

"Rum and Coke," Joseph said to the sergeant tending bar. He eyed the two suspiciously.

"Same," echoed Umbriago.

The bartender took note of Joseph's bursting bomb insignia. "Gotcha Gunner," he smiled, pouring into an overflowing shot glass. Drinks in hand, they melted into the crowd, but their way was blocked by a trio of navy nurses jiggling the ice in their drinks.

"Get you a fresh one?" Umbriago volunteered to a tall, willowy blond.

"Well, where did you two come from?" she cooed.

"Just back from patrol," Umbriago lied.

The women appeared to welcome the young party crashers after trying to make conversation with fawning field grade officers.

"You look like you've been in some rough battles," the blonde said, scrutinizing Joseph.

"My battle was with dengue fever," Joseph answered.

"But it looks like you've seen some horrible things," she pursued. Nurse Blanche all over again, Joseph thought.

A light colonel walked up, tipped his glass, and said "Happy New Year." Although he meant it to be sincere, his words had a meaningless, hollow ring. With the 3rd Division approaching its most horrific battle, Happy Doomsyear might have been as appropriate.

"Happy New Year," the group responded. Joseph's drink was giving him a pleasant buzz, and he began to relax. He had just helped himself to the canapes, when General Graves B. Erskine approached, his steely blue eyes making contact with Joseph's furtive glance. "Here we go, Umbriago," Joseph said under his breath. But the general simply gave a curt nod and walked past. Erskine had recently taken command of the division after serving as chief of staff to General Howling Mad Smith, commander of all the marines in the Pacific. Not that he needed it, but apparently a lot of Smith's toughness had rubbed off on Erskine. His reputation as a no-nonsense disciplinarian and fearless leader was well known.

A couple of drinks later, Joseph and Umbriago jubilantly emerged from the nipa hut, feeling no pain and full of stories to brag about.

Rapidly, Guam was transformed into a major base. Neat camps of Quonset huts housed support troops. Admiral Chester Nimitz set up headquarters on the lofty perch of Adelup Point. A giant air field occupied the area near Finegayan, where Joseph had knocked down trees for a battery position. Tumon Bay was cleared of its tank obstacles and barbed wire. Air force officers and nurses sunned themselves in the white sand near a beach club.

Meanwhile, the 3rd Division still lived in muddy camps with patrols wearily searching out Japs. They did not know it, but their fate had already been decided. The air force had begun bombing Japan with B-29s from bases on Guam and Tinian. But the 1,200-mile return trip was taking its toll on damaged bombers, many of which were forced to ditch hundreds of miles from home.

Almost exactly halfway between the Marianas and Japan was a string of islands, called shotos in Japanese. Among the Volcano Islands was an infinitesimal speck called Iwo Jima, meaning Sulphur Island. A U.S. airfield on Iwo Jima would make a perfect emergency landing field for stricken bombers. The air force had to have it.

Eleven

Iwo Jima: Black and Red Sands —February 1945

Apra Harbor was bustling with activity in mid-February. Dockside cranes were hoisting vehicles, equipment, and ammunition into the gaping holds of ships, Where was the *Mormacport?* Joseph inquired of the crew of a small boat that had just tied up. The coxswain pointed to an unimposing vessel riding at anchor amid a fleet of transports and supply ships. Yes, they would give him a lift to the ship. He handed over his pack and other belongings and soon was enjoying a breezy ride over choppy waves on his way to the ship.

Mormacport had been a Dutch motor ship of the Moore McCormac Line. It had a crew of navy reservists, including the captain and officers. She was fairly new, in trim shape, and sported a new paint job. Joseph would ride her to wherever, along with troops from the 12th Regiment headquarters. She was already loaded and killing time while awaiting orders. Joseph reported to the troop commander, then found his bunk and stowed his gear. Later he went back topside and, with permission from the officer of the deck, boarded a landing boat for a last visit ashore.

Near the waterfront stood an expansive galvanized metal building that was the navy officers' club. Soon Joseph had joined a crowd slaking their thirst with cold beer and discussing the forthcoming operation.

The conversation centered on the Palau Islands where the 1st Division had recently fought a bitter battle on Peleliu. Unlike previous battles, the Japs on Peleliu adopted a come-and-get-us-defense. Instead of wasting troops in banzai charges, they stayed in their pillboxes until routed out in close combat or fried by marine flame throwers. The Peleliu defenders also employed the heaviest mortars, up to 320 millimeters, and rockets that fired 550-pound projectiles. Nothing like this had been experienced by marines in the Pacific.

Joseph was drinking with a marine infantry lieutenant and a navy ensign. They became hungry, but no food was to be had at the bar. "My ship is in dock," the ensign said. "I can get us some chow." By now the trio had consumed several beers and were feeling no pain. With thoughts of the upcoming battle, they were in a foreboding mood. Live it up, they'd say, the hell with tomorrow. By now it was dark.

They followed the ensign to the dock and began climbing a long, steep gangway. Must be an aircraft carrier, Joseph thought. After finally reaching the top, they found themselves looking down an abyss some five stories below. Nestled at the bottom was a corvette dwarfed by the gigantic floating dry dock she rested in. The ship was bathed in the lights of the dry dock. They made their way down the ladder and boarded. The ensign led them to the wardroom and began foraging for food in the pantry.

Finding nothing immediately edible, he went into the cooler and came out with three frozen beef steaks. Meanwhile, the marine lieutenant was fiddling with the glass door of a gun case that held a row of Thompson submachine guns. The lieutenant had to have one. Their host had begun frying the steaks, and the marine looey was extracting a Tommy gun from the rack when the skipper of the ship, a lieutenant commander, barged in. "Just what in the hell is going on here?" he shouted. The ensign shrank as the skipper launched into a tirade. "You two get the hell off my ship," he bellowed, unnecessarily because Joseph and the looey were already beating a retreat for the gangway. Gathering their breath at the top of the drydock, the lieutenant lamented, "Boy, I could use that Tommy gun in my platoon. What good is it doing in that glass case? Those swabbies wouldn't know what to do with it anyhow."

"Yeah, well I can still smell those steaks," Joseph groaned.

Next day the *Mormacport* hoisted anchor and fell in with the convoy. The ship's speaker summoned the troops to the number-one hatch cover where a major waited to begin his briefing. He unrolled a rubber relief map and flopped it on the hatch. "This is Iwo Jima," he announced, to no one's surprise. "Only 620 miles from Japan."

Two other marine divisions, the 4th and 5th were on their way from Hawaii. They would be the assault troops. The 3rd would be held in floating reserve.

"From the pounding they've been getting the 3rd probably won't be needed," the major opined.

Indeed, navy carrier planes and air force bombers had been plastering the island for months. But after a recent raid, one bomber pilot had found the anti-aircraft fire had actually intensified. This indicated that Iwo's defenders were burrowed deep underground. The raids weren't killing many of them.

The island, shaped like a pork chop, was only four and one-half miles long and two and one-half at its widest. It was dominated by a 550-foot extinct volcano at the southern extremity, Mount Surabachi. At the narrow neck at the base of the mountain, barely a half-mile of coarse, black volcanic sand separated the beach on the east from the one on the western side. To the north, a rock-strewn plateau rose to an elevation of 380 feet. It was a jumbled landscape, interlaced with chaotic gorges and ridges. Gnarled bushes and stunted trees struggled to survive in the barren environment.

In a letter home before the battle, a Japanese soldier described Iwo as "a place where no sparrow sings." There was no ground water; the troops and civilians who lived on the island depended on rain water that was stored in cisterns. Annual rainfall averaged sixty inches.

Lying just north of the tropics, Iwo had a cool season from December through April, during which temperatures ranged from sixty-three degrees to the low seventies. After years in the tropics, the 3rd Division troops would find the weather on the chilly side, particularly when it rained, so they had been issued green lightweight jackets. In New Zealand, Joseph had scrounged a tank jacket—a valued item of clothing issued only to tank crews—that was lined with wool felt. He had eschewed the lightweight army issue jacket and, instead, stuffed the tank jacket in his pack. It would turn out to be a mistake.

From the warmth of his bunk in the predawn hour of February 19, Joseph became aware that the screws of *Mormacport* had ceased turning. Then came the rattle of the anchor chain clanking noisily on its way down. They had arrived. On deck, the air was cool and breezy. The ship was anchored about 1,000 yards from the island.

Daylight revealed hundreds of ships of all sizes lying off the eastern and western shores of the island. At 6:30 A.M. the battle fleet thundered into action. Six battleships and five heavy cruisers, each assigned a sector, hammered away until a pall of smoke and dust obscured the features of the island. Joseph's old C.O., Colonel Donald Weller, had been transferred to General Holland Smith's staff and was the naval gunfire officer for the Fifth Amphibious Corps.

From commanding a battalion of 75-millimeter "peashooters," Weller had planned and coordinated the bombardment of a powerful fleet, firing shells from 5 to 16 inches. After an hour and thirty minutes, the surface bombardment ceased, and seventy-two fighter and bomber planes roared in to attack the landing beaches and the mountain with rockets and bombs. Then came a swarm of forty-eight fighters ravaging the same areas with more rockets, napalm, and machine gun fire. It appeared nothing could survive the savage bombardment.

At 0900, the first waves of armored amphibian tractors labored across the black beach. Reaching the loose dry sand, some hung up on their bellies. Unpredictably, the steep gradient of the dune terrace obscured their view and line of fire. Troop-carrying amphibians followed close behind to disgorge the assault troops.

From the rail of *Mormacport,* Joseph trained his binoculars on the beach. The scene spread before him was like a giant museum canvas depicting an epic battle. So compact was the battlefield as seen through the lens of Joseph's binoculars, it could have passed for a life-sized diorama. Suddenly the beach erupted into a holocaust. Shells and rockets rained down on the assault waves. Bodies of marines were flung upwards like rag dolls by the explosions.

For what seemed like an eternity, the assault troops were trapped by the unrelenting rain of iron and steel. Their forward movement was hampered by the loose sand that sucked at their feet. "Poor bastards," a sailor muttered, echoing the thought in Joseph's mind.

Still, more troops now arriving in Higgins boats were being deposited on that killing ground. Ever so slowly, a thin line of green-clad marines inched toward the crest of the dune line through the unabated enemy bombardment. By midmorning, eight assault battalions were on the beach, about 8,000 men.

In the wardroom of the *Mormacport,* radios crackled with transmissions between ships and shore commands. A coded message from the beachmaster to an LST asked about the availability of landing craft.

"I have twelve sardines," the answer came, nearly drowned in static. "Five in cans, seven opened." The translation: Five armored amphibians, seven amphibian troop carriers.

A war correspondent attempted to dictate a radio story. He began his lead in flowery prose . . . "Gallant marines under heavy fire stormed ashore this morning on the tiny Japanese island of Iwo Jima . . . " Before he could continue, the jabber of a Japanese voice on the same frequency would drown out the correspondent's transmission. Patiently, he would wait for the Jap to shut up, and then he'd resume. "Gallant marines under heavy fire . . . " The game continued until the frustrated correspondent gave up. He probably missed his deadline.

As hopeless as the situation appeared, advance elements of General Keller Rocky's 5th Division pushed their way across the narrow neck of the island. After having been battered by mortars and rockets on the beach, they were raked by machine guns and rifle fire as they crossed the terrace. John Basilone, a hero at Guadalcanal, was killed. His machine gun had shredded Colonel Ichicki's regiment on the Tenaru River and won him the Congressional Medal of Honor. Basilone had voluntarily left a cushy assignment on a war-bond tour in the States to return to combat.

On the right, the 4th Division of General Clifton B. Cates was making even slower progress, repulsed by heavy fire from bunkers and pillboxes on the rocky northern plateau. By nightfall, the marine 0-1 line, the objective for the day, began like a noose around the base of Surabachi, snaked northward across part of airfield numbers one, and was anchored at the East Boat Basin. The troops dug in and made preparations for a counterattack. There was none. General Tadamichi Kuribayashi's 22,000 defenders were staying put underground. His strategy was not to waste his men and to make the marines pay with their lives for every yard gained.

The D day casualties of the marines were placed at 2,400, of which 500 were killed. To say the generals were "pleased" by the figures would sound insensitive. But they had prepared for heavier casualties, up to five percent of the landing force.

On D day plus one, the 28th Regiment prepared to assault Surabachi as the Japs on the mountain continued to rain explosives on the marines at the base. On the right, the 4th Division had breached Jap defenses around airfield number one, but became stymied by stubborn resistance in the vicinity of a stone quarry on the east side of the island. The casualties mounted, up to thirty-five percent in some units. An average of three men per minute were being hit. The 4th and 5th Divisions needed reinforcements from the floating reserve.

Aboard their ships the 3rd Division's 21st Regiment was alerted. On the third day, the regiment was boated. The rain came and the surf rose. For the better part of the day, the boats carrying the 21st circled around and around over rough water. The men were seasick, cold, and hungry. Joseph had developed a theory about assault landings: Make the troops as miserable as possible so when they're finally turned loose ashore, they'll be fighting mad. Finally the 21st was ordered in, occupying a position in the center of the island between the two stalled divisions.

Aboard *Mormacport,* the speaker announced a Catholic mass in the number-two hold.

Joseph made his way down the ladder to where a makeshift altar was set up on the hatch cover. Men with weapons slung over their shoulders gathered around a young priest with a crew cut. Joseph, who had served as an altar boy, noted half-comically that the priest was wearing a pair of worn and scuffed sneakers. They contrasted grotesquely with his colorful satin vestments. Father Allen in Lake Tarsa always wore polished Florsheims. The priest offered a brief mass. With bowed heads, the men received communion wafers as the priest murmured their last rites.

Back on the topside, groups were climbing down the nets into waiting boats. Joseph was still without orders. Someone on shore would eventually decide he was needed and where. He was sure it would be as a forward observer with the infantry. As he gazed absentmindedly on the island, the air suddenly erupted with the hoarse roar of thousands of voices. It was like the home team had scored a touchdown. All eyes were on Surabachi. There, at the very peak on a makeshift pole, rippled the American flag. Ships blared their horns. The air was electric with the current of uplifted spirits.

No human with a drop of American blood would ever bring himself to burn or desecrate his country's flag had he witnessed that scene.

Flag raisings in war usually mean the seizing of the objective and successful culmination of a battle. For all the boost in morale the Surabachi flag-raising had given the marines, it meant one battle had been won. The main event was yet to play out over the rest of the island.

Later in the day as Joseph was maintaining his surveillance of the battle and awaiting orders, a plane suddenly approached the ship from the island, flying low and trailing smoke. It was a navy TBM Avenger, a torpedo plane off a carrier. Because of their slow speed, some carried naval gunfire spotters. The plane was some 300 feet above the water when it burst into flames and headed straight for the *Mormacport*. On the ship, men froze in place. Three bodies trailing burning, half-opened chutes dropped from the plane. At the last instant, it veered and crashed only yards from the port bow of the *Mormacport* and quickly sank in a circle of blackened water.

A haunting thought crossed Joseph's mind. Lieutenant John Friday, a fellow officer formerly of Easy Battery, was a naval gunfire spotter. On Guam, he had applied and been accepted for the naval gunfire spotter school in Hawaii. Could he have been one of those three men who plunged to their death in flames? Later it was confirmed that Friday was missing in action.

In their first action, the 21st suffered heavy casualties fighting through the dunes between airfields number one and number two.

Shortly after noon on the fourth day, a radio message came, ordering Joseph ashore with a couple of regimental communications men, a wireman, and a radio operator. He was to replace Lieutenant Millsaps with the 2nd Battalion, 21st. Millsaps had been wounded the evening before. Sergeant Gregory, his team scout, was killed. As the landing craft grounded ashore, Joseph saw at close hand the wreckage of boats and amphibian tractors that he had viewed through his binoculars. Except for occasional mortar bursts, the beach was quiet.

He led his men up the black, sandy ridge and through the dunes until he sighted the yellow canvas sign of the 2nd Battalion command post. His wireman connected one end of the lightweight combat wire on a spool to the battalion's switchboard and began reeling off the wire as they continued toward the front line. They arrived on the apron of the airfield runway just as Lieutenant Raoul Archambault was leading K Company in an assault across the airfield. The objective was a tawny bluff of earth a few yards square and twenty feet high that marked the intersection of two runways.

Twice, Archambault's men had been repulsed. Now they charged a third time. A trench behind the bluff swarmed with Japs. Breathless, after racing 200 yards across the fire-swept runway, Joseph arrived as Archambault's men were engaged in hand-to-hand combat in the Jap trenches. Archambault, Joseph decided, was one hell of a leader and the bravest marine he had ever met.

A wild-eyed young private, exuding adrenalin, emerged from the melee with a smoking BAR and the brim of his helmet partly sawed off by a Jap automatic. Exhilarated and incoherent, he attempted to describe how he had dispatched a half-dozen Japs.

Quickly, Archambault's men took over the bluff and set up their own defense. It was now late in the day. Joseph climbed to the top of the bluff and surveyed the front. He drew a sketch of the terrain and plotted likely enemy troop concentrations on his map. He watched for signs of enemy mortars but saw nothing. The Japs used smokeless powder.

As dusk was enveloping the battlefield, a bulldozer towing a trailer with containers of hot chow from a field kitchen in the rear was stopped as it was about to pass the front lines. The driver was unaware that he was about to enter no-man's land. He wasn't sure who was supposed to get the chow. Warrant Officer George Green of Fox Battery and a forward observer with the 3rd battalion, 21st made the decision. He was among the first on the scene with his mess kit at the ready. "Hot chow, guys, come get it," Green called out while spooning up a helping of hot slum gullion. To his regret, Joseph was too occupied with his cranky radio to partake of the feast. It would be his last chance for a prepared meal in the next three weeks.

After a quiet night, compliments of General Kuribayashi, the 21st anxiously made preparations to be relieved by the 9th Marines who were just coming ashore. Some companies of the 21st had lost nearly half their men, and every other original company commander had been killed or wounded. As the 9th deployed at the apron of the airfield and prepared to cross, the Japs opened up with mortars and artillery. Showers of shrapnel shrieked, and the ground shook. Joseph's fragile communication wire had been cut the night before and the radio operator was unable to raise the artillery positions to call in counterfire. The difficulty was that none of the 12th Regiment (artillery) had yet come ashore, and artillery support for the 21st was coming from the 13th and 14th Regiments of the 4th and 5th Divisions. The radio net was hopelessly jammed with the transmissions of three divisions and the Japanese. No one was getting a word in edgewise.

"Where's the goddamned artillery support when we need it?" the voice of Lieutenant "Red" Egan shouted above the din. "We're getting the shit cut out of us." Egan had recently become a company commander. The helpless and frustrated forward observer could only shrug in disgust. Joseph had a pretty good idea where the Jap rocket and mortar fire was coming from; he had plotted suspected locations the evening before. But he was incommunicado.

The situation was grim. The 9th was pinned down on the opposite side of the runway. Until they moved up, the 21st would have to stay put. Finally, an air strike was called in. As a swarm of Hellcats from carriers out at sea bombed and strafed the Japs, the 21st pulled back and the 9th took up the attack. It was an ignominious beginning for Joseph, and he vowed to prove to Egan and the 21st that the artillery could be counted on.

After reaching the relative safety of the fallback area among the dunes, he contacted Easy Battery, which had just come ashore, and demanded a reliable radio and a complete F.O. (forward observer) team. He was not denied. Up came Sergeants Andy Sabol and Frank Dilger along with a new radio man and a wireman lugging a spool of heavy communication wire. Now he had a complete F.O. team. Sabol, a muscular Pennsylvania steel worker, was the communication sergeant for the battery. But the situation at the gun position being static, he wanted action and insisted on joining the F.O. team. Dilger came up as scout sergeant.

The exhausted men of the 21st were flopped in foxholes, as crowded as a colony of nesting sea birds. None of them were aware of the graying, robust figure slowly picking his way among the foxholes.

Joseph at once recognized General Erskine, the division commander. His command post must have been near by. Strangely, he was not accompanied by an aide. The last time he had seen Erskine was when he and Lieutenant "Umbriago" had crashed the general's New Year's party on Guam. He approached the general and saluted.

"Good morning, sir. Can I help you?"

"Good morning," the general replied gruffly. "Who are these men?"

"Twenty-first Marines, sir. We just came from across the airfield."

Erskine uttered a satisfied grunt and stalked off.

His reputation as division commander was yet to come. From the moment he had established his command post ashore, he was determined to drive a wedge through the center of Kuribayashi's main defenses all the way to the north end of the island and the sea. Soon the troops in the front lines would be repeating an adage, "We got Japs in front and Erskine behind. Better move out men."

Nicknamed "The Big E," Erskine made good his intentions to use his two regiments as a spearhead up the center of Iwo. At times he risked the exposure of the division's flanks, where the 4th and 5th Divisions lagged on each side.

With barely enough time to regroup and refill its ranks with replacements, the 21st was back on the attack, this time abreast of the 9th, its sister regiment. They entered Motoyama Village, or what remained of it.

Concrete rubble and sheets of corrugated roofing were the only recognizable signs of the village. Its residents had been employed in a sulfur mine and some grew sugar cane. Dwarf trees that had once provided some shade around the houses were in splinters. Here, the 21st encountered the heaviest mortar and rocket fire of the battle. Joseph caught a glimpse of an object the size of a twenty-five-gallon garbage can tumbling earthward. He dove into a shallow hole, but the concussion levitated him two feet upward and deposited him out of the hole.

They were being hit with the 320-millimeter mortars so much had been heard about. Next came the 500-pound rockets, resembling flying acetylene bottles. They came whooshing from behind an outcropping of rocks not more than 100 yards ahead. One flew barely ten feet above their heads and traveled two miles before exploding near the artillery positions back on the beach.

Joseph led his men behind a crumbled stone wall. Sabol hooked up the phone. No sooner had he cranked it, when the operator in the Easy Battery fire direction center answered excitedly.

"We're getting rocket fire here. Can you see it?"

"What the hell you think we're getting here, confetti?" Joseph replied. In a more serious voice he began, "Fire mission! Target area 218 Uncle. Mark with one round of smoke."

"One round smoke on the way," came the FDC.

"Everyone watch," Joseph called to his men, a single 75-millimeter shell burst being difficult to spot amid all the other explosions. Even white phosphorous. They saw nothing.

"Repeat smoke, battery one around in target area 218 Uncle," Joseph called. Again they waited.

"There it is, Gunner," Dilger shouted. The rounds were considerably left of the target area shown on Joseph's map. "Right 400. Down 100. Shell HE," Joseph called.

A volley of high explosive shells whistled overhead and fell close to where the rockets were coming from. A minute later, another rocket blasted off.

"Repeat range. Fire for effect," Joseph called.

"On the way," came the FDC.

Yet another rocket came flying over. Joseph turned to his men.

"We're hitting them right where the flash is coming from, they must be underground."

The duel became a personal confrontation. The Japs lowered their launcher and aimed point blank at the troops in the town. Joseph decided the danger was more from the concussions than from the shell fragments. The rocket casings must have had thin walls stuffed with TNT. They were dropping a mere fifty yards behind the infantry line. Mercifully, the Japs were prevented by a bluff that concealed them from lowering their aim directly on the front-line marines.

Joseph conferred on the phone with Captain McElroy at the battery position. "They must be operating from a cave," he said. "They're in the ground by the time our rounds land."

They decided to hold the guns loaded and ready. Joseph had timed the frequency of the rocket firings at about every four minutes.

He would try to guess when the Japs were in the act of firing the next missile. With luck he'd catch them in the open. Three times at random, Joseph called "fire." After the third volley, there was no answering rocket. "Cease fire, mark it down as probable." Joseph said to McElroy ten minutes later.

The fighting in Motoyama Village was as fierce as Joseph and his F.O team would experience. The Japs must have felt a special attachment to what had been a community, and they gave it up grudgingly. Men were dying every minute over this worthless pile of rubble.

While trying to get a bead on the rocket launcher, Joseph had been forced to crawl to different positions for better observation. With each move, snipers' bullets cracked over his head.

Sabol observed that Joseph was wearing his fancy tank jacket. It even held his name in gilt letters on a cordovan leather patch over his breast, crafted by a New Zealand artisan. Although the day had gotten warm, he had been too busy engaging rockets to remove the jacket.

"You're drawing fire with that fancy jacket," Sabol shouted. "They recognize you as an officer."

Heeding the warning, Joseph took off the jacket. From that moment he would only wear it after dark. A chill wind arose after nightfall. It moaned softly through the lifeless trees and rattled a sheet of corrugated metal. The sky was bright with stars.

From a distance, the familiar taunts of Japs were heard, "Marine, you die."

A nervous 4th Division company commander on the right trying to contact the 21st somehow got patched to Joseph's F.O. phone line. His platoon on the left was unable to make contact with the 21st and he feared having his flank exposed. The infantry always made it a point to "tie in" for the night. Could Joseph contact the 21st and get them to close the gap?

"Anyone moving about now will get shot," Joseph replied. "We'll try to pass the word."

With that, he called out in a muffled voice to a mortar section nearby. They had a phone to the company C.P. and forwarded the message. Joseph heard no more from the 4th Division.

The morning began with what would be a daily routine: An air strike followed by an artillery barrage. Then the infantry would "jump off." As the routine played out, there would soon come cries of "Corpsman!" Stretcher bearers would emerge struggling to carry out some unlucky grunt whose number had come up. The attack might go a hundred yards before bogging down. Marines would silence a pillbox and move on only to be attacked from the rear. The Jap defenses were so connected with a maze of tunnels that it was like putting out a brush fire. It might spring up anywhere.

When the attack finally pushed through Motoyama, Joseph's F.O. team came upon a disabled rocket launcher and the bodies of its three-man crew.

The launcher was a crude device of heavy lumber supporting a wooden trough about four feet high. It rode on rails in and out of a cave. Joseph's "kill" was noted by a combat correspondent and reported in press releases Stateside, including the Lake Tarsa weekly.

Each day Erskine's wedge drove deeper into Kuribayashi's midsection. The division was two-thirds of the way up the island, having reached a plateau with outcroppings of rock that resembled the Badlands of South Dakota. The infantry battalion now had its second commander. At his age, Major George Percy had no business on Iwo Jima. The graying middle-aged reserve officer had quit his Wall Street brokerage firm and finagled an overseas assignment. He was a familiar figure running about the front lines in a crouch lugging a carbine. His utility jacket was stained with blood where he had been nicked on the shoulder by a shell fragment.

Percy would sidle up to Joseph's observation post, slap him on the back, and inquire "How's the artillery, Gunner?" Joseph would usually reply, "Major, if your guys will find those Japs for us, we'll do the rest." Finding Japs wasn't easy. They were seldom caught in the open, and their smokeless powder made it hard to detect the muzzle blasts of their mortars and artillery. The Japs wore beige uniforms which blended in with the terrain. The marines, except for their mottled camouflage helmet covers, wore the green utilities that had been suitable in the jungles. On treeless Iwo, they struck out like sore thumbs.

It was two weeks since the landing when all eyes were riveted on a crippled B-29 cautiously making its approach to airfield number one. It would be the first of hundreds of emergency landings by shot-up superfortresses returning from bombing runs over Japan, twenty-six in March alone. The chance of fliers making it back to their ice machines, cabanas, and nurses on Tumon Beach were greatly enhanced by Iwo's airstrips paid for with marine lives.

As the infantry was digging in late one afternoon, the F.O. team found and occupied a large square pit a few yards ahead of the company command post. It was deep enough to stand in and long enough for the lanky six-foot Dilger to stretch out full length. The pit gave an unobstructed view of the terrain to the front. One hundred yards behind were the infantry mortars. When they had registered the battery on a rock pinnacle and plotted likely targets, Joseph and his two NCOs unburdened themselves of their equipment and stretched out side by side. In adjoining foxholes were the radio and wire men.

When darkness came, U.S. destroyers began firing 5-inch illumination shells, a nightly routine. As the magnesium flares swung back and forth on parachutes, the light created sinister shadows formed by the boulders and outcroppings of rock across the battlefield. Tired eyes could easily be deceived into believing the eerie shadows were Japs running back and forth.

Suddenly they heard the unmistakable flutter of a mortar round directly overhead. They flinched. There was a thud, and Joseph's head and face was sprayed with dirt. He reached back and touched the hot fins of the mortar round, not six inches from his head. Dilger was also reaching.

"Leave it alone," Joseph yelled. Too late, Dilger had grabbed and flung it out of the hole. Still, it did not detonate. The three climbed out of the hole and cautiously examined the dud in the dim light of a flare. They made out the yellow markings of the U.S. Army ordnance. It was a "friendly" 60-millimeter shell, a short round.

Joseph waited for the light of a new flare and made his way to the company C.P. He had already decided the short round was not an error of siting. The mortars were too close to lob a shell into their pit no matter how grievous the gunner's error in elevation. "When's the last time your mortar tubes were swabbed?" he asked the C.O. He knew that under continuous firing, unless periodically cleaned, the tubes would become clogged with a sticky residue of gunpowder that resulted in the loss of range. A second lieutenant summoned from the mortar section stammered and couldn't remember for sure when his tubes had last been cleaned.

"Until you do so, we're not going back out there," Joseph announced.

In an odd way, Joseph and his NCOs owed their lives to a gummed up mortar tube. The round had emerged so sluggishly, it had not achieved the velocity needed to arm the fuse. In mortar and artillery shells, fuses were actuated by the set-back force as the shell overcame inertia when fired. Once the fuse was armed, the shell would detonate upon striking the ground or a solid object. An abnormal velocity was not sufficient to arm the fuse.

With the assurance that the mortar tubes would be promptly swabbed, Joseph and his crew returned to their hole. Under cover of a poncho, Joseph and Dilger lit cigarettes. Sabol didn't smoke.

"Don't ever pick up a dud," Joseph admonished Dilger. "Some of those things can lie for years until some boob picks one up and then, bam, he's gone."

Even as a dud, Joseph reckoned, his skull would have been crushed had the missile struck him in the head or face.

As the three reflected on the incident, Joseph wondered aloud if Dilger would have qualified for a medal had he thrown himself on the shell instead of disposing of it as he had.

Did it have to explode to qualify as a heroic deed that saved men's lives? Heroes who fell on grenades and gave their lives to spare others automatically qualified for the Congressional Medal. Joseph put the questions to the two men: If you fell on the shell that just landed, not knowing it would be a dud, wasn't it your intention to sacrifice your life and therefore an extreme act of heroism?

"Hell, it wouldn't be the man's fault if the damned thing didn't go off," Dilger chortled. "He should get some medal, maybe not the big one."

They decided only philosophers could answer the question.

As the battle progressed, the days became blurred. They lost all track of time. One evening, the battalion set up in an area of loose sand that emitted hot sulfurous fumes. The vision would have fit into Dante's image of the Inferno.

Cans of rations were heated by burying them in the ground. A canteen of hot coffee could be kept warm through the night. Sleeping in foxholes scooped from the sand was like a rotisserie, though not quite as hot. The side of the body on the ground would become uncomfortably warm while the other side needed a blanket to ward off the night chill. One had to keep rotating.

Occasionally, when all was quiet, a three-quarter-ton truck equipped with a rocket launcher would back up near the front lines. "Not here," the grunts in the line would yell. "Go somewhere else." (Original NIMBYs?) Unheeding of their pleas, the crew quickly would fire off a rack of 4.5-inch rockets, raising smoke and dust visible for miles, and promptly, the Japanese would answer with a barrage of their own. By that time, the truck launcher had scratched out and barreled for safety leaving the poor grunts to weather the return barrage.

A briefing of front-line officers was called by the 21st Regiment C.O. A haggard group of mostly unfamiliar faces squatted or sat in front of an easel with a situation map overlaid with acetate. As the intelligence officer was about to begin, an agitated lieutenant rushed in. Joseph immediately recognized Tom Pottinger, a Fox Battery F.O.

"The Chief . . . Scondras, just got his head blown off," he blurted. Recognizing Joseph, he continued, "He was standing right next to me and . . . " here he broke down. "His head was gone."

Respectfully, the colonel at the easel lowered his pointer and waited. The assembled officers stared hard at the ground. Lieutenant Scondras was a full-blooded Indian. He had been a versatile athlete at Dartmouth and was one of the best-liked junior officers in the artillery battalion. He and Pottinger were sharing an O.P. when he was decapitated by an artillery round. Pottinger had emerged unscathed.

The battle was winding down; fewer bodies were coming by on stretchers. But increasingly, a more distressing phenomenon was occurring: small knots of men, supported by corpsmen, straggling to the rear and sobbing inconsolably. Combat neurosis, they called it, or fatigue. In Hollywood flicks of World War One, it was called "shell shock." It was unnerving to see these men who had lived in fear and horror until they could no longer take it. They cracked. Joseph saw their reddened eyes and flowing tears, eyes that had witnessed the death or maiming of too many buddies. Yet, except for the compassionate corpsmen, they were shunned like lepers for fear the trauma was contagious. Deep inside the psyche of the toughest men, the notion was ingrained that marines didn't cry.

Flights of air force Mustangs were now making bombing and strafing runs ahead of the battalion. That meant the fighter strips in the rear were operational. The sleek fighters flew just above ground level, in and out of gorges, following the contours of the terrain. The marines held their breath. Could air force pilots be trusted with close air support missions? Did they know the exact location of friendly front lines? They had faith in the navy Hellcats and marine Corsairs.

Soon the Mustangs would be fitted with spare fuel tanks and escort the B-29s to and from Japan.

Finally, near the end of the third week of the battle, the infantry battalion reached the edge of a steep cliff, 200 feet high. From their lofty perch they could see the end of the island and the sea. Kitano Point lay a half-mile away, at the far end of a desolate, plowed up patch of ground. Giant boulders had been cracked apart from naval shells. Not a single bit of vegetation was to be seen. Joseph searched the ravaged terrain with his glasses but saw no sign of activity. It was obvious the battle for Iwo Jima was petering out.

A patrol from the 1st Battalion worked its way down the cliffs and reached the beach. They filled a canteen with sea water, which eventually made it to Erskine's CP. It was labeled, "Not for consumption. For inspection only." The canteen validated Erskine's boast to drive to the sea.

Joseph's field phone buzzed.

"Tom Belzer here Gunner, Got any targets?"

It was Lieutenant Colonel Thomas Belzer, the operations officer of the 12th Regiment. They were acquainted, Major Belzer having served as the "Three," operations officer, of the 2nd Battalion before his promotion. Staff officers were identified as numbers. Battalion One was administration: Two, intelligence; Three, operations; and Four, supply and logistics.

Belzer went on: "You are the only F.O. in the division with a view of Kitano Point. I have every available gun in the regiment and corps artillery tied in and ready to shoot. Give us some targets."

Joseph swallowed hard. From not being able to fire a single shot at airfield 2 to help extricate the 21st Marines from their firestorm, he was being offered more guns than he had use for: thirty-six 75-millimeter pack howitzers; twelve 105-millimeter howitzers; and twenty-four 155 millimeter howitzers, a total of seventy-two tubes.

As he talked on the phone, Joseph again panned the barren landscape with his glasses. There was no sign of any human activity.

"There are friendly patrols in the area, Colonel," he explained. "We haven't drawn any fire, and we're sitting on top of a cliff in plain sight. I don't see anything to shoot at except broken rocks."

Belzer sounded disappointed. His fire direction team had cobbled together enough artillery for a barrage sufficient to blow up what was left of the island, and now he was being told there was nothing to shoot at. Like being all dressed up and no party to go to.

"You sure?" he quizzed.

"Colonel, my four men are searching the area," Joseph answered. "The company commander here also doesn't see anything. But I will call it at the first sign of any activity."

"Okay, but I can't hold these battalions forever," Belzer ended.

A feast or famine, Joseph said aloud.

They spent a quiet day on the cliff except that occasionally they would feel a rumbling deep in the bowels of the earth. Could another volcano be in the making? Next to Joseph's observation post was a heavy, water-cooled machine gun in a sandbagged pit with a crew of four men. Mail had arrived, and they were engrossed in reading letters from home. Suddenly from underground, there was a terrific blast directly under the gun crew. Three men were killed and their gun disabled. Opened letters that held comforting news from mothers and fathers, girlfriends and wives fluttered about speckled with blood.

Nothing was fair in this damned war, Joseph thought.

Far below, at the foot of the cliff, in large caves was a Japanese ammunition dump. Earlier in the day, a marine flame thrower had worked his way to the mouth of a cave and squirted a lethal tongue of jelled fuel. It had set off a chain of explosion that culminated with the big blast that blew all the way up through the top of the cliff.

"The truck will be there soon," Captain McElroy announced on the phone the next day. Joseph's F.O. team was being pulled out. The artillery war was over; now it remained for the engineers and pioneers to seal up the caves.

Joyously, Joseph's crew clambered aboard the four-by-four for the three-mile ride back to the beach, exhilarating in their freedom. But as the truck passed through a narrow cut in a bluff, a high velocity round struck the embankment. The Japs had this pass well zeroed in. A single piece of shrapnel struck Sabol in the leg, sending blood gushing through his utilities. The driver tore onward, not stopping until they reached the artillery aid station.

After seeing that Sabel was going to be okay, Joseph found his way to a large pit covered by a tarp.

It had served as a sort of "dormitory" for the junior grade officers of the artillery battalion. Joseph was warmly welcomed; acclaimed a survivor. He had been with a front-line infantry company for twenty-one days. Ronnie Stillman had also survived as an F.O. with another battalion.

"Got any souvenirs?" someone shouted from the far end of the pit. "Only my dog tags," Joseph answered.

He consumed a miniature bottle of medical brandy, compliments of the battalion surgeon, and experienced a feeling of well being like he'd never had before. There was mail awaiting, several letters from Cara. She was still waiting. There were a couple from his parents with the bad news that his grandmother in Lake Tarsa had died. Funny, Joseph thought, he had expected to be the first of his extended family to die.

Floating about from one hand to another under the tarp was a recent, but already dog-eared copy of *Time Magazine*, a lightweight overseas edition.

The cover captured Joseph's attention. It was the flag-raising over Mount Surabachi. Though hardly a student or connoisseur of art, Joseph was captivated with the drama of the picture. Even an untrained eye could recognize that the moment captured by Joe Rosenthal with his cumbersome four-by-five-inch speed graphic camera was a masterpiece.

They were on the beach, preparing to board Higgins boats for the ride to their transport, when McElroy approached Joseph.

"The battery has been authorized to award two Bronze Stars," McElroy began. "Obviously, your F.O.'s deserve them. You can take one for yourself and give the other to one of your team."

"Are you recommending me for a Bronze Star?" Joseph asked.

"Like I said, if you think you deserve a medal, it's yours," McElroy continued.

"All of my men have risked their lives time and again, especially the wireman," Joseph said. "Sergeant Sabol certainly deserves one. Either of the other wiremen should have the other."

At that, Joseph turned away. He had given away his medal, but he felt no great loss.

*   *   *

"Uncommon Valor was a Common Virtue."

That was how Admiral Chester W. Nimitz eloquently characterized the fighting on Iwo Jima.

Twenty-four Congressional Medals of Honor were awarded. On the home front as more gold stars were displayed in cheerless windows by grieving mothers, the navy parried press criticism by justifying the heavy loss of life on Iwo Jima as a favorable tradeoff. While 5,885 marines and 433 navy men died seizing the island and 17,272 were wounded, they had potentially saved the lives of 24,761 airmen.

It was a stretch of figures which assumed that every crew member of the 2,251 Superfortresses that made emergency landings on the island would otherwise have perished.

Back on Guam, the 3rd Division's information section published a two-page special edition on the battle, classified as "RESTRICTED" and not to be mailed out. On heavy yellow paper, the bulletin chronicled stories of the battles as related by troops. One article told of the heavy casualties inflicted on the enemy by the 12th Regiment's artillery bombardments. The 12th was credited with inflicting sixty percent of the enemy casualties.

One quote caught Joseph's eye. It was from Lieutenant Joseph "Red" Egan, a company commander of the 21st Marines, who said of the 12th: "Their guns saved our necks plenty of times. Every time we needed artillery support, it was right there. Thank God."

While indulging in the compliment, Joseph chuckled to himself, remembering how Egan had stood over his foxhole on airfield number 2 in a withering fire storm and screamed, "We're getting the shit cut out of us. Where's the goddamned artillery when we need it?"

Twelve
Reunion with Cara—1945

"Hello."

He had forgotten the sound of Cara's voice. It was warm and soft. His heart was pounding.

"It's me, I'm back . . . in San Diego."

"What took you so long?" she asked.

He had written her from Guam a month before that he was on his way home but, at the time, didn't know it would be aboard an LST, the slowest ship in the navy. It had taken twenty-seven days. While they were at sea, the war in Europe had ended and President Franklin Roosevelt had died. Harry Truman was the new president.

"It's a long story. I'll explain later." He only had a couple of nickels left to feed the pay phone at the Marine Corps base.

So began the cautious process of reconnecting after a separation of nearly thirty months.

Following her instructions, he was soon on the Greyhound bus for the short ride to Oceanside. She was waiting at the station with her vintage Dodge, the "Green Hornet," as she called it.

Cara shared a duplex in town with another school teacher. In the tiny front room, Althea pulled up a chair. She wanted to share in the reunion and hung on every word. When Joseph glanced her way, she was staring at him with her mouth agape. He was already nervous and didn't need an audience. He was relieved when finally Cara said it was nearing time for him to catch the last bus to San Diego.

"I'll be back tomorrow night," he said at the station after an overdue kiss.

The Reclassification and Distribution Center was a model of efficiency. In two days, the eleven officers in Joseph's returning group had been paid, fitted with new uniforms, given physical examinations, assigned to duty stations across the country, and issued priority train tickets. A disappointed Joseph studied his orders. After a thirty-day leave, he was to report to the Marine Detachment, Naval Retraining Command, Williamsburg, Virginia. He had hoped for assignment on the West Coast. Instead, he was going to be a continent away from Cara.

"Williamsburg is a nice place," Captain Mike Crocker said, in trying to console Joseph. Mike had been the survey officer in their artillery battalion. "I've been there. It's very historical. It's been restored by the Rockefeller Foundation."

Back in Oceanside that evening, Joseph shared the news with Cara and then blurted an awkward proposal. To his immense relief, she accepted without raising a single question. Her school term would soon end, after which she would make plans for the trip east to get married. They were leaving to have dinner at the Carlsbad Hotel. Cara appeared in a red dress, and in an apologetic tone asked if he minded.

"Mind what?" Joseph asked, thinking how great she looked.

"My red dress."

"Of course not," he said. "I like it."

It dawned on him that here was a most considerate woman, a side of her he had already discerned from her letters. The Oceanside area was swarming with marines from the giant Camp Pendleton base, and the sight of women in red dresses had been known to trigger their worst behavior.

Joseph had one last piece of business to take care of before his departure from San Diego. Some five years earlier, when he had been promoted to corporal, he had opened a savings account with a bank in the Hillcrest district of East San Diego. Planning on a college education at the end of his enlistment, he had taken out an allotment with the Marine Corps that deposited a major percentage of his pay into the account each month. But he had never heard from the bank after the first year.

He approached a teller at the Bank of America, stated his name and inquired about the balance of his account. The teller went to his files and began a search. He returned with a puzzled expression and asked for details. Soon, other bank clerks were checking records, but no trace of Joseph's account could be located. Joseph's face flushed with a mixture of panic and anger, and he demanded to talk to the manager.

"Are you sure it was this bank?" the manager asked.

"I'm sure," Joseph replied.

"Are you sure it wasn't the bank down the street?" continued the manager.

"I don't know of another bank on this street," Joseph answered heatedly, as he now believed he was being snookered.

Meanwhile, the original teller he had talked to had been on the telephone. He hung up the receiver and called out to Joseph. "The First National has your account. They're expecting you. It's on the corner of the next block." he said pointing in the direction. Stammering an apology, Joseph was off for the other bank.

"Man, we've been wondering about you all this time," a teller at the First National said, after checking Joseph's ID card. "The Marine Corps never told us where you were." He produced a passbook and entered the current balance. It was nearly $5,000, a small fortune in 1945, particularly for a marine. Practically walking on air, an elated Joseph departed with an updated bank statement securely in his breast pocket. Cara wouldn't be marrying a pauper.

The long train ride east was slow and boring. In the diner, Joseph was amused to hear a middle-aged woman complaining to the steward that there was no sugar bowl on her table.

"Only men in uniform get sugar, ma'am," the steward answered polite.

America was still nursing a hangover after the V-E Day celebration, yet the invasion of Okinawa was just underway and Japan had shown no inclination to surrender.

The skipper of Joseph's homebound LST, a young navy lieutenant, had expressed his feeling about the duration of the war as they were leaving Guam. He figured it had a long way to go. It was their first night aboard, and after dinner as they were having a second cup of coffee, he broached the subject.

"Why should we be in a hurry to get back to the States," he stated rhetorically. "They will give us sixty days, at the most, and then we'll be out again for another operation. Unless you object, I'm going to take my sweet time getting back."

There having been on objection, he pointed his slow boat towards Eniwetok in the Marshall Islands. He took on fresh water, although it wasn't needed, what with only forty men and eleven officers on his troop manifest. Next, he made for Kwajalein, only a two-day sail even on the slow boat. A bit of R&R was in order. On Kwajalein, there was a nifty little O-club on the water's edge, crafted of nipa palms by the natives. Joseph struck the jackpot on a ten-cent slot machine. He poured out his winnings on the bar, two handfuls of dimes, enough to pay for everyone's drinks the rest of the evening.

Next came Pearl Harbor and a major disappointment. The ghostly masts and superstructures of sunken battleships jutted like tombstones from the inky waters off Ford Island. The sidewalks of Honolulu were pulled in at sundown, and the whole city was blacked out. Joseph's group wandered into the deserted lobby of the Royal Hawaiian Hotel. The dining room and bar were already closed. They boarded the LST a little more eager to complete the last leg to San Diego.

It was a navy custom for ships returning from the war to fly victory pennants from the main mast. Their multicolored signal pennants were strung one after the other like the tail of a kite. From the mast of a stately carrier or battleship entering San Francisco's Golden Gate the pennant was a spectacular sight whipping smartly in a strong breeze.

Rounding Point Loma and entering San Diego Bay, the LST skipper gave the order to break out the victory pennant. Flown from the squatty LST with its short mast and not much of a breeze, the effect was quixotic. The ship made its triumphant return with the tail of its reluctant pennant dragging astern in the water as though they were trolling for tuna. Unfazed, the young skipper lit a cigar and savored the occasion.

*   *   *

Four days after leaving Los Angeles, the Southern Pacific squealed to a stop at the Dennings station in the dead of night. Joseph heard his heavy metal trunk clatter down the iron steps of the baggage car, suspended at the end of the porter's arm. He eased it down to the graveled railroad siding and dropped it. The locomotive belched a cloud of steam and resumed its journey, leaving Joseph with his thoughts in total darkness.

He was at the end of a long journey begun seven years ago in this very place. The train had continued to New Orleans and was probably the one that had taken him to join the marines in 1938.

Joseph dragged his trunk to the station. A sleepy stationmaster, most likely the same one that had sold him a one-way ticket to New Orleans, called a cab. On the empty concrete road to Lake Tarsa, the driver lowered the windows letting in the cool night air and a few insects that avoided splattering against the windshield.

In Lake Tarsa, Joseph banged on the back door until a sleepy Ornas turned on the kitchen light and unlatched the screen. His father had never been one to lose much sleep. After a joyful, but short, reunion, he was back in bed leaving his son all to Clarissa. She told him they had known he was on Iwo Jima by the article in the weekly paper that reported his encounter with the rockets in Motoyama Village. All during his absence, she had kept repeating the beads of her rosary until they were worn shiny.

The town bustled with prosperity. Men and women were making good wages working in war-related industries in Lake Charles and Lafayette. Everyone had money but there was not much to spend it on, what with rationing in effect. Meats, gasoline, tires, sugar, and alcoholic spirits were in short supply, but not beer. Saturday nights, Ornas's bar was jammed with customers sucking on long necks of Dixie and Jax.

Wearing his new tan gabardine summer uniform, Joseph was having a beer with a friend, when a customer asked Ornas, "Who is that marine officer over there?"

"Oh, that's not an officer. It's my son," Ornas replied innocently. He had never taken note of Joseph's letter telling of his promotion to warrant officer. Nor was he the least bit knowledgeable, or concerned, about military rank insignia.

Joseph was bored and longed to be out of Lake Tarsa soon. He kept thinking of Cara and wondering if she would succeed in securing train passage to Williamsburg. He stayed two weeks, mostly out of respect for his mother who wanted him close as long as possible. Her gumbos, jumbalayas, and crawfish etouffes didn't hurt her cause.

Joseph spent two days in New Orleans. He sampled the Ramos gin fizzes in the bar of the Roosevelt Hotel, where he was staying, and the restaurant fare in the French Quarter. In a jewelry store on

Canal Street, he bought a set of rings for Cara. He knew nothing about diamonds or gold and cautiously settled for an inexpensive set. He promptly mailed the engagement ring to Cara. She was thrilled with the ring, she wrote him in Virginia. Just like her.

The Naval Retraining and Distribution Center was at Camp Peary on the banks of the York River forty miles up from Norfolk. In historic Williamsburg, Joseph found himself transported back into colonial times. Residents went about their business wearing colonial costumes. The town was a life-sized replica of an American village 170 years earlier. Never had he seen so many antique brick buildings. Like Mike Crocker had said, the Rockefellers had poured millions of dollars into the restoration of Williamsburg.

Joseph settled into the BOQ and his duties with the marine detachment, whose purpose was to retrain and rehabilitate the navy's general court martial prisoners. About 1,000 of them were incarcerated in what resembled a POW camp. It was surrounded by a ten-foot barbed wire fence and sentry towers manned by armed marines. In reality, it was a boot camp in which marine drill instructors attempted to instill some semblance of discipline and respect for the navy among the incorrigibles, most of which had jumped ship at some port or other.

Back in San Francisco, Cara's dad, Kelly, was working his connections, which were well placed in the Bay Area, arranging transportation for her trip east. Rail travel in war times was restricted mainly to the business of war. Only civilians with essential business to conduct were accommodated. As a management consultant and public relations advisor for the California employer's council, Kelly had butted heads with the Bay Area's most obnoxious union leaders, including the notorious communist, Harry Bridges, who held enough power to freeze war materials on West Coast docks.

Before long, Kelly secured tickets for Cara, and she began her own "Sentimental Journey" aboard the Southern Pacific.

After a tiring trip of seven days—the route took her through Chicago—she disembarked into the wilting July heat of Virginia. She wore a stylish, light-blue gabardine suit, not suited for the weather but most becoming in Joseph's eyes. He checked her into a room at the Williamsburg Lodge, and soon they were discussing their marriage. There were problems of religion, she being a Protestant, and they decided on a civil marriage.

Captain Butterworth and Lieutenant Stepanovich picked them up at the hotel in the military green Marine Corps panel truck. It wasn't until they entered the office of the justice of the peace on Duke of Gloucester Street that Stepnaovich, who was as nervous as Joseph, discovered he had forgotten the belt to his uniform.

Big Herman Schweidman, a navy lieutenant who played pro ball for the Chicago Bears before the war, sent up a bottle of champagne to their room. Williamsburg was an ideal place for a honeymoon, quiet and fashionable, even in wartime, but the newlyweds decided they should go somewhere. With their choices limited by a three-day leave, not to mention the difficulties of traveling, they boarded a Greyhound bus and went to Richmond. The bus was packed, and they stood the whole hour of the trip. Typical honeymooners, they saw very little of the city, rarely venturing from the venerable Richmond Hotel with its bronze statue of Stonewall Jackson on the grounds.

Back in Williamsburg they moved into a rooming house near the campus of William and Mary College. Joseph bought a car from a marine corporal who was being tranferred. It was a 1938 Buick coupe. Cara promptly christened it the "Black Bullet." The car had been well kept and needed only new tires. Lieutenant Schweidman was on the ration board at Camp Peary, and Joseph didn't have to wait long before "Black Bullet" was wearing a new set of rubber. The car was a godsend. Joseph no longer had to bum rides to and from camp or rush to catch the bus. By managing their gasoline ration stamps, he and Cara explored Jamestown and other historical sites of Tidewater, Virginia. They often drove to roadside restaurants for dinners.

August 6, 1945, they were walking hand in hand on Duke of Gloucester Street on their way to dinner. From inside the stores and shops, radios were blaring the news of a mighty new U.S. bomb that had obliterated Hiroshima, Japan. The atomic age had been born, and the end of the war was imminent. Joseph would soon have been heading back to the Pacific for the invasion of Japan, but the bombs had changed everything. Still, he had misgivings about the air force ending the war with two bombs. His comrades had sacrificed their blood in securing air bases for the B-29s carrying the A-bombs. They had taken off from Tinian and flown a course over Iwo Jima, their haven in the event of a mishap. It was a silly thought, he knew, especially when he felt the warmth in the hand of his new bride. Yet, in the immediate postwar years, the prophecy of Joseph's fears nearly came to pass when a miserly Congress, at the urging of President Truman—an army veteran of World War I, who was outspoken in his dislike for the Marine Corps–all but dismantled the corps. Who needed an amphibious force, was the thinking in Washington, when the air force had the atomic bomb?

As they studied the menu in the dining room of the Williamsburg Lodge, a waitress began filling their glasses with champagne. "Turkey dinner for servicemen is on the Rockefellers tonight," she announced.

They found an upstairs apartment in town, and Cara was soon enjoying the social life with navy wives in the building. They spent their first Christmas together. Cara baked a duck. They had cruised the countryside in the Buick and bought the bird from a farmer whose wife had dressed it out. Joseph relished the occasion, thinking back on the many lonely holidays he has spent in the Pacific.

He had gotten over the nervousness of his first several weeks after returning from the war. But, Iwo Jima still haunted his mind. Some nights he would awake from a recurring nightmare that he was caught in the open with bombs and shells falling. He would be comforted by Cara's soft breathing and soon drop back to sleep. Some days his stomach wouldn't hold food despite Cara's best attempts to nourish him properly. She was a bride who knew how to cook. Not so with a young navy wife in the apartment building. In her genteel Southern upbringing, servants did all the cooking. Her husband, a dentist, bought a pressure cooker, and they subsisted mainly on his pot roasts. After a botched-up attempt at brewing coffee in a Silex, she put the coffeemaker away—for good—in the pantry with the wet grounds still in the glass.

From the apartment building, Joseph and Cara graduated to a cozy little garage apartment. Cara's mother came to visit from San Francisco. To his relief, Joseph passed inspection. They liked each other. Cara's mother had been reluctant to see her daughter travel 3,000 miles to marry a marine she had never met. Now she was reassured.

Camp Peary was being phased out, and Joseph was expecting orders. They were no long in arriving. His temporary appointment to warrant officer was being terminated. He was given the option of remaining in the corps with the rank of master sergeant or of accepting a discharge. He opted on a discharge.

In New Orleans, Joseph's appointment to warrant officer was terminated. Returning to Lake Tarsa had never been an option in Joseph's mind. While in New Orleans, he interviewed for a job with the U.S. Immigration Service, but it didn't pan out. Neither did their search for an apartment. They soon tired of New Orleans and the humid heat and headed the Buick for San Francisco where Joseph's chances for employment would be more favorable.

They stopped over in Lake Charles to have the valves ground on the car. After the operation, the "Bullet" ran like new, but the mechanics warned Joseph that he would have to drive slowly for the next 500 miles—no more than 35 miles an hour—to break in the valve job. Driving at top speeds across Texas in August would have been bad enough, but at 35 miles an hour, it was a purgatory, especially without air conditioning. To avoid the heat, they would hit the road at daylight and drive 100 miles before stopping for breakfast.

By three in the afternoon they were looking for a motel.

As a precaution against overheating, they bought a canvas water bag, which they slung on the front bumper. Gasoline was again plentiful at double-digit prices. In the pre-interstate driving days, a stop at a gas station was somewhat like the pit stops in stock car racing. No sooner was the ignition off when an attendant would fling open the hood and reach for the oil dipstick. A second attendant would insert the gasoline nozzle and clean the windshield while the gas was pumping. A third man would be on his knees checking the air pressure in the tires. It was full service in the real sense of the word at no extra charge. Joseph and Cara patronized the gas stations likely to have the cleanest rest rooms, usually Gulf and Texaco.

The journey west was like a second honeymoon. At the Grand Canyon, they found accommodations in the Bright Angel Lodge and spent a day gazing in awe at the ever-changing colors of the canyon. They had planned to cross Death Valley early in the morning. But after overnighting in Las Vegas, which was then better known for its "quickie" divorces of Hollywood movie stars than for its gambling casinos, they reached the eastern approach of Death Valley early in the afternoon and decided to continue on. All went well until they reached the first of the terraces that elevated them from the lowest point in the United States—below sea level—to the foothills of the Panamints and Sierra Nevadas.

Three times the Bullet overheated, each time conveniently near one of the water barrels placed on the roadside by the California Highway Department. Joseph would pull over and with a wadded rag cautiously turn the radiator cap releasing the steam. When Bullet stopped regurgitating, he slowly poured in water, and they would resume the climb. At Bishop, where they stopped for the night, they were invigorated by the alpine climate.

They reveled in the scenery of the Sierras, occasionally stopping to soak their feet in the cold rushing steams along the roadsides. Crossing the Bay Bridge into San Francisco, Cara perked up, reinvigorated by the chilly fog rolling in from the Pacific. Shivering in his lightweight civilian clothes, Joseph was reminded of a remark by Mark Twain that the coldest winter he had ever spent was August in San Francisco.

The battle over, author (left) poses with Ronnie Stillman, a fellow forward observer on Iwo Jima.

Joseph and Cara shortly after their wedding in Williamsburg, VA, 1945.

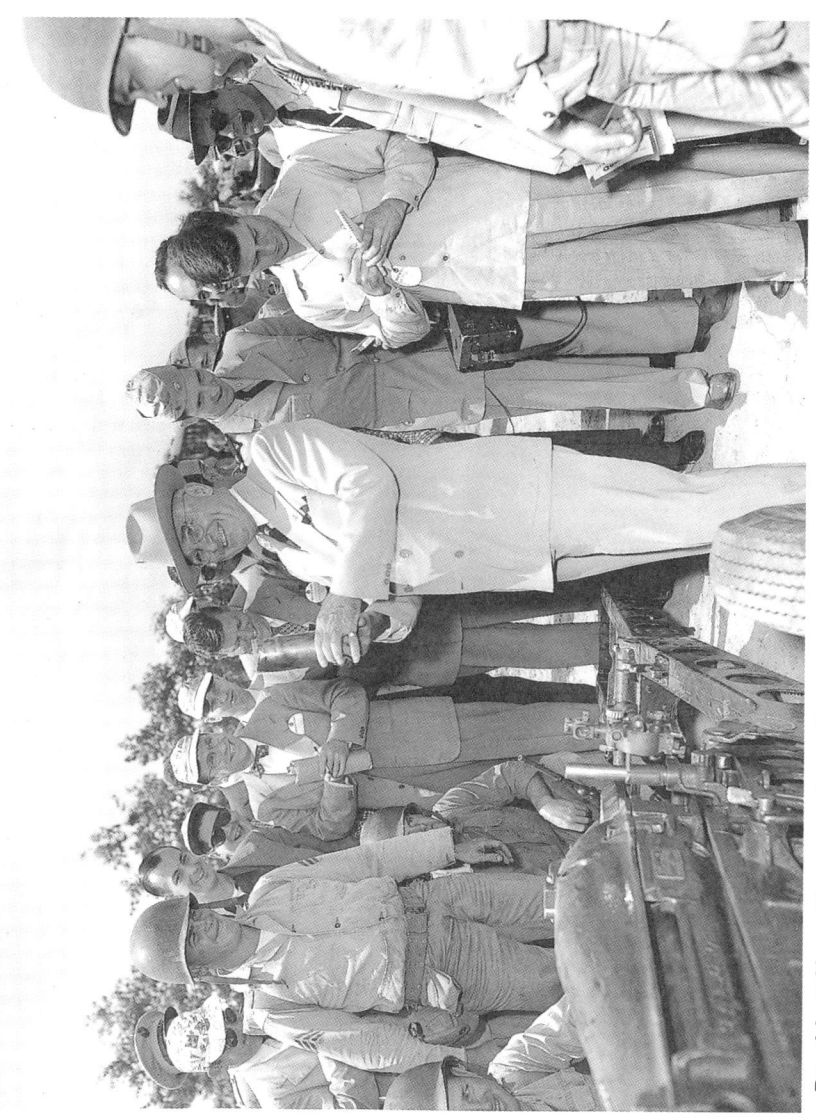

President Harry Truman jokes with reporters and the crew of Marine howitzer in Quantico, VA, 1952.

Joseph's able Battery of 105s delivers fire on Chinese positions during the Korean War, December, 1952.

Artillery crew tidies up after bombarding Chinese positions, Korea, 1952.

Author, headed home from Korea 1953.

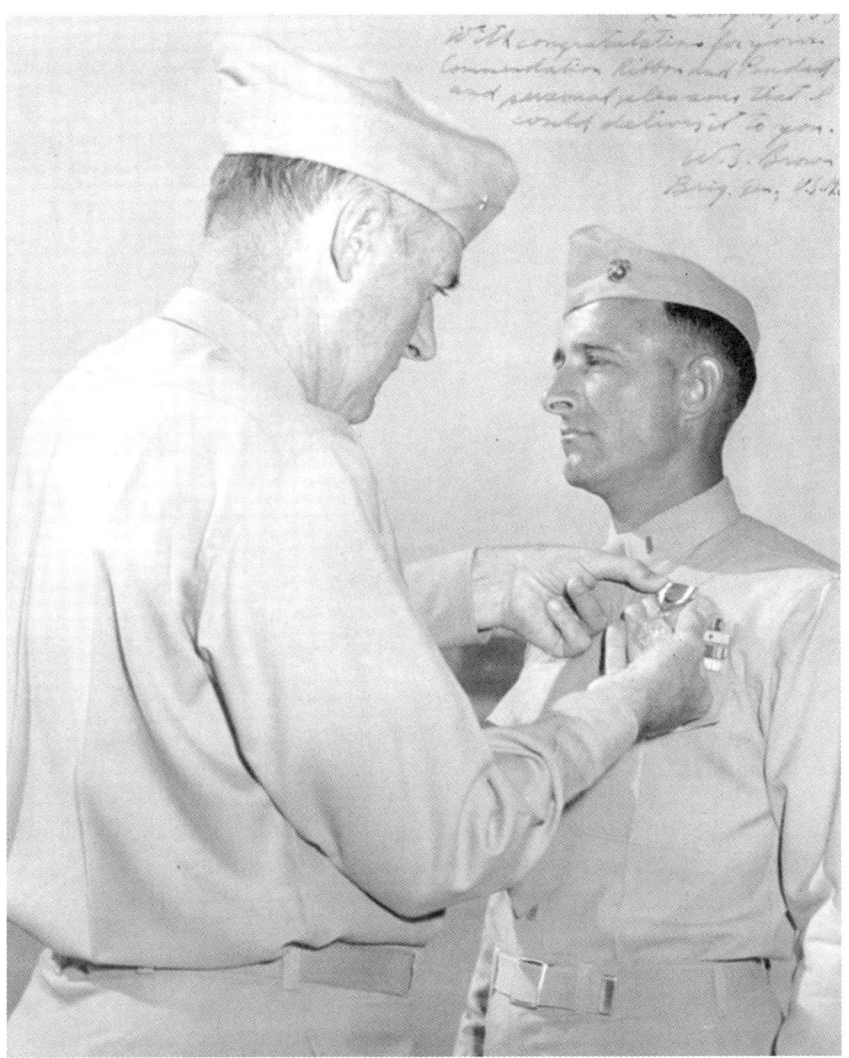
Author receives medal from General W. S. "Bigfoot" Brown, Camp Pendleton, Ca, 1953.

Author gets a pat on shoulder from Philippine President Ramon Magsaysay after rendering honors during dedication of the Cubi Point Naval Air Station, Subic Bay, 1956.

Author, Subic Bay, Philippines, 1956.

Cara (center, right) holds up party favor at the floating restaurant in Hong Kong, 1956. Author is third from left. Sam and Ann Houston are at right.

Joseph hangs it up after 22 years. He is congratulated by Col. Fredrick Karch.

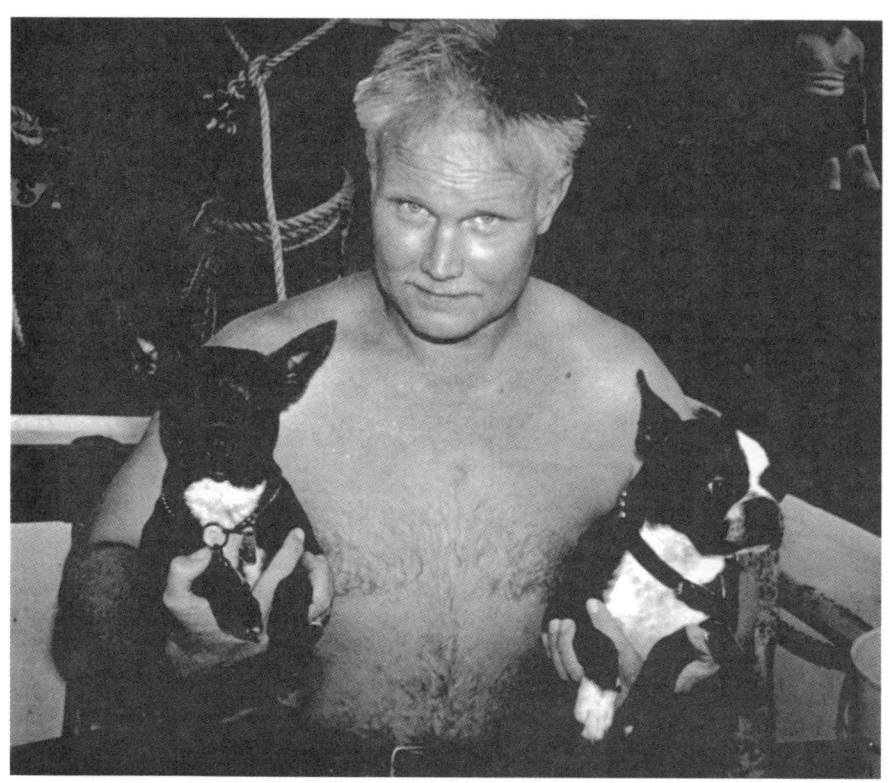

Joseph's photo of rescued boatman and dogs at Cedar Key, Fl made national news in 1961. Joseph was then a journalism student at the University of Florida.

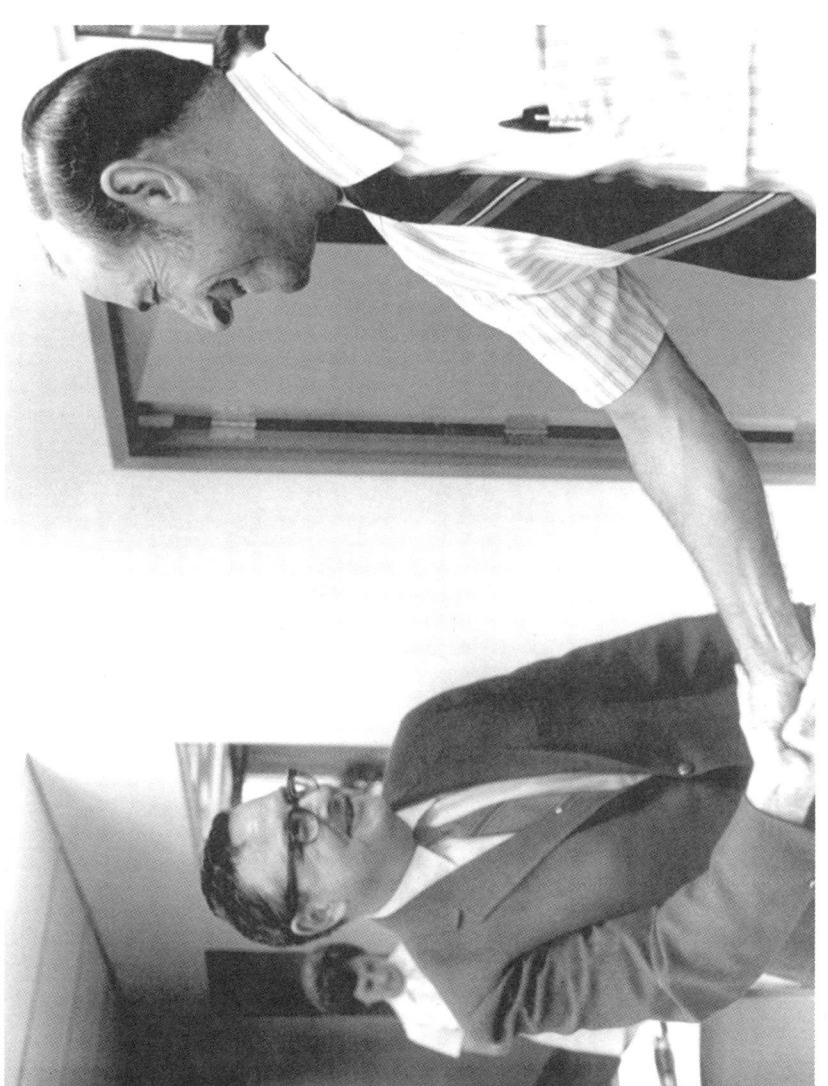

Author (right) congratulates his former professor, H.G. "Buddy" Davis, the day Davis won a Pulitzer Prize for editorial writing in 1971.

Springtime at Hoot 'n Hollow

Author (at left) in Moscow during the Cold War.

Thirteen
The New Civilian—1946

Joseph shifted uncomfortably in his chair as the frowning counselor opposite the desk studied and shuffled a sheaf of papers.

"Your scores don't point closely to any direction," he said after clearing his throat. "You show a variety of ... of possibilities, but none of any substantive strength. I don't think your scores are good enough for college."

Along with thousands of GIs returning from military service, Joseph had taken a battery of tests at a veterans vocational center in San Francisco in hopes of finding a niche in the civilian world.

Veterans were swarming into colleges under the G.I. Bill and buying homes with guaranteed government loans. Joseph, and marines in general, disliked the very term GI. In army slang, it was the nickname for enlisted men. In actuality, it stood for government issue. In the Corps, where everyone was a marine, officer or enlisted, G.I. was what you called a garbage can. "Hell, I wasn't issued, I was born," marines would scoff.

Joseph had hopes of entering college, with or without a G.I. Bill, but wasn't surprised at the counselor's bad news. He had been out of high school eight years and the curriculum at Lake Tarsa hadn't been anything to shout about. The only encouragement he had ever received in high school was from his English teacher, who praised his essays.

"You really should go to the university and take journalism," Marie Gross had said to him, pronouncing it univoisity and joynalism in her genteel north Louisiana drawl.

"So ... where does that put me?" Joseph asked the counselor after an awkward spell.

"From what I read in your scores, you must have been a helleva good marine," came the answer. "You have eight years of service and a top enlisted rank. If I were you, I'd go back."

Joseph wasn't sure whether he should accept the counselor's advice as a compliment or as bad news. He had been given ninety days to return to the corps with the rank of master sergeant. He still had time and continued to look around. He applied for the civil service, which gave veterans a priority in hiring, and was offered a job at the Ammunition Depot in Hawthorne, Nevada.

Cara never interfered with his decisions, but it was plain she wouldn't be happy in the isolation of Hawthorne in the Nevada desert. On the other hand, she seemed quite satisfied at the prospect of continuing as a marine wife.

Joseph put off his decision. He took in baseball games at Seals Stadium, shivering in the evening fog. September ushered in a glorious fall season in California, and he went to football games in Kezar Stadium, across the street from Cara's old high school. He watched college teams from Santa Clara and St. Mary's and a nascent San Francisco Forty Niner team playing in the All America Conference.

Then one day, he drove to the marine recruiting office, presented his discharge papers and reenlisted for three years. He was appointed a sergeant major. He didn't argue about the rank but would have preferred to be a master gunnery sergeant. He was a field marine, not a pencil pusher. The marine detachment at Treasure Island, where he was assigned, already had a sergeant major, and he greeted Joseph with suspicion. Two sergeants major meant one would be transferred out.

Treasure Island, in the middle of the bay, formerly Goat Island, had been the site of the 1939 Golden Gate Exposition. A leg of the Bay Bridge rested on its southern extremity. The navy had taken it over, and the marine guard detachment had a casual company that processed marines returning from the Pacific. Joseph was given a desk in a corner of the office, from which he supervised a half-dozen clerks typing up discharges and reassignments. It was a boring eight-to-four job. Joseph commuted in the Black Bullet from the upstairs, cream-colored stucco apartment just off Geary Boulevard he and Cara were living in.

Joseph and Cara became charter members of the Marines' Memorial Club in downtown San Francisco. In 1946, the Corps was deliberating on a monument to commemorate the marines who died in Pacific battles. It would be built using profits accumulated by post exchanges in the Pacific. A committee headed by Colonel Evans Ames, who had commanded the 21st Marines at Bougainville, decided on a living memorial. They purchased a twelve-story building in downtown San Francisco, which originally had been a woman's club and, during the war, housed female members of the Marine Corps and navy.

Its 137 rooms were available to marines en route to and returning from Pacific bases.

Today the Memorial Club flourishes as a haven for active members of all the armed services and a favorite gathering place for retired military personnel. Its skyroom bar and dining room afford a spectacular view of downtown and the bay area beyond. Marine Corps memorabilia are impressively displayed in the lobby, the corridors of the hotel, and in a large museum room. The artistry was created by Dixon Poole of Peoria, Arizona, a former marine who served as NCO with Joseph's guard company in Subic Bay, the Philippines. In 1946, Joseph never imagined the modest beginning of the club would evolve into a showpiece for the Corps that it became.

All the while his conniving co-sergeant major was being ever alert for an opportunity to get him transferred. His prayer was answered in the form of a Marine Corps bulletin. The First Marine Division, on occupation duty in North China, needed a sergeant major. Soon, orders came, directing Joseph to proceed via FAGTRANS—the first available government transportation—to Tientsin, China.

With feigned regret, his opposite number handed Joseph the orders. But on a closer reading, the orders directed that he first be completely immunized against a range of diseases that were rampant in postwar China. It would take several days before Joseph would complete the series of shots. In the meantime, his travel orders were canceled, and he was back in limbo.

The irony continued. Another bulletin arrived from Headquarters Marine Corps. Joseph had been reappointed to warrant officer. The First Division needed junior grade officers more than sergeants major, and he would still have to go to China. He chuckled as the reigning sergeant major showed him the bulletin.

"You will need to take a physical exam before your appointment is official," he said.

"You mean SIR, don't you?" Joseph said with a mocking smile.

"Yes, SIR," came the reply dripping with sarcasm.

It was coming on to the Christmas season. The department stores downtown glittered with lights, and Union Square was decked in gold and silver tinsel and striped candy canes. Cara, never one to pass up a tradition, broke out a tiny crepe paper Christmas tree and set it in the bay window.

Joseph reported to West Coast Marine Headquarters at 100 Harrison Street for further orders. All along, he had thought his departure would be delayed until after the holidays. To his dismay, his orders were endorsed and his departure set for the following day. He would join a draft of officers reporting in from all over the country for transportation overseas. The week before, he sold the Black Bullet. Parting with the car had been a sad occasion, but not nearly as painful as would be leaving Cara at Christmas time.

The Cold War was chilling up and there was no telling how long the 1st Division would be kept in China. Mao Tse-tung's Red army had taken over the interior and was closing in on the Nationalist Army under the corrupt Generalissimo Chiang Kai-shek which occupied the coastal cities.

On their last night, Joseph held Cara closely in his arms as she sobbed softly. It would be their first time apart as husband and wife. The following morning, Cara and her mother drove him to 100 Harrison Street. From there the draft of about fifty junior grade officers and a couple of field grade officers boarded buses and were driven to the Alameda Naval Air Station. They sat around the officers mess most of the afternoon, enjoying drinks and an early dinner.

The draft was split for the flight to Honolulu. To his delight, Joseph was assigned a seat on the *Marianas Mars,* one of the navy's four huge flying boats. The world's largest seaplanes, designed by Glenn J. Martin and built by his company, had a wing span of 200 feet. Originally designed as long-distance bombers, then converted to transports, the planes' two passenger decks had plush, black leather lounge chairs. After takeoff, a flight nurse walked the aisles, handing out sandwiches and fruit and pouring hot coffee from a stainless steel urn. In its day, it was the ultimate in military air transportation.

The giant PBM taxied to the far end of the bay, pivoted to the north, and began its long takeoff run. Its chunky whalelike hull shouldered aside the choppy waves, sending up plumes of white water. After a run of a mile or so, the four powerful Pratt and Whitney engines wrenched the flying boat out of the water and sent it soaring over the Bay Bridge cluttered with late afternoon holiday traffic.

With a hard turn to the left, it flew over Alcatraz and headed over the Golden Gate Bridge. Bathed in the setting sun, the rouge-colored cable towers of the bridge rendered a warm translucent glow. The plane followed the sun until it dove behind a gray horizon. Joseph dozed, dreaming alternately of Cara and China.

They spent Christmas Day in a dreary BOQ in Pearl Harbor, wondering why the Marine Corps had snatched them from their families in such a hurry. Nothing had changed, Joseph thought. In the military, it was always hurry up and wait. The next day at Barber's Point Marine Corps Air Station, they boarded a C-54 transport plane for the long flight to China. It was a far cry from Joseph's cushy ride on the *Mars*. On each side of the passenger and cargo cabin was a row of canvas bucket seats, uncomfortable and impossible to recline in.

Not long out of Hawaii, they landed for fuel on tiny Johnson Island. Its runway was merely the size of an aircraft carrier, and aluminum carcasses of wrecked planes shone beneath the shallow waters at each end.

The C-54 droned on hour after hour to Kwajelien. Joseph thought of his last visit to the island on the LST returning from Guam two years before, when he had hit the jackpot on a slot machine and paid for the evening's drinks. They laid over for the night. The officers' club was a shambles from a holiday party the night before.

The next day, they touched down at Tsingtao in North China. Before the final short flight to Tientsin, they were taken to the officers' mess at the Marine Corps air station for the evening meal, the serving of which had all the aspects of a ceremony. The officers filed in and stood at their tables until the "Old Man," the C.O., took his seat. At that moment, the double doors to the galley burst open, and in shuffled a column of Chinese servers in lock step, each carrying a serving tray of food over his shoulder. The only sound came from their sandals gliding over the polished floor.

As the meal progressed, empty dishes were held up to subservient waiters for refills with the command "hop to" or "chop chop." However demeaning the American attitude was toward their Asian allies of World War II, the stoic Chinese showed no resentment. They were grateful for the few dollars they earned and for first dibs at the leftover food. There was a famine in the country.

Division headquarters was inside the city of Tientsin. Joseph presented his orders and was assigned to the 1st Battalion, 11th Marines, a 105-millimeter howitzer battalion. On the jeep ride to join his new outfit outside the city, he got his first close view of North China. It was a bitterly cold winter and not a tree or sprig of grass was to be seen across the barren countryside.

Women bundled in quilted jackets and head shawls, some with babies strapped to their backs, scratched the lifeless earth for twigs or anything useful as firewood. Men, who had apparently scavenged farther out from the city, were more successful. They pushed wheelbarrows laden with branches and sticks tied into bundles. A pall of gray smoke blanketed the city. The pungent smell of burning coal filled the air, and cinders coated people and buildings. Men on bicycles pedaled along, wearing white surgical masks over their faces, apparently to filter the gritty air and perhaps protect against germs. Judging from their Western clothes and topcoats, they could have been white collar workers and professionals.

The peasants, those who would soon be welcomed into Mao's communist ranks, wore blue-gray quilted clothing and no surgical masks.

Upstream from the bridge over the solidly frozen Hai Ho River, work gangs with timber saws were harvesting blocks of amber-colored ice. In the warmer months, the water must have been the same color with the silt it carried from the interior uplands. Two-wheel carts drawn by ponies wearing shaggy winter coats waited on the banks to be loaded. Joseph cringed at the thought of seeing chunks of that dirty ice in his lemonade. More likely the ice would be stored in caves and used to preserve perishable foods in the summer months.

Joseph's new battalion was quartered in a former U.S. embassy compound outside the city. The trim, red-tiled, two-story brick buildings might have been taken for a college campus but for the six-foot-high brick wall around the perimeter and the absence of trees and shrubs. The buildings appeared none the worse after the period of Japanese occupation since the Americans departed in November of 1941.

In the colonial period preceding the war, the imperial powers, namely Japan, Great Britain, Germany, France, and Italy, in addition to the United States, enjoyed *concessions* wrung from the Chinese government for commercial purposes. Each maintained large legations and troops, which protected and catered to the interests of their national corporations doing business in China.

The 1st Division had been sent to North China shortly after World War II to disarm and repatriate the Japanese army in the region. Their mission completed, they were being kept as logistical support for the Chiang government. As Mao's Red legions marched inexorably from Manchuria toward the Nationalists, their presence became ever more menacing to the marines standing between the two warring factions. Marine infantrymen rode shotgun on U.S. supply trains moving between the capital city of Peking, formerly Peiping and now Beijing, sixty miles inland, and the coastal cities of Chinwangtao, Tsingtao, and Tienstin. The marines also guarded vital roads.

The Chinese Reds, vastly superior in numbers and weapons, more or less tolerated the Americans, considering them more a nuisance than foe. There were occasional confrontations, but for the most part, the Reds kept their distance.

Ongoing negotiations between President Harry Truman's envoys and the warring factions had the effect of making the American troops neutrals. All the while, hard liners in the U.S. Congress ranted that the Truman administration was "losing" China. The fact was no amount of diplomacy, or even force, could have stemmed the Chinese hordes from their goals of a Communist nation.

From what Joseph and his marine associates observed, the Chinese people would have been better off under communism, certainly no worse than their fate under the corrupt government of Chiang Kai-shek.

The battalion's 105s were parked in a corner of the compound next to the motor pool, icicles dangling from their muzzle covers. The six-by-sixes and jeeps were under constant surveillance both from the sentries that guarded them and the thieving neighbors in the village beyond the brick wall. The thieves were experts at draining gasoline from vehicles and stripping them of batteries and tires. They did it with such stealth and speed that often they were back across the wall with their loot, undetected.

One morning at daybreak, the compound was awakened by the chug chugging of a Browning Automatic. Lieutenant Feldman, the officer of the day, had chanced to be inspecting sentries as thieves were passing jerry cans of gasoline over the fence. Feldman raced to the guard house and grabed a BAR. By the time he returned to the scene, the thieves had disappeared into the village. Undeterred, Feldman jumped on the bed of a truck, hoisted the cumbersome weapon at hip level, and sprayed houses with .30-caliber bullets until the magazine was empty of its twenty rounds. It was the stuff that international incidents are made of, but thankfully no innocent inhabitants of the village had been hit.

Jeeps driven to the city and parked in the street were fair game, certain to be stolen or stripped. For a while, drivers thwarted hijackers by removing the rotors from the distributors. It didn't take the hijackers long to catch on. Soon, rotors were hot items among the thieves who carried them ready to install. Drivers sometimes returned to find their jeep sitting on axles stripped of wheels and tires.

Joseph made trips to the city to buy souvenirs, always accompanied by one or two companions. They always made sure to have the driver, armed with a .45, remain with the vehicle.

Filled with curiosity, they walked past sidewalk kitchens that sold watery soup ladled from steaming cauldrons. Men—never any women—sat shoulder to shoulder at long tables with their chopsticks beating streams of the hot liquid from bowl to mouth.

They strolled uneasily among the throngs, wary of pickpockets that stalked them. Once an emaciated woman trotted alongside Joseph for a block, thrusting a sickly baby at him and imploring him to take it. It was a scene he could never dismiss from his mind.

To escape the streets, they'd duck into the safety of a merchandise store. Proprietors didn't allow street people inside. Welcoming his customers with folded arms and a bow, the merchant would unlock massive wooden chests to reveal colorful bolts of silk and stacks of satin gowns and robes. The bargaining would begin.

"Twenty dolla', 'Melican," he would say holding up a garment.

"Five, U.S.," would come the counteroffer.

The haggling would continue until the price was right for both parties, although the merchant would put on a hangdog face as though he had given away the ranch. Jewelry, vases of cloisonne and porcelain, fancy lacquered boxes, and carved statuettes were touted as "very old, very dear," always dating to some ancient Chinese dynasty.

For ten dollars, discounted from fifty dollars, Joseph bought a "genuine" ruby for Cara. Back in San Francisco, a jeweler declared it fake, but the imitation was of such high quality as to be worth much more than ten dollars.

One day a marine supply truck with a work detail of several men was surrounded by a mob in the street. Some of the crowd of demonstrators held mops dipped in a vile smelling substance into the faces of the men. A few of the marines fingered the trigger guards of their carbines, but remained calm. Among them were veterans of the bitter fighting on Okinawa. After a few tense minutes, the driver blew the horn and eased the truck forward. The mob parted, but the incident was a sign that the division's days in China were numbered.

After a private from the artillery battalion was charged with beating a Chinese pimp, Joseph was sent to the precinct police station by his C.O. to apologize and assure the police that proper disciplinary action would be taken.

"Just say we're sorry and that we'll punish the man," the colonel instructed.

At the station, a sullen group of police was huddled around a potbellied stove, thrusting their hands and feet toward the heat. They stared expressionless at Joseph when he asked if anyone spoke English. Joseph cursed to himself that he had been the emissary when Chinese interpreters were sitting on their butts at division headquarters.

He became uncomfortably warm in his greatcoat and fur hat. After an agonizing silence, a police lieutenant with a smooth, clean-shaven skin arose and spoke up in halting English.

"What is it you have to say?" he asked.

"That we regret our man broke your law and that he will be punished," Joseph replied, hoping to sound properly officious. At the same time he wanted to avoid any sign of kowtowing, the ancient Chinese custom of submitting to a superior.

The lieutenant glared at Joseph.

"Is that all you came to say?" he asked.

"Yes, that's all. We regret what happened. Our man will be punished," Joseph repeated.

With that, he planted the toe of his right shoe directly behind his left heel, did a crisp about-face and marched out, knowing that his diplomacy had not scored any points.

"What'd they say?" the colonel wanted to know when Joseph reported back.

"Nothing, sir," Joseph answered, "but I got the feeling our man better not show his face in town again. "Especially in a whorehouse."

Slowly, the battalion began moving its artillery ammunition from the old French arsenal on the other side of the city to a dump nearer the coast. It was an indication that the division was beginning preparations to leave China. Apparently the ammo was being given to Chiang's army. Joseph was put in charge of a convoy of trucks hauling wooden crates of 105 shells.

Although spring was approaching, the temperature remained frigid. Sitting in the cab of the unheated six-by-six for seven hours, Joseph had never been as cold in his life, not even in Iceland. Heeding the advice of a fellow officer, he had slipped a small flask of brandy in his parka before leaving quarters. Halfway to the new dump, he shared the last of the brandy with the driver. The winter clothing they'd been issued, parkas, rubber shoe packs, mittens, and fur caps was the same as in Iceland, but not sufficient to ward off the frigid air that descended from Siberia and Manchuria. Joseph was sure his toes would be frostbitten, but they thawed after he had parked his feet close to the stove when he had returned to quarters.

Not long afterward, the 11th Marines loaded their guns and vehicles on flatcars and their men in ancient railroad coaches for the trip to Chinwantao, where a troopship awaited. Working parties worked around the clock loading equipment on the ship. On the dock, the cold was brutal.

A couple of American missionaries in clerical robes and flowing white beards boarded the ship to have dinner with the ship's captain. Finding converts would become more difficult in Marxist China.

As the loading was completed, a Coast Guard ice breaker appeared on the scene. With powerful thrusts, the ice breaker's sloping bow would mount the ice sheet until the weight of the ship broke it up in chunks. The process was repeated until a channel was opened for the troopship. The broken ice floes, a couple or more feet thick, clunked off the hull of the troopship as it gathered speed. They were the color of amber, like the slabs of ice Joseph had seen being harvested on the river.

Freed of its icy straitjacket, the ship turned south and entered the open water of the Yellow Sea, which was indeed yellow. History had been made. China was officially "lost" and the final memory for the marines was of bobbing ice floes far astern.

Fourteen
Prelude to Korea

In their anxiety to escape the cold in China, the 11th Marines had given little thought of where they were going. Logically, it might have been Japan, Okinawa, or the Philippines. But it was Guam they headed for.

They docked and unloaded at familiar Apra Harbor, which was nearly deserted. The 105s were limbered to the six-bys for the trip up the hill to an old Quonset camp. It was not a joyful homecoming. The jungle had begun to reclaim the camp. They chased out the rats and toads from the huts, swept out the dust and cobwebs, and moved in. There was no sane reason to maintain an artillery regiment on Guam, and boredom quickly set in. While in China, Joseph had been plagued with a nasty cold that clogged his head and chest. A swim in the warm waters of Pago Bay was the remedy. Joseph dove enthusiastically into the breakers. He felt gobs of phlegm dislodging from his chest and head, induced by the therapeutic effects of the salt water. China was out of his system.

Joseph bunked in a hut with some twenty junior grade officers. Bob Huff, another warrant officer, occupied an adjacent bunk, and they became close friends.

Huff had survived the bombing and sinking of the battleship *Oklahoma* at Pearl Harbor. He had later fought with the 4th Marine Division in the Marshall Islands and at Iwo Jima. The two kept a safe distance from a gang of sophomoric lieutenants in the hut, who consumed cases of warm beer, argued, and brawled through the evenings. They were an embarrassment, and being around them was the low point of Joseph's career as a warrant officer. With morale at rock bottom, it was clearly time when the regiment was ordered back to the States after only a month on Guam.

Joseph's eyes strained for the first sight of Cara when the *Cavalier* eased into a berth at the foot of Broadway in San Diego. She wasn't there. They had miscommunicated. She was taking the train down from San Francisco and had gotten off in Carlsbad where they'd planned to meet in the hotel. It all ended well, and they spent another honeymoon at the hotel. It was to become a habit.

The 11th Marines, along with returning units of the 1st Division, occupied barracks at Camp Pendleton, just up U.S. 101 from Carlsbad. Joseph was assigned quarters on the base, another Quonset. The village for married men was nestled among the brown hills of Pendleton, formerly the huge Santa Margarita cattle ranch. The nearest neighbors resided on the hillside just out the front door: burrowing owls, foxes, coyotes, skunks, and rattlesnakes. The wildlife, snakes excluded, provided entertainment in the halcyon pretelevision days.

Joseph bought a used car, a yellow Chrysler two-door sedan in which he commuted to and from camp. Before long, the First Battalion was assigned to temporary duty at the Marine Corps Supply Depot in Barstow, 100 miles east in the Mojave Desert. The corps was mothballing vehicles and other rolling stock and parking them in the desert. The vehicles were drained of fuel, motor oil, and hydraulic fluids, chained in groups of five and towed along U.S. Route 66 to the parking area.

On weekends when Joseph wasn't able to return to Pendleton, Cara would come out, and they would stay in a motel. On Saturday nights, they enjoyed an unforgettable experience dining in a ranch house among the Joshua trees and yuccas, where a concert pianist from New York grilled steaks and played classical music. The pianist had moved to the desert for his health, and three times a week turned chef for a limited number of guests. He served "Moscow Mules" in frosted brass mugs and cooked his steaks in an old iron wheelbarrow directly on a bed of fiery coals. None ever tasted better. After the meal, the host entertained at the piano.

The battalion returned to Pendleton to find that the division had a new commanding general, Graves B. Erskine who had ramrodded the Third at Iwo Jima. Peacetime had no definition in his vocabulary. He sent his troops on one rigid field exercise after another. Although equipment was aging and spare parts scarce, Erskine demanded full participation in maneuvers.

In Washington, the Corps was battling for survival. All that remained of the nearly 400,000-man wartime corps were the skeletons of two divisions at Pendleton and Camp Lejeune, North Carolina.

Because of the wartime buildup under Franklin Roosevelt, it was assumed that Democrats were the friends of the military, while Republicans, particularly a handful of right wing isolationists, were out to gut the armed forces. So when Harry Truman ran for reelection in 1948, Joseph, voting for the first time, enthusiastically cast his vote for Truman, as did a majority of marines.

But Truman was no FDR. Neither was he, a World War I Army captain, much of a friend of the Corps. Urged by Truman, the Secretary of Defense, Louis Johnson, began slashing army and navy budgets while maintaining the fair-haired air force at near peak level. After all, reasoned Truman and Johnson, had the air force not ended the war in Japan? The U.S. alone had the atomic bomb. There would be no more conventional wars, certainly none that required massive amphibious operations and divisions of marines.

In February 1945, Defense Secretary James Forrestal had gone ashore on Iwo Jima with Admiral Nimitz as the flag was raised on Mount Surabachi. In the euphoria of the moment, Forrestal exclaimed, "That flag insures that there will be a Marine Corps for the next 500 years."

But now Forrestal was dead, a suicide victim. Suffering from depression after leaving the government, he had jumped from a sixteenth-floor window of the Bethesda Naval Hospital. Comparing him to Louis Johnson, there was general agreement in the marines that the wrong man had jumped.

In that postwar political environment, Erskine's pared down division plugged along with shortages and bailing wire.

On New Year's Day, Joseph and Cara attended a reception by General Erskine at the officers' club. The general walked by their group, smiled, and wished all a Happy New Year. Joseph remembered Erskine's New Year's Day party at Guam that he and Lieutenant "Umbriago" had crashed. Did the general recall seeing him there? Joseph mused. The last and only time he had spoken to the general was on Iwo Jima when the "Big E" stumbled on his battle-weary group of 21st Marines near airstrip number 2.

Occasionally, when the navy found enough fuel for a transport squadron to cruise a few miles, the division made practice landing exercises at San Onofre Beach on the Pendleton reservation.

One such exercise was made on a windy day when the surf was ideal for surfboards but not landing craft, and several amphibian tractors capsized off shore, spilling seabags and packs into the water.

A reporter from the *Examiner* in Los Angeles, covering the exercise, filed a front-page story that hundreds of marine bodies were floating in the sea. The fact was that two marines had drowned in the mishap.

On another landing exercise, when Joseph's jeep bounced ashore off the ramp of an LST, he spotted Cara, nearly nine months' pregnant, standing on an embankment off the beach, snapping pictures.

Joseph waved and continued his dash to the battlefield to take on an imaginery Red force that was threatening the U.S. oil supply in the Middle East.

Joseph and Cara had just moved out of the Quonset into an apartment in a federal housing project in Oceanside, when little Annie arrived. She weighed six pounds five ounces, and with a mop of brown hair was the sweetheart of the maternity ward. She'd been delivered in the Oceanside hospital. The bill came to $68.15.

Joseph's C.O. was an avowed bachelor, who hated married men or, at least, made a good pretense of it.

"Always wanting time off because of wives and kids," he would carp.

After one field exercise, the troops had been given a long weekend starting Thursday afternoon. Annie was delivered on Friday, and Monday, when Joseph returned to duty, Major Kafka began his usual harangue at a meeting of battery officers.

"I suppose you'll be asking for some time off when your wife has that baby," he chortled at Joseph.

"Have a cigar, Major," Joseph answered. "It's a girl. She was born on my time, not the Marine Corps'."

Annie joined the postwar generation that decades later would become the Baby Boomers, when demographers observed a spike on the census graph in the decade of the 1940s. The marines were doing their part. Rows of diapers flapped on clotheslines at Sterling Housing. Strollers cluttered the sidewalks between the pale green stucco buildings. Among Joseph's and Cara's circle of friends, the Huffs—Bob and Alice—welcomed their second child. Louise Moran, Roy's wife, gave birth to a boy.

The Morans had married a bit late in life, and Louise thought it comical when she became pregnant. The Ettenboroughs, in the apartment adjoining that of Joseph and Cara, had a baby boy.

Little feet were pitter-pattering throughout the project. But the bliss of parenthood was missing in the household of Walt and Winnie. Walt was a warrant officer, a seasoned veteran nearing his fortieth birthday. Winnie was several years younger. Try as they did, she wouldn't conceive. Finally they consulted a gynecologist. Following his advice they altered their mating hours: mornings instead of evenings, mornings and evenings, and even at midday when Walt would sneak home for lunch and a "nooner." Still no luck. Walt elevated the foot of the bed with wooden blocks so that they did it downhill, so to speak, after which Winnie would remain tilted and motionless for an hour.

They abstained for periods of time, then resumed the effort well rested. Still, Winnie didn't conceive. All through the experimentation, she wore a serene expression, gay and carefree, while Walt became drawn and haggard. He was giving it his all while suffering the jokes of his parented colleagues who teased him about "shooting blanks."

Adding to his fatherless woes, the poor guy had the bad judgment to buy a Kaiser/Frazer, which had just debuted on the car market. The nondescript sedan was painted a red-lead, like that of Henry Kaiser's Liberty ships. An auto shop's labor-in-waiting, it was the first and last of Kaiser's cars. When Joseph last saw Winnie and Walt, before his reassignment to the East Coast, the couple was talking of adopting a baby.

The Corps had fought all its battles of World War II in the tropical Pacific. As the cold war continued to escalate the navy and marine brass in Washington decided some practice in a cold environment was in order. At Pendleton, planning began for an extended winter exercise on Kodiak Island off the southern coast of Alaska. Special fuels and lubricants would be tested, along with "slave" units that blew heated air on engines for cold weather starting. Winter clothing and enriched field rations would also be tested.

Ironically, in January 1949, as the convoy cruised northward out of San Diego, the brown coastal hills of Southern California became dusted with white dandruff from a freak snowstorm.

"We could've stayed here and trained instead of going all the way to Alaska," was the comment of the day on Joseph's LST.

Navy screwups provided comic relief on the trip up. The LST flotilla was commanded by a reserve flag officer who had been grandfathered with the obsolete rank of commodore. A control freak, he burdened his ship captains with a constant barrage of conflicting radio messages. Upon entering the narrow channel into Juneau, the commodore unexpectedly released the skippers from his flagship control with an order to revert to individual ship navigation. At that point, he might as well have signaled "every man for himself."

The LSTs broke from the column and scattered about seeking anchorage. Commander Green, the confused skipper of Joseph's LST, grounded his ship on a sand bar. Meanwhile, the commodore's radio crackled with a barrage of messages and invectives directed at Green's vessel. Innocent as he was of the botched-up situation, the poor guy was promptly slapped with the sobriquet "Sand Bar Green." Liberty in the quaint capital of the Territory of Alaska was delayed on Green's ship until the next rising tide had refloated it.

The commodore called a meeting of skippers aboard his flagship. Green sent his executive officer in his place with instructions to tell the commodore he had more important business to take care of.

The exec, a young lieutenant, returned an hour later, his notebook filled with criticism directed at Green. Green gathered his ship's officers and chief petty officers in the wardroom to hear the lieutenant's report.

"The commodore said if you had paid closer attention to orders——"

Green angrily pounded the table and cut him off.

"You go back and tell the commodore I said for him to kish my ash." It wasn't clear whether his slurred words were faked or caused by loose dentures.

The cruise took on more serious aspects entering the Gulf of Alaska where the convoy ran head-on into a fierce north Pacific storm. Mountains of waves tossed the shallow-bottomed LSTs about like corks.

In the tank deck were all the vehicles of Joseph's battery, secured with chains and cables. A bulldozer tore loose and, with each yaw of the vessel, slid back and forth on the steel deck. Like a giant pinball, it went crashing into vehicles on each side. If the wrecking monster wasn't brought under control, the trucks would soon be crushed like tin cans.

Joseph's crew of truck drivers, largely through the efforts of Corporal Lang, finally brought the bulldozer under control by trapping it with heavy timbers thrown down in its path to act as buffers. It was dangerous work for the men who balanced precariously in truck beds above while poised with sixty-pound timbers as the ship listed and pitched in the angry sea. One slip and fall into the path of the 'dozer could be fatal.

Lang was a diligent, hard working Marine. Within two years, he would be killed during the fighting at the Chosin Reservoir in Korea when the Chinese ambushed his truck convoy. Joseph often wondered if Lang had been killed while driving one of the trucks he worked so valiantly to protect on the LST.

Kodiak proved cold enough for the purpose intended. The winterized vehicles performed up to par, and the troops enjoyed the snow, a new experience for many. In the field, they learned to sleep warmly in burrows scooped in the snow. They'd line their holes with pine branches or cardboard from C-rations cases before crawling in with their sleeping bags. Of no small concern were the huge Kodiak grizzly bears that prowled around. Sentries armed with blunt-nosed "bear" ammunition were kept posted around bivouacs, and in the mornings, it was not unusual to find bear tracks a foot wide around encampments.

The popular "Weasel" a lightweight tracked vehicle that scooted around at high speeds over the snow, provided the fun of a new toy. It carried small loads and towed light supply trailers.

Although it could never have entered the minds of the Marines at the time, within two years, the lessons learned in Kodiak would prove valuable during the fighting in the frozen North Korean hills.

Upon returning to Pendleton, the troops took a week off from normal duties for annual rifle and pistol qualification. Joseph commuted to the rifle range in a remote canyon in his used Chrysler that had an erratic fuel gauge. While returning from firing one day, he ran out of gas. He knew the troops would soon be following in trucks, so he got out, lit a cigarette, and waited for the first truck which might have a spare jerry can of fuel. As his mind drifted aimlessly, a shot cracked.

"What the hell's going on?" he shouted at a sergeant who came running up the road with a smoking M-I rifle.

"A mountain lion," the sergeant said excitedly. "He's down there at the bottom of the hill and was stalking you, so I jumped off the truck and took a shot."

"Bull," replied Joseph, but at that moment he caught a glimpse of the big tawny cat making tracks through the creosote bushes in the ravine. He thanked the sergeant.

"But how'd you happen to have a live round?" Joseph asked, hinting at regulations that ammo was not to be taken from the range.

"It was in the pocket of my jacket; didn't know it was there," the sergeant replied with a sly grin.

New cars were gradually appearing in showrooms after the wartime hiatus. While having his fuel gauge repaired, Joseph fell in love with a gleaming new maroon four-door Windsor sedan in the Hannah Chrysler showroom in San Diego. Was it available?

It was, for just over $2,300. Joseph went to the bank, drew out enough for a down payment from his savings account and drove back to Oceanside in his new car. Cara promptly christened it "Big Red."

Joseph got orders in the summer of 1949. He was to report to the Marine Corps base at Quantico, Virginia. The packing crew from the base supply depot came to the apartment and stuffed their meager belongings in barrels and crates for storage. With Annie in a makeshift play pen in the back seat, they motored to San Francisco, where Cara would stay with her mother until Joseph found a place in Virginia.

As Joseph was driving through Colorado on his way east, he did a double take while passing a truck on the highway. Emblazoned on its sides in large letters was the word "Hadacol." *Mon Dieu*, "Couzin" Dudley J. LeBlanc was peddling his potent health tonic all across the country. In the Depression years, the Lafayette entrepreneur and politician began promoting his elixer to radio listeners in southwest Louisiana, singing Cajun songs and making his sales pitch in French.

Joseph remembered seeing farmers on their Saturday shopping days loading cases of Hadacol in their wagons along with the groceries. The stuff had an alcohol content enough to provide a good buzz.

LeBlanc's commercial programs had the effect of awakening interest in the vanishing Cajun culture. Later he founded the Council for the Development of French in Louisiana. CODAFIL, as it is called, remains a strong influence in preserving the Cajun heritage and renewing ties with its Canadian homeland.

LeBlanc served with distinction in the Louisiana legislature, but twice, his efforts fell short to unseat the Huey Long regime from the governor's office in the skyscraper capitol in Baton Rouge.

The motel age was underway, and on his journey, Joseph found comfortable new lodgings all across the country, especially in the West. The South still lagged behind with many motels renting rows of little cabins.

He stopped in Lake Tarsa for a short visit with his parents. The town had a new look. The streets were cleaner. The city park had been spruced up, and the broken-down wharf on the lake repaired. Returning war veterans were governing the city and, with youthful energy, striving to restore its pre-Depression era pride.

Ornas had a new car. The little Chrysler two-door sedan was only the second one he had ever owned. The first was in a 1925 Model T Ford that he bought for $500 while still farming rice.

To get from the farmhouse to the gravel road leading into town, they had to pass a rutted, often muddy, country lane. Dressed in their Sunday clothes, the family would climb the running board and slide into the black imitation leather seats, Joseph and Mae in the back and Clarissa in the front with Ornas. If after a heavy rain, they got stuck, which happened several times, Ornas would go back to the barn and harness a team of mules. Straining the traces, the animals would pull the machine from its muddy grip, Ornas remaining in a foul mood in his muddy shoes.

When he had mastered the ornery machine, Ornas decided to teach Clarissa how to drive. With a firm grip on the wheel, she kept the car moving smoothly at slow speed. Up ahead, a big jersey cow was ambling across the road. Clarissa stayed the course. She had forgotten where the brake was and broadsided the poor animal. The car stalled and milk from the cow's swollen udder flew into the windshield. With a baleful look at the car, the cow staggered off the road, presumably not seriously hurt. Without a single word, Clarissa slid out from behind the wheel never again to drive a car.

Marines referred to Quantico, forty miles from Washington, as the "country club" of the corps. The leafy post on the banks of the Potomac River had spacious brick barracks for the enlisted men and comfortable quarters for officers and NCOs. There was the appearance of permanence about the base, as opposed to Pendleton and its temporary wooden buildings. The recreation facilities were first class and included a golf course, swimming pools, and riding stables. The post exchange was like a department store.

There were no combat units stationed at Quantico. The troops, mostly combat veterans, performed specialized duties, such as testing experimental equipment and putting on demonstrations for junior grade and field grade staff officers' schools. There was an officer candidate school for second lieutenants, so rigorous that it had a fifty percent dropout rate.

With the close proximity of the base to the nation's capital, the troops were often called on for parades and ceremonial duties when foreign heads of state visited the White House. Joseph was assigned to the artillery battery in the Schools Demonstration Troops which familiarized infantry officers with fire support techniques.

While on the waiting list for post quarters, Joseph found an apartment in the country and sent for Cara. She flew over with seventeen-month-old Annie on an American Airline plane to Washington National Airport, where Joseph met them.

It wasn't long before they moved into an apartment in a section of the base nicknamed "Whiskey Gulch." Annie was toddling about and beginning to talk. She became a favorite with a Colonel Totman, who lived across the street and whom she called Curley Totman, no disrespect intended. The colonel was bald as a door knob.

Joseph and Cara grew tired of their cramped little apartment, and he applied for larger quarters. He was offered a rambling old ranch-house that had served as a guard house during World War I. They loved it and moved in.

The East Coast Railroad ran through part of the base and their back yard was within a stone's throw of the tracks down in a ravine. When trains roared through, the house would shake as in an earthquake. It was joked about that the most pregnancies in quarters along the tracks had their origins with the 2:00 A.M. passage of the New York to Miami Silver Meteor.

Early one morning, they were awakened by a commotion on the tracks. A freight train had derailed, scattering boxcars for a hundred yards. A derrick on rails was called in to lift the boxcars and replace them on the track. Some tank cars containing whale oil had ruptured, and it was weeks before the smell of fish oil had dissipated, to the disappointment of the many cats in the neighborhood.

President Truman's favorite relaxation from the stress of the White House was cruising the Potomac aboard the 244-foot presidential yacht, *Williamsburg*. On weekends he gathered his favorite D.C. cronies for a leisurely cruise featuring poker games and, reportedly, straight bourbon. Often the boat tied up for the night at the Quantico dock where the president delighted in giving the slip to his bodyguards and taking brisk walks on the base unaccompanied. It became a familiar and somewhat amusing sight to see overweight secret service men huffing and puffing to catch up with the president. If he vanished on Sunday mornings, they would find him sitting in the back pew of the chapel singing hymns with the congregation.

The base commander would have a paroxysm when he'd learn that the president was loose on the base. A standing order at the guardhouse specified that the officer of the day notify the general. Then all hell would break loose. Security at the main gate was doubled, and sentries raced to man check points and crossroads lest some threat to the president arise.

Joseph was in charge of firing salutes when honors were rendered for visiting flag officers, members of Congress, and heads of state. Once after Joseph's crew on the twin five-inch naval guns had flawlessly cranked off twenty-one rounds for the president, his entourage drove by on its way off the base. Truman, who appeared to have a genuine interest in guns dating to his experience as commander of an artillery battery in France, ordered his car stopped. In front of the guns Joseph and his men were frozen at attention.

Gollee, I'm about to meet with prez," thought Joseph. Truman stared owlishly through the thick lens of his spectacles. He touched his fingers to the brim of his hat in a salute and nodded to indicate a "well done." Joseph responded with a crisp salute.

"I got to salute the president twice," he joked back at the office. "Once with twenty-one rounds and once with my hand."

Truman was an observer a couple of times when the Quantico Marines demonstrated the latest battlefield techniques. He accompanied a contingent of arms merchants and Pentagon brass that President Dwight Eisenhower later pegged the military-industrial complex. The joint civilian orientation exercises became known for its acronym, JCOX.

The Marines were experimenting with helicopters in the tactical concept of vertical envelopment. Joseph's outfit had developed the technique of moving guns by helicopter. Lifting a trussed up howitzer with a cable, the helicopter would carry it, swaying back and forth, and lower it to the desired firing position. Crews would land from other helicopters and race against a stopwatch to set up their guns and commence firing.

After observing the demonstration, Truman walked up to one of the howitzers with a swarm of reporters and photographers in tow. He chatted with the crew, expressing mild disappointment that no one was from Missouri. An AP photographer with a bulky speed graphic camera called out, "Mr. President would you look into the muzzle of the gun, please."

"Only a jackass sticks his face in the muzzle of a gun," the president shot back. The cameraman cringed with embarrassment as Truman and his entourage guffawed. Truman then stepped to the other end of the gun where the breechblock was open. "Here's how you do it," he said to the cameraman. "Get your camera ready." With that, he peered into the breach while the mollified cameraman got his shot.

On the artillery range, a wooden grandstand had been set up for large observation classes. During one exercise, a battery of 105s was emplaced some 2,000 yards behind the stands fully occupied by a class of new lieutenants. The impact area was another 1,000 yards directly in front of the stands. The officers were going to experience the sound of artillery shells fluttering over their heads.

Through an unexplainable, nearly fatal, error on the plotting board in the fire direction center, the opening volley fell 500 yards behind the grandstand. The lieutenants were jolted in their seats by the *CUR-RUMP* behind them. They turned around in time to see six rising clouds of black TNT and dust. The instructor, a light colonel, was aghast, and Major Anderson, the battery commander, who was narrating the scenario, nearly had apoplexy.

His battery had come within a few hundred yards of wiping out an entire class of company grade officers. Quickly the fire direction center corrected the range and sent the next volley on target 1,000 yards ahead of the grandstand.

The lieutenants applauded, believing the first volley had been intentionally fired behind them as part of the demonstration. Major Anderson sheepishly went along with the deception, and the firing proceeded without further incident.

During the summer months, battalions of reserves came to Quantico for two weeks of field training. In June 1950, Joseph's battery was at Camp Goettge, deep in the piney woods, supervising a 155-millimeter howitzer battalion from Birmingham.

On Sunday, the twenty-fourth, when training was suspended and everyone was lazing away the time, Joseph picked up a copy of the *Washington Post.*

North Korea had invaded South Korea, the headline shouted. In all likelihood, the United States would come to the aid of its South Korean friend. Radios blared news accounts that the United States was again at war.

Marine reserve units had an advisory staff of regular officers known as the inspector-instructor (I&I) staff. The Birmingham advisor in charge was a gung-ho lieutenant colonel. Immediately, he assembled the reserves in the recreation building, leaped on the stage, and attempted to whip up enthusiasm for the war. He assured them that the battalion would stay intact and not be broken up and parceled out to regular units.

"We are going to fight as the Birmingham battalion and nothing else," he exhorted.

Instead of the cheering he expected, there was only silence. The reserves had wives, families, and jobs in Alabama. They weren't ready to go to war by a long shot.

When they were dismissed, a serpentine line formed for the one pay phone in camp. Before long, the reverberations reached Washington, and soon the senior senator from Alabama, John Sparkman, arrived with assurances that the battalion would return home and be allowed time to get their personal affairs in order before being called to active duty.

Except for the acceleration of officer training, Quantico remained far removed from the war.

By August, the First Marine Provisional Brigade, including the 1st Battalion, 11th Marines, Joseph's old artillery outfit, had taken a defensive position on the Pusan perimeter in South Korea.

In Washington, a California congresswoman reacting to the shabby treatment the Corps had been getting from the Pentagon, thought the time was right for Truman to appoint a marine general to the Joint Chiefs of Staff. In addition to his worries about the war in Korea, the president was dealing with a hostile Republican Congress.

Testily, he responded to the congresswoman's suggestion. "As far as I'm concerned, the Marine Corps is the Navy's police force, and as long as I'm president, that's what it will remain."

If that wasn't enough of an insult, Truman continued, "The Marine Corps has a propaganda outfit equal to (Joseph) Stalin."

The *Washington Post* chronicled the quotes in headlines. At last Truman had unburdened himself of his true feelings for the Marine Corps. But his timing could not have been worse. The Marine brigade had already distiniguished itself at Pusan and proved an inspiration to the beleaguered Army troops who had retreated into a cul-de-sac on the Korean peninsula. With the firestorm raging over the president's ill-advised comments, he summoned Marine Commandant Clifton B. Cates and personally handed him a written apology. Then he hastened to the Mayflower Hotel, where the Marine Corps League, an influential civilian lobby, happened to be holding a convention and there apologized a second time.

Truman's peccadilloes didn't stop there. He sent a threatening note to the music critic of the *Post* after Paul Hume had panned daughter Margaret's performance in her debut as a classical concert singer. He wrote that if they ever met, Hume might be needing a face lift and a supporter "below."

Spirits were lifted in the Marine Corps when the 1st Brigade landed at Inchon in a brilliant and audacious counterattack designed by General Douglas MacArthur. On the outskirts of Seoul as the marines were launching an assault to recapture the South Korean capital, MacArthur wrote: "I have just returned from visiting the marines at the front, and there is no finer fighting organization in the world."

No argument there.

Quickly, MacArthur's 8th Army surged past the 38th parallel, the boundary between North and South Korea, and captured the enemy capitol of Pyongyang. Optimism soared, and the Stateside media predicted that the boys would be home for Christmas.

But MacArthur had gone one ridge too far in the snowy hills near the Yalu River, which separated Korea from Chinese Manchuria. The egomaniacal general had brushed aside warnings of massive Chinese troop movements near the river. By the hundreds of thousands, the Chinese were pouring into North Korea. Taken by surprise, MacArthur's 8th Army was overwhelmed and retreated in disarray. The promising autumn had suddenly turned into a winter of despair.

The marines were caught in a trap near the frozen Chosin Reservoir and suffered heavy casualties. Putting an optimistic spin on a grim situation, the happy warrior, Colonel Lewis "Chesty" Puller, the Corps' most decorated marine, told his British commando counterpart, Colonel Douglas Drysdale, "They got us surrounded, but they won't get away this time."

To a combat correspondent who noted that "retreat" was a new word in the marine vocabulary, the sagacious General O. P. Smith, who commanded the marine division, replied, "Hell, we're not retreating, we're attacking in another direction."

In an epic struggle that would take its place in the pantheon with Belleau Wood, Guadalcanal, and Iwo Jima, Smith's marines clawed their way from the jaws of annihilation, bringing their equipment, their wounded, and their dead. The bloody trail from Chosin to Hungnam became the Via Dolorosa of the Korean War. But the brigade lived to fight another day.

Christmas in Quantico was not a happy occasion. The thoughts of everyone were with the marines in Korea fighting for their lives.

In April, Truman bit the bullet and faced another firestorm of criticism when he relieved the charismatic Douglas MacArthur. On the radio, Joseph listened to the general's dramatic, "Old soldiers never die," speech before Congress. When the passions had subsided, the American troops in Korea faced the hard reality of a long struggle in a landmass, not the kind of war the marines preferred to fight.

Quantico continued to produce platoon leaders and train field commanders. Soon, the first of the 11th Marines to be rotated from

Korea joined the demonstration troops, and Joseph heard firsthand of the fighting.

The war had placed new demands for company grade officers, more than the Corps was producing in its school. To fill the shortage, headquarters in Washington invited warrant officers to apply for commissions as second lieutenants.

Joseph, who was now a WO-3, one step removed from the top warrant grade, always considered becoming a lieutenant as a demotion. But Major Anderson persuaded him to apply.

"You're just over thirty, and I believe too young to remain a warrant officer," he counseled.

"You're not too old to be a lieutenant, and you'll have time to advance."

Reluctantly, Joseph applied for a commission and quickly received his gold bars. He was a "shavetail." Soon after his promotion, he was ordered to the Army Field Artillery Officers School in Fort Sill, Oklahoma.

Upon completion of the three-month course, he was to report to Camp Pendleton for further assignment to the 1st Marine Division in Korea. After the army's debacle in Korea, marines were not enthusiastic about going there to fight. Truman had coined the expression "police action" to describe the conflict. The euphemism created a sense of apathy on the home front and bitterness among the families who had lost their sons in the fighting. Like it or not, career marines did as they were told and did their best.

Leaving Annie in Florida with her grandmother, who now lived there, Joseph and Cara set up temporary housekeeping in a garage apartment in Lawton. Among Joseph's class of one hundred officers were a half-dozen marines. The curriculum was heavy with mathematical problems, particularly trigonometry, and Joseph was thankful that he had completed a correspondence course in math with the Marine Corps Institute.

"It's a beautiful day in Oklahoma," the army captain sang out with sarcasm.

They were on a hilltop OP on a raw, wintry day with the wind tearing at maps and papers on clipboards. Joseph heard the instructor call his name above the gale. "From the dark pile of rocks to our front at a range of approximately 3,000 yards go right and down until you see a ravine with a dead tree at the bottom. There is an enemy tank stalled there. Your problem, mister."

Joseph tracked the target description with his binoculars and quickly spotted the white branches of the dead tree. "Fire mission," he yelled to the telephone operator. "From check point Kilo, right 400, up 300. Enemy tank. One round HE."

From an unseen battery of 105 howitzers behind the OP came a round that threw up a puff well to the right and above the target. "Left 300 down 200," he commanded. The idea was to bracket the target until the bursts came within 50 yards in range and deflection, and "fire for effect" would be ordered. Then all six guns of the battery would cut loose.

To clobber a target after a minimum of searching rounds was challenging and satisfying. In the classroom, the routine dwelt heavily on surveying and fire direction techniques. The students would be assigned "homework" involving the plotting of map coordinates on a blank chart, which would be brought back to class and used in problem solving. Joseph taught Cara how to do the plotting, which freed him to concentrate his study time on logarithms and trigonometric functions.

The instructors always complimented Joseph on the accuracy and neatness of his plotted charts. As much as he would have liked to, Joseph never revealed the secret of Cara's handiwork, but she took satisfaction knowing she was contributing to his success as an artillery officer.

Actually, she contributed in other ways. Once she went shopping in Wichita Falls, Texas, an hour's drive south from Lawton, with several requests from Joseph's friends to buy them a fifth of whiskey. Oklahoma was "dry" in more ways than one. Troopers were known to stop cars at the state line and conduct searches for contraband alcohol.

On the trip back, a windstorm turned the sky red with Oklahoma dust, reminiscent of the Depression days when farmland was stripped of its productive soil by windstorms and destitute "Okie" families fled to California. Visibility was so poor that Cara drove with the headlights on in full daylight and was unaware that she had crossed the state line without incident and safely with her alcohol.

Time flew and Joseph graduated. He placed near the head of the class and was the top marine. Then it was on to Pendleton to join a draft of officers going to Korea.

Fifteen
The Forgotten War—1950–1953

After another painful farewell with Cara at Oceanside, Joseph was aboard a C-54 air transport, making his fifth crossing of the Pacific. Approaching the Marine Air Station at Atsugi, Japan, the pilot discovered that he had lost hydraulic power in his landing gear. Would it lock properly in the landing position? To burn up fuel in the event of a mishap, he circled for nearly an hour over the countryside, where Japanese were stooped in rice paddies planting seedlings and never looking up at the plane. The troop passengers began to have doubts that they'd make it to Korea. As it turned out, the landing gear functioned properly.

Joseph was curious about the Japanese people, his limited knowledge of them having come from the battlefield. He joined a small group of marine officers going to Yokohama for the evening. They rode a high-speed train crowded with Japanese commuters, who lowered their gazes at the Americans. How could the people appear so docile when so many of their sons had been killed in fighting the Americans? How could they conceal their bitterness?

The next day, the group would be facing uncertain futures in Korea, so they enjoyed a lengthy Japanese dinner served by geishas, during which they consumed quantities of sake and Asahi beer. Early the next morning at Atsugi, they were routed out of bed after a few winks of sleep, fed breakfast, and herded on a transport plane.

At Kimpo airfield at Seoul, they were issued field equipment and weapons and assigned to units of the 1st Marine Division. They said farewells and wished good luck to new friends now going separate ways. Joseph boarded a truck for the twenty-mile ride to the 11th Marine headquarters.

Driving past the outskirts of Seoul, Joseph was awed by the devastation from the fighting. Four times the city had changed hands, and each battle added to the destruction. Skeletons of hollowed-out buildings were all that stood. A bridge lay broken across the Han River, its ribs blackened by fire.

The June sun beat down relentlessly, and the humidity was stifling. The sake and beer of the previous evening conspired with the heat to bring on the worst of hangovers. The convoy crept along a dusty, narrow road choked with military trucks and Koreans pushing two-wheeled carts. Their truck halted abreast a procession of "honey" carts, filled with human excrement destined for the rice paddies. Joseph got a whiff of the stench and leaned over the side to vomit.

They soon drained the lukewarm water in their canteens. Water discipline, so strictly emphasized in the Pacific fighting, would have to be learned all over. They welcomed a brief thundershower, which drenched and revived them in the open truck.

At regimental headquarters, Joseph was assigned to the First Battalion. He passed up the evening meal. He awoke early the following morning feeling refreshed and ate a decent breakfast in the field mess. Then it was a jeep ride to the battalion at the front.

"We haven't had any incoming back here in some time," the driver said. "The firing batteries up front get it now and then."

The traffic thinned out the nearer they got to the front. They passed a railhead with several Pullman cars parked on a siding.

"War correspondents," the driver informed, pointing to the green cars. Joseph saw several figures through the windows of the car hunched over typewriters. He wondered what there was to write about. The war had stalemated into a siege with both sides hunkered down in trenches and bunkers.

They crossed the Imjin River on a rickety pontoon bridge and arrived at the 1st Battalion, which occupied positions on the north bank of the river. At the battalion, C.P., Joseph met Colonel Jones, his new C.O. Jones was an affable officer and chatted with Joseph at length. "For the time being, you'll be the battalion munitions officer," he said. "Gunner Reardon will show you around. He'll be here shortly."

Reardon was a muscular warrant officer, his face tanned nut-brown from the Korean summer. He was awaiting rotation back to the States. He escorted Joseph to a sandbagged pyramidal tent that hugged the side of a hill. Joseph dropped his gear on an empty canvas cot. His utilities were soaked with perspiration, and he wiped the sweat from his eyes.

"We're still in the dry season," Reardon said, "but the monsoons will start any day now, and when it rains it doesn't quit."

Joseph eyed another cot with a crude table alongside made of ammo crates. On the table were several photographs of a woman.

"The chaplain's wife," Reardon explained. "He's also due for rotation. Doesn't spend much time up here; goes to regiment or division every day in his jeep."

The chaplain, Joseph soon learned, had a fear of getting killed in the remaining days of his tour. It was not too unusual with short timers.

Back in the States, Dwight Eisenhower had been nominated as the presidential candidate of the Republican party with a promise to end the Korean War. Can't happen too soon, Joseph thought.

It was another scorching day when he hiked to the ammunition dump a half-mile away. In the wide, saucer-shaped depression among the hills were stacks of 105 shells in crates.

A rotund gunnery sergeant met him, and the two began walking among the stacks. He noted that the stacks were well dispersed and sandbagged. A hit from an enemy round would not likely set off another stack. The shells were familiar to Joseph except for one pile with the word "propaganda" stenciled on the crates.

"They're hollow shells," the gunny explained. "We stuff them with leaflets that are scattered all over when the time fuse goes off. It tells the Chinese what good guys we are and how well we'll treat them if they surrender."

When Joseph had finished his inspection and his questions answered, the gunnery sergeant led him to a bunker dug into the hillside. Outside the entrance was a tent fly that provided shade. Under the fly were several "lounge" chairs built from ammo crates. Two NCOs who had been sitting got to their feet and saluted. The gunny introduced his assistants.

He motioned Joseph to one of the chairs. They sat gazing absently at the heat waves shimmering across the scarred earth laid bare by bulldozers in building revetments. The gunny broke the silence.

"Would you care for something cold, Lieutenant?"

"Cold? Out here?" Joseph replied.

"I guess you wouldn't say anything to anyone, so we do have a cold one for you."

With that, he ducked into the bunker and emerged with a tall bottle of Japanese beer. Cold beads of moisture clung to the bottle.

"Jeez that hits the spot," Joseph said after chugging away at the cold, frothy beer. "But where'd you get the ice?"

"Division morgue," the gunny answered. "They throw it out when they're done with it. Nothing wrong with it after it melts a little," he added, after noticing the lift in Joseph's eyebrows.

Joseph finished his beer and decided not to ask any more questions.

Dog battery, in position just ahead of headquarters, took a hit from an enemy artillery round, killing two men and wounding several. The battalion surgeon was slow in responding and Captain Ezell furiously berated him.

Before long, Joseph was assigned to Charlie Battery as executive officer. The guns were emplaced in an open area, under camouflage nets and surrounded with sandbag revetments. There wasn't much firing, as the Chinese to their front didn't move around much. At night the battery fired interdicting missions hitting trails and crossroads used by the enemy.

Artillery positions in Korea, though barely a mile from the front lines, were much like the rear area camps of the Pacific war. The men slept in canvas cots under pyramidal tents.

Each battery had a field galley that prepared three hot meals a day, including fresh beef once or twice a week. Occasionally there were fresh eggs for breakfast. Hot coffee was available throughout the day.

The infantry up front roughed it by comparison. In the MLR, the main line of resistance, they lived in bunkers fortified with logs and sandbags. Units were frequently rotated to rear areas, where they enjoyed the same comforts as the artillery men.

Once or twice a week, Joseph took his men for a dip in the Imjin. It was a wide, shallow steam, but a steady current kept the water cool and refreshing. After washing off the dust that coated them, the men would dress and mount the trucks to become coated with new dust on the ride back to the battery.

Twice a month a mobile PX came by and set up for business in the battery area. Besides the usual candy and cigarettes, there were watches, cameras, and cheap Korean souvenirs available. Almost every man acquired a quality German or Japanese camera.

As Reardon predicted, in July the monsoon rains arrived. Water had to be bailed out of gun pits, and the whole area became a quagmire where the earth had been rearranged in carving out the battery position. A road across the valley to their rear became a causeway and then slowly disappeared altogether beneath the flood. A column of infantry, cautiously making its way to the front, lost a man when he stepped off the road and was drowned.

Coincidentally, the mail deliveries slowed down. Joseph had not heard from Cara since he arrived in Korea, and he was worried. The miserable weather added to his anxiety.

The Armed Forces radio station in Seoul, which should have played uplifting tunes, contributed to the ennui by airing depressing country music, including one song that went, "I got the ro-oh-oh ta-a-a shun blue ooz." Joseph had eleven months before he could even think of Stateside rotation.

The MLR stretched across the waist of Korea hugging the 38th parallel for some 120 miles. The chain of trenches and bunkers zigzagged according to the terrain, going slightly above the 38th in some zones to take advantage of dominating hill masses and ducking below the parallel where the Chinese were most firmly entrenched.

Peace negotiations were under way between the United Nations and the Chinese and North Koreans. The two sides met once or twice a week and haggled in a designated no-fire zone near the village of Panmumjom. Charlie Battery was emplaced nearest and immediately to the right of a narrow corridor that led to the truce village from the U.S. lines.

This restricted the traverse of the guns to the left, and six-foot stakes were driven vertically into the ground to stop gun barrels from being cranked too far left. Despite the precaution, an occasional stray round found its way into the corridor, and the Chinese would threaten to call off the talks. Under a flimsy truce that set the rules of engagements, neither side could seize and hold ground from the other. Infantry ground action was limited to patrols. Fighting a war from trenches was not in the style of marines, and frustrated infantry commanders often sent out entire battalions on patrol. Aroused Chinese troops, believing a full-scale attack was underway, would leave their holes like a disturbed nest of fire ants only to be caught in the open by the 105s and 155s of the 11th Marines. Marine fighter planes from Kimpo would join in the killing spree with 500-pound bombs and napalm.

One such fight occurred on hills with the code names Carson and Reno. Both were in disputed territory, and when the Chinese and North Koreans attempted to occupy them in force, the marines counterattacked and drove them off. In that fray, the 11th Marines fired continuously throughout the day.

Joseph's "cannon cockers" were happiest when working off their frustrations and boredom by cranking off round after round. Swabbing their gun bores afterwards and disposing of small mountains of shell cases kept them busy for a day or two.

The Korean terrain is mainly vertical, with steep, knobby hills everywhere. Moving about always meant a climb, whether going to the galley, the head, or the fire direction center. A few weeks in Korea was all it took to develop strong leg muscles.

The long hot summer was finally eased out with a glorious spell of fall weather. In the early mornings, the crisp air energized the troops. The cadence of performing routine duties accelerated. Scrub oaks on the hillsides turned a russet brown. Field jackets were issued.

On November first, Joseph received his promotion to first lieutenant. Colonel Jones summoned him to his hillside hutch to break the good news. There was more to come.

"How would you like to have a firing battery?" Jones said. "Captain Brown in Able Battery is due for rotation, and I think you can do a good job. The outfit is getting a bit rusty and needs a little shaking up."

One didn't refuse the opportunity of being a battery commander, particularly a brand new first lieutenant. The next day, Joseph began the process of assuming command of "Stable" Able Battery and its 160 men. He gathered the officers and NCOs around, introduced himself and gave a short talk. He carefully avoided any mention of Colonel Jones' reference about the battery being a bit rusty.

Enlisted men generally described their C.O.s in three categories: "Good guy," which meant an easy going officer and usually a sloppy outfit; "tough guy," which described an officer that insisted on things being done "strictly by the book," and last, "horse shit."

This was reserved for a martinet, who lacked compassion and inflicted misery on his men for his perverse pleasure.

Joseph decided he would combine strictness with fairness. He would go by the book but make allowances for human nature. He conveyed this to his senior NCOs. Without their respect, he would have a tough row to hoe. From experience he knew that NCOs preferred discipline to laxness. If it came from the top, it made their job easier, as they would have solid backing in dealing with "gold bricks" and screw-ups.

As NCOs went, gunnery sergeants were the key to good leadership, the salt of the earth in the Corps. While the first sergeant was the ranking NCO, he was too often immersed in paperwork and other administrative duties. The "gunny," on the other hand, was constantly circulating among the troops, maintaining discipline and setting a good example by his demeanor and dedication. Able Battery had a competent gunnery sergeant.

It was early December when the first snows of winter had begun and Able Battery was ordered to displace to an alternate firing position. The move was to be done at night under blackout conditions. As darkness set in, they fired several parting salvos from the old position. Salvo meant each of the six guns firing in sequence at five-second intervals, as opposed to volleys when the guns fired simultaneously.

Meanwhile, working parties were striking tents, and loading the mess sergeant's field ranges and cooking equipment.

"Don't expect any hot coffee any time soon," grumbled Sergeant Gladys, the mess sergeant.

Finally Joseph gave the command, "CSMO," meaning close station, march order. Quickly the guns were placed in the towing position and the prime movers backed up to the gun pits. Ammunition was loaded in separate trucks. The new position had been prepared beforehand and Joseph had reconnoitered the route. The comm (communication) section had wired in the new position and a survey team had located and staked out gun positions and orienting points.

Guided by miniature green lights on the front and rear of each truck, the convoy fell in line and the march began at a snail's pace. The night began clear, with the stars giving off a bit of light. Joseph in the lead jeep had closed his eyes at intervals to become accustomed to the darkness.

That afternoon he had posted guides at crossroads to make sure no vehicle strayed from the route.

It was a lesson he had learned while executive officer of Charlie Battery. On a similar night march, the battery commander had failed to post guides along the way and, in his lead jeep, took a wrong fork in the road. After traveling for nearly an hour, they finally reached a village occupied by an army unit.

"What town is this?" the battery commander inquired of a sentry.

"Oujongbu," the sentry replied.

"OUJONGBU?" the battery commander shouted in disbelief. It meant they were nearly twenty miles from their objective and faced an all-night ride backtracking.

Joseph's convoy stayed the course and arrived at the new position without incident, although the clear night had given way to low scudding clouds, which usually meant snow. Quickly, the guns were unlimbered and emplaced. Aiming stakes, a pair for each gun, with red and green lights at the top, were set out obliquely from each piece, the first at thirty paces and the second at sixty. Each gunner directed the placement of the stakes until the two were in perfect alignment with the vertical crosshair of his optical gun sight. They then became the reference point for all lateral, or deflection, shifts.

The battery executive officer laid the guns in the predetermined compass direction with an aiming circle. Meanwhile the fire direction center crew had set up their tent, tied down the sides so no light could shine through, lit the Coleman lantern, and set up the plotting tables. Within an hour, Able Battery was awakening the Chinese with hot steel from an unexpected position.

"Got some hot coffee, Skipper," came the voice of Sergeant Gladys in the darkness through the wind and snowflakes. His cooks had set up the mess tent, fired up their oil-burning ranges, and brewed a cauldron of hot coffee, not without a fair amount of grumbling. There was more truth than fiction in Napoleon's dictum that an army traveled on its stomach. And there was no mistaking the uplifted spirits of Joseph's cannoneers resulting from the hot "joe" they were sipping from canteen cups in the now-swirling snowstorm.

One of the duties Joseph looked forward to was visiting his forward observers in the front lines. Peering through a telescope that poked above their bunker he observed targets the battery had previously engaged. Joseph saw the enemy for the first time. In a trench that zigzagged 300 yards away, he saw the conical Chinese helmets bobbing up and down as soldiers went about improving their positions. Shovels of dirt flew from trenches like prairie dogs digging new burrows.

"Why aren't we firing at them?" Joseph asked Lieutenant Brown, the F.O. "Looks like a good target for VT fuses."

Variable time fuses had tiny radar units that sent out radio waves. As the shell neared the ground, the waves bounced back and intensified until the fuse ignited and the shell burst in the air just above the ground.

"Yeah, I agree," replied Brown, "but the battalion commander wants to leave them alone for the time being to see what they're up to."

Forward of the MLR some three or four hundred yards out, the infantry maintained listening posts usually manned by a squad. A scout corporal from Lieutenant Brown's F.O. team had gone out with the infantry and decided to stay. Although the squads were rotated frequently, he refused relief. He claimed to have been nicked eight times by enemy mortar shells and hand grenades but refused to come out for medical treatment. Joseph decided the corporal needed psychiatric treatment more than bandages for his superficial wounds.

Joseph went forward on payday with military script for his men. Everyone was paid except the eccentric corporal on the outpost. The company command post nearby had a phone line to the outpost, and Lieutenant Brown called to tell the man his battery commander was waiting at the company C.P. with his money. The corporal wouldn't budge. He expected his C.O. to come to him with the money. Joseph couldn't leave the money with the lieutenant. Regulations required that each man sign his name on the payroll at the time of payment.

There were certain risks that weren't worth taking, and running a gauntlet behind enemy lines to pay a man of questionable mentality was one, Joseph reasoned.

"I'm not about to crawl out there through barbwire just to pay that idiot," Joseph said to Brown. "Tell him when he wants his money to look me up."

Eventually, the corporal ran out of cigarettes and returned from the outpost wearing his bloodstained utilities as a badge of honor. Joseph reassigned him to a gun crew.

At the extreme western sector of the MLR on a bluff overlooking the Han River near where it flowed into the Yellow Sea, the 11th Marines maintained a gun position. Batteries alternated in occupying the position for six-week periods. In mid-December, Joseph's battery was ordered to occupy the position. The battery would be on its own with the nearest friendly unit, the amphibian tractor battalion, farther downstream.

The gun position was well maintained, and Joseph's battery settled in. They enjoyed being out from under the daily supervision of battalion headquarters.

Oil-burning mountain stoves were issued and set up one to a tent. With a good supply of rations, fuel, and ammunition, Joseph looked forward to ending the year on the Han.

It was a distance of several thousand yards across the river and rarely were enemy troops sighted. Previous firing batteries had carefully plotted targets at every possible crossing point.

With a limited daily allowance of ammunition, Able Battery had to be content with firing harassing missions at suspected points across the river.

Joseph's orders read that all Korean civilians had been warned to clear the area. Anything moving was to be considered military in nature and to be engaged with artillery fire. Korean peasants customarily wore white clothing, and enemy soldiers were known to wear white camouflage over their uniforms to move about freely near American lines. Many U.S. men had been shot in the back during the conflict by this treachery.

One day, Joseph was summoned to the O.P. by a report that "many people" in white were observed across the river. Joseph peered through the BC scope, making out twenty or thirty white-clad figures at work with implements. It was too late for the harvest season and certainly not the time of planting. Quite possibly they were soldiers preparing positions from which to attack. With some hesitancy and reluctance, Joseph nodded his approval when the forward observer sent back the fire commands. The initial rounds landed well beyond the figures, which scattered and headed for safety behind a hill. "Cease fire," Joseph ordered when the figures had disappeared. "I doubt they'll come back, but if they do, let 'em have it again," he added. That was the end of it. No more activity was observed.

Christmas approached with mail deliveries bringing in food packages and gifts from home. Joseph got cookies, a tin of smoked oysters, and oranges from Cara, who was in Florida with her mother and Annie. From his mother in Lake Tarsa came a roasted wild Louisiana duck she had canned at the parish home demonstration center in Dennings. Joseph shared the bounty with the lieutenants in his tent, along with a nip from the bottle of Old Forester from Ornas that miraculously made it through the mail unscathed.

Able Battery's troops salvaged tinsel and colored wrapping from packages and used it to decorate a small pine tree growing in the middle of the battery position. They added spare red and green night lights from their aiming stakes, producing a reasonable Christmas festive setting.

To ring in the New Year, Joseph had squirreled away a few rounds of high explosives. Targets had been selected during the day and Able's guns lit up the sky with air bursts at the stroke of twelve.

"The Chinks have their own new year, different from ours, don't they, Skipper?" The gunnery sergeant noted above the din.

"Yep, but they celebrate with firecrackers," Joseph replied wryly.

One day, the assistant division commander appeared for a surprise inspection. The battery exec spotted the jeep displaying a single star on a red plate. The general's bladder was badly in need of relief after bouncing over miles of rough Korean roads, and he made a beeline for one of the two urinal tubes in the open on each side of the battery area. The tubes were empty fiber cases that shells came packed in. They were buried upright in a bed of sand and gravel with a funnel on the receiving end, fashioned from ration cans.

As the brigadier was relieving himself, the overzealous exec raced up and popped a salute. The surprised general shifted his hold that was controlling the stream from his right hand to the left and awkwardly returned the salute. In the process, he sprayed his boots.

"Cripes sakes, couldn't you wait until he finished taking a leak?" Joseph scolded his eager subordinate when the general had departed. Fortunately, the battery position was shipshape, and the general was satisfied with what he had seen.

Able Battery maintained a two-man listening post near the bottom of the bluff overlooking the river. One night, the gunnery sergeant made his way down to check on the men and found only one on duty. He said he had been asleep and did not know his companion had disappeared. From down below, the gunny heard Korean voices. He rang the field phone to the battery exec, gave his report, and requested a detail of three armed men.

Silently the four crept downward to the river bank and found their man in a makeshift camp, where a flourishing black market was operated by Korean rogues. There were two women in the group, confirmed by the wayward sentry as prostitutes.

Under questioning by Joseph, the sentry lied that he had gone to the river to "investigate noises" and that he was not involved in any illegal activity. Joseph had no choice but to charge the man with deserting his post. In the court-martial at headquarters, his defense counsel, the battalion adjutant, got the charge reduced to unauthorized absence, and the man escaped with a slap on the wrist. Joseph promptly had him transferred to headquarters battery away from the temptation of rogues.

The six-week tour on the river Hans having passed, Able Battery returned to its old position with the battalion.

Gradually, winter passed, and the first signs of spring appeared with the blossoms of wild plum followed by the wild azaleas, which turned the hillsides purple.

Passing abandoned farmhouses along the roads, Joseph often wondered what tragedies had befallen the families that were uprooted and scattered like leaves in a tempest. With their rotting roofs of rice thatch, they stood as stark reminders of the cruelties of war. Broken windows and sagging doors that swayed with the wind presented a haunting picture. On one house strings of dried red peppers and garlic remained where months before they were hung out on the weathered wall of the back porch. Among the tall weeds in the yard, a solitary rose bloomed.

In the "Land of the Morning Calm," the armies of the North and South had surged up and down four times through the peninsula. Like flood tides, they had driven families to wander aimlessly in search of safety, food, and shelter.

Joseph pitied the gaunt-faced Koreans who waited patiently near the garbage cans at the end of the chow line where his troops emptied the scraps from their mess kits. Only when the mess sergeant nodded his approval did they begin sifting through the garbage for morsels.

Before General Kim Il Sung sent his North Korean soldiers and Russian tanks across the boundary into South Korea, egged on by China and Stalinist Russia, Korea had lived under the brutal oppression of a Japanese occupation since 1910. In 1945, what began as an agreement between the U.S. and the USSR to jointly remove the occupation army of Japan resulted in a North and South Korea with opposite ideologies and political forms of government.

For U.S. troops, the Korean conflict had turned into a war of disgust by 1952. The generals recognized that their troops had to have a diversion from the grinding repetitions of combat or morale would deteriorate. After six months, every man became eligible for a week of R&R in Japan in special rest camps. Joseph's turn came late in February and he boarded a C-54 transport plane at Kimpo for a flight to Kyoto. The pilot invited him into the cockpit. He was amazed at the mountainous topography of Japan that unfolded beneath them.

Kyoto, the original capital, had been spared from the destruction of other large Japanese cities. A few bombs had been dropped in 1945, but the ancient Buddhist shrines, shogun castles, and Zen temples had been spared. As the center of Japanese culture, Kyoto offered a panoply of colorful sights that Joseph recorded in abundance on his new thirty-five-millimeter camera. It was his first experiment with color slides that he and Cara would enjoy viewing when he returned home.

When he tired of eating Japanese food in his hotel and in restaurants, he returned to the R&R camp where the mess offered good American food, including steaks, fresh fruits, and milk.

Back in Korea, Joseph was reassigned as C.O. of Service Battery. Officers were rotated customarily to give them a variety of command responsibilities. As logistics officer, he was responsible for procuring and distributing the bullets, rations, and fuel for the battalion. It was a boring job, and he used his jeep to break the monotony with personal forays, including a sightseeing trip to Seoul and a visit to the Black Watch Scottish battalion that occupied a sector of the MLR nearest the marines.

A Scots lieutenant invited him for a drink in the officers' mess. It was under a sprawling circus-like tent that had all the amenities of a British pub, except for the out-of-place Korean bartender in a white jacket, the mahogany bar, and the Oriental carpet spread over a plywood deck.

Almost as feared as an incoming round was the hemorrhagic fever that was fatal to many of its victims. Doctors traced it to mites from rats that infested bunkers and underground fortifications.

Joseph's anticipated rotation came in late May when he was ordered back to the States.

Eagerly, he broke in his replacement. His NCOs threw a surprise going-away party that featured a guitar-playing sergeant who ad-libbed ribald songs about Joseph.

The next day he was in Ascom City, an Army logistics camp at Kimpo that processed incoming and outgoing troop drafts. There he was examined by a team of doctors, and specimens of his feces and urine were scrutinized under the microscopes of laboratory technicians. He was herded under a gang shower that sprayed powdered DDT on him that would take care of any mites or lice.

The entire process was viewed with alarm lest some physical problem be discovered and his return home delayed or canceled. All went well and he soon trooped aboard the U.S. Navy troop transport *General M.C. Meigs* along with nearly 4,000 returning veterans. There was one last bit of anxiety to be sweated out by the returnees. Chinese prisoners began rioting in U.S. POW camps, and it was feared they would be recalled to quell the uprising. As a condition of the armistice that was being worked out, the United States insisted that North Korean prisoners be given the option of staying in South Korea. Communist ringleaders threatened them, and when too many prisoners were opting for asylum, they instigated the riots which turned bloody.

On June 23, the *Meigs* slid under the Golden Gate Bridge and tied up at Fort Mason. If the Korean War was an unpopular one in the minds of many, such was not the case in San Francisco. As they disembarked, the veterans on the *Meigs* were greeted with a band playing martial music and professional entertainers singing songs of welcome. The effect was a tonic for the men who had feared their sacrifices on the battlefield would not be appreciated.

Joseph was met at the dock by the Giffens, long-time friends of Cara, and welcomed to a place of their dinner table for a long-awaited home-cooked meal.

American Airlines was advertising nonstop flights to Florida, and Joseph bought a ticket at the downtown office. The flight took off late at night and to everyone's surprise soon landed in Phoenix. The "non-stop" flight also put down in Dallas and New Orleans.

From Tampa, the following day, Joseph boarded an old amphibian commuter plane for the short flight to Orlando. Greeting him at the airport, Cara looked radiant with her Florida suntan. His heart swelled with pride at the sight of his beautiful young daughter. He missed a whole year of seeing Annie grow.

Sixteen
The Peacetime Corps—1953–1959

Joseph's leave time quickly evaporated in a fortnight of family outings and sight-seeing in Florida's laid-back pre-Disney World days. They loaded their suitcases in their gray DeSoto and headed back to California and Camp Pendleton. Joseph had traded in the Chrysler in Oklahoma while attending artillery school.

They motored leisurely westward, enjoying the scenery and stopping frequently for sightseeing attractions. Cara could never get enough traveling. Every highway was a happy trail, and she relished the prospect of what lay beyond. Her botanical courses in college became an education for Joseph in the flora and fauna of the passing countryside.

"Pretty wild flowers," he might remark.

"Lupine," Cara would respond. "Or bluebonnets."

Fondly, she often referred to the California redwood tree by its genus, Sequoia sempervirens, without a trace of pretentiousness. She had been born in the very shadow of those majestic giants in the tiny northern California lumber town of Scotia where her father was personnel manager for the Pacific Lumber Company.

Astronomy fascinated her. She'd scan the skies at night and point out the stars and constellations. Though a practical homemaker and innovative cook, she welcomed every opportunity of getting out of the house and way from the kitchen stove. She would study the menu of a roadside hash house with the same scrutiny she might in a five-star restaurant.

While in Korea, Joseph had formed a casual friendship with a major in regimental headquarters. His tour was ending, and he had been reassigned to the detail section in the personnel office at Headquarters Marine Corps. In his capacity, he would be in charge of posting artillery officers at stations throughout the Marine Corps.

"If there's anything I can do for you, don't hesitate to write me," he said to Joseph on his leave-taking.

Joseph hoped to avoid being assigned to the 2nd Marine Division at Camp Lejeune, so as his own time for rotation neared, he wrote his major friend at Marine Corps headquarters:

"I have never sought favors in the corps, but since you so kindly offered your help, I do so now. Please reassign me to any place but Camp Lejeune."

He got his wish, and a set of orders to Fleet Marine Force Troops at Camp Pendleton. There, he joined the 155-millimeter gun battalion. Nicknamed the "Long Toms," the 155s were the largest weapon in the corps' arsenal, capable of hurling a 95-pound projectile a distance of twenty-five miles. Pendleton's artillery range was too small to accommodate the 155s, but the corps had recently acquired 932 square miles of choice terrain in the Mojave Desert. Joseph's new outfit moved to Twentynine Palms, forty miles north of Palm Springs as the crow flies.

Before the move, Joseph received the Navy Commendation Medal for his actions as a battery commander in Korea. Along with several other recipients on the dusty parade ground at Pendleton, his medal was pinned on by Brigadier General W. S. "Bigfoot" Brown who wept as he affixed the decorations on the shirtfronts of the men. On Iwo Jima, Joseph had rejected a Bronze Star when he felt the citation was impersonal and lacking in sincerity. This one was heartfelt and, in his perhaps immodest way of thinking, well deserved.

The Mojave is the hottest and driest desert in North America and, combined with its remoteness, a perfect location for a Marine Corps facility. A permanent camp had just been completed at the base of the Bullion Mountains.

Not entirely by coincidence, a developer from San Bernardino was building a tract of family homes between the base and the small town of Twenty-nine Palms. Sun Gold Hills he named it, in the fanciful appellation typical of developers. With financing from the Veterans Administration, married men in Joseph's battalion bought homes sight unseen while still at Pendleton. Families were left behind in quarters at Pendleton when the battalion moved to the desert. On weekends, Joseph brought home samples of floor tiles, formica countertops and paint cards, from which he and Cara made the choices for their $10,000, air-conditioned, three-bedroom, one-bath home, with garage attached. The air conditioning was adapted to the dry desert air. Water piped to the roof cascaded through a set of wooden vanes. An electric fan inside pulled the air cooled by the water and circulated it through the house. It was an efficient and economical method of cooling a house.

In the evenings, Joseph busied himself polishing floors and cleaning windows. Cara and Annie arrived ahead of the van carrying the furniture, which had been stored at Pendelton. Alas, the kitchen décor was not what Cara had selected, in particular the tomato red formica countertops and coral pink wall. The substitute changes had not bothered Joseph, but Cara was bothered a whole lot. "I'm the one who's going to be in the kitchen, and that wall has got to be repainted." Repainted it was, a harmonizing gray to her liking, but the countertops were there to stay.

They not only became accustomed to the desert but fell in love with it.

Their new home had a window wall in the living room with a view that looked past the cactus and greasewood bushes to a large mountain in the distance. By day, Cara kept her corduroy drapes drawn tight to ward off the blazing sun. After sunset the drapes would be pulled just as the shadows were turning the mountain to a purplish hue. With a highball in hand at day's end, Joseph would gaze transfixed at the beauty of the softening purplish color of the mountain where an hour earlier the sun had fiercely beaten upon the earth.

Cara accepted a job teaching second graders at the small school on the base. Annie was enrolled in kindergarten. One of Cara's teacher friends was an unmarried, strikingly attractive young brunette who had eligible lieutenants standing on their heads vying for her attention. A free spirit, she once attended a PTA meeting wearing her mink coat and nothing else.

Joseph received his promotion to captain and was given command of a firing battery. He invited the officers of the battalion to his house for a celebration that included the traditional "wetting down" ceremony. In the initiation, he had to down a highball glass of straight bourbon until his new captain's tracks were high and dry at the bottom.

The battalion frequently took to the field for firing exercises, towing their big guns with Caterpillar tractors. Simply setting one up in the firing position was a project. Gunnery procedures were basically the same as with smaller calibers, except that weather balloons were launched prior to firing to check wind velocity and direction, which would affect the projectile in its long flight to the target. Powder temperatures were also factored into the firing data.

To load the gun, two men hefted the fused projectile on a tray to the open breach. A third crew member with a ramrod shoved the round into the chamber until the lands of the bore bit into the soft copper rotating band of the shell. Powder bags were placed behind the projectile and the breach block closed. A brass primer cap was inserted in the breach block. When the lanyard was pulled, the firing pin struck the primer, igniting the powder bags. The resulting explosion would rock the desert floor, raising a choking cloud of sand and dust.

During one night exercise, a crew member was driving stakes in the ground for the camouflage net. Reaching into a bush with his stake, he felt a stabbing pain and was sure he had stuck his hand on a cactus. But his section chief's flashlight revealed the puncture marks of a rattlesnake. The battery corpsman performed first aid and immediately evacuated the victim to the base infirmary. By the time he arrived, his hand and lower arm were swollen grotesquely. He made a successful but painful recovery.

"Stay away from the bushes at night," Joseph cautioned his men, tardily.

On one extended exercise, Joseph was in charge of the OP on a mountaintop some five miles from the battalion's gun positions.

At the end of the day's firing, a truck arrived to take the several officers and men who had been conducting fire missions back to camp.

"I've got to be here early in the morning," Joseph said, not relishing the dusty, bouncing ride to camp and back. "I think I'll just spend the night here. Bring me some chow when you come back in the morning."

As the truck started down the hill, a sergeant threw out a folding cot, apparently intended for the colonel. "So the rattlesnakes won't crawl over you, Captain," he called out.

When the truck was out of sight, Joseph promptly set up the canvas cot, silently thanking the sergeant, and stretched out just as a full moon was rising over the Bullion Mountains. It began as an orange ball then faded to a platinum silver as it ascended. He had never before seen the moon in that brilliance. It illuminated the desert floor below making it seem like broad daylight. Neither had he ever been so much alone. But as the night wore on, he heard sounds indicating he had plenty of company. Coyotes yipped in the distance and the ground below him came alive with small creatures rustling among the cactus and greasewood. He imagined the chirping as coming from tiny kangaroo rats fleeing sidewinders. He knew there were scorpions and tarantulas nearly half the size of his hand and was even more thankful for the twenty-four inches the skinny wooden legs of his cot separated him from the ground. He drew some comfort from the .45 and clip of bullets he had in case a rattler got too bold. Feeling forsaken in the moonlight on a mountaintop five miles from the nearest human, he couldn't decide whether to howl or crank the field phone and talk to anyone at the base camp.

But *they might think I'm scared,* he thought. The air turned chilly, and he wished he had a blanket. With all the dried sticks and branches around, he thought of building a campfire, but quickly banished the idea when he remembered his own admonishment to his gun crews to stay away from the bushes at night. He fished out his poncho from his gear, threw it over his head to ward off the glare of the moon and finally dropped off to sleep.

The groaning of the truck laboring up the mountain trail in the morning awakened him.

"How was it, Captain?" a lieutenant called out.

"Great. Slept like a log," Joseph said, rubbing his eyes and stifling a yawn.

Summer temperatures consistently dipped well above the one-hundred-degree mark, so training was abbreviated to a five-hour day, beginning at 7:00 A.M. It was impossible to touch the metal of a gun or vehicle after midday without being burned. Training was also canceled when high pressure over the desert incubated winds that howled through the area, stirring up sand storms. Santa Anas, they were called, as they rushed westward towards the California coastal areas fanning brush and forest fires along the way. Joseph's

DeSoto was parked in the open on the base and caught the brunt of a Santa Ana.

Within minutes the side of the car exposed to the wind was sand-blasted to bare metal. His insurance company agreed to pay for a paint job, but only once. He followed the adjuster's advice and waited until he had orders out of the desert before having the car repainted.

One winter a freak weather front dropped several inches of snow over the desert. Children frolicked in the snow with their dogs. In the higher elevation, icicles hung from the bayonets of Joshua trees.

Joseph and Cara set about landscaping the big sand box that was their backyard. Joseph wrestled barrel cacti from the desert ground and transplanted them in the yard along with two dollar-leaf eucalyptus trees bought from a nursery. They found colorful flagstones at the base of a mountain and laid them down into a neat patio. Cara planted snap dragons, and from the coast, Joseph brought in ice plants, mesembryanthemum, Cara called it. The only encouragement the plants foreign to the desert needed was a bit of water.

Next, Joseph bought a load of redwood planks from a lumber yard in San Bernardino and set out building a fence around the yard. It had become a necessity to keep out the next door neighbor's two rambunctious boys, who'd go racing through the yard knocking over patio furniture and trampling the plants. He got the job done but not before suffering a painful case of bursitis, digging postholes with an augur.

Their backyard at 22 Yucca Street was a labor of love, and they took pride in entertaining friends and grilling steaks in the evenings.

But as was always the case in the Marine Corps, just when they were beginning to enjoy the fruits of their labor, Joseph was ordered to the Philippines. He was to report to the commanding officer, Marine Barracks, U.S. Naval Station, Subic Bay. He and Cara immediately set about making plans for the move. They put the house up for sale. Family quarters were not immediately available at Subic, so Cara and Annie would have to remain for the time being. They got a couple of nibbles on the house but that was all, so Cara would be saddled with closing the deal when she found a buyer. Joseph reported to Travis Air Force Base near San Francisco on May 6, 1955 for transportation to Manila and his seventh crossing of the Pacific.

After arriving at Clark Air Force Base on Luzon two days later, he flew in an old navy amphibian across the Zambales Mountains to Subic. The "gooney bird" circled the cobalt waters of the bay and gently splashed down three hundred yards off shore. It taxied to a boat dock, where a crewman deposited his trunk and a sack of mail. The tropics were by no means new to Joseph but, coming from the dry desert air, he felt the oppressing humidity through his gabardine summer uniform.

A jeep and driver waited to take him to the BOQ, where he would park his trunk before reporting to his new commanding officer. A row of coconut palms on the waterfront leaned toward the bay. They passed Tappan Park profuse with royal poincianas, pink and purple bougainvillaea, and scarlet hibiscus. The fragrant air reminded him of New Caledonia.

Except for a four-year period of Japanese occupation in World War II, Subic had been in U.S. hands since 1898.

In the battle of Manila Bay, Commodore George Dewey had calmly given the order to his gunnery officer, "Fire when ready, Gridley." It is unlikely the outcome of the battle would have been different had Captain Gridley asked for five more minutes. But ready he was, and soon the fleet of Admiral Patricio Montojo lay at the bottom of Manila Bay. The Philippines remained a U.S. possession until granted full independence following World War II. There was a catch, one that the Filipinos would come to regret. The United States was to be granted ninety-nine-year leases on military bases of choice. They picked Subic Bay, Clark Air Force Base and the old Cavite navy yard. Subic's main function was operating a ship repair facility and dry dock which serviced the Asiatic fleet.

The marine detachment was housed in a large, two-story prefabricated, metal building at the far end of the naval station. Offices were upstairs. Downstairs were instructional classrooms and NCO quarters. Across from a gravel parade ground was a row of Quonset huts where the troops lived.

Colonel G. G. Williams greeted Joseph warmly. "Been expecting you," he said, waving Joseph to a chair in front of his desk. The flash of his gold ring and blue stone of the Naval Academy caught Joseph's eye. Williams assigned him as commander and training officer of the guard company.

"He's a stickler for rules and regulations, but fair," said Captain Davis out of the colonel's hearing. Davis was the administrative officer of the barracks. "Don't try to pull anything on him, he's wise," Davis cautioned.

Joseph's impression of his new C.O., stated in the terse language of an officer's fitness report, would have been: Studious, officious, considerate, not given to jocularity.

The marines were responsible for the security of the base, and sentries were kept posed twenty-four hours a day at key locations on the perimeter, which fanned out for miles in all directions. They also maintained martial law in the town of Olongapo, just outside the main gate where thousands of Filipinos lived, many of them employees of the base. A fetid canal separated the town from the base. Rickety shanties of rusted corrugated tin hovered on stilts over the banks of a river whose dark water flowed sluggishly past the town. On the crooked, dusty main street, jeepneys in gaudy decorations raced back and forth, loaded with passengers, some hanging on the outside of the vehicles. There was an open market and at least a dozen bars where painted girls plied their trade with sailors and marines.

Joseph put his name on the waiting list for quarters and was told not to expect anything for six months. He mentioned it casually while talking to Colonel Williams a day later. Suddenly, the colonel's eyes widened behind his gold wire-rimmed glasses, and he sat up in his chair. He had just remembered something.

"Didn't you say your wife was a schoolteacher?" he asked.

Joseph nodded.

"They need teachers at the base school," Williams continued. "If your wife wants to teach, you can get priority on the quarters list."

With that, he picked up his phone and called a navy commander in charge of the school for dependent children. Ten minutes later, Joseph was in the commander's office.

"How soon can she be here?" he asked.

"She's got to sell a house in California first and then arrange for transportation."

Joseph cabled the news to Cara. She answered with news of her own that she had found a buyer for the house and was about to close the deal. She would also have to close out all her records at school; store the furniture, get the DeSoto to the port in Oakland for shipment to the Philippines, and herself and Annie to San Francisco to await the next navy ship. Cara was experiencing the trials and tribulations of a marine wife in a big way. But as it were, she wasn't just an ordinary marine wife, but a schoolteacher wife, and the school at Subic Bay needed her immediately. After a flurry of preparations and transactions, she and Annie were in San Francisco staying with a friend while awaiting the next ship to the Philippines, when a radio message from COMNAVPAC arrived at the Marine Corps Department of the Pacific on 100 Harrison Street.

The commander of naval forces in the Pacific at Pearl Harbor directed Cara to report to Travis immediately for Priority-One air transportation to the Philippines.

Joseph, meanwhile had been temporarily assigned to the quarters recently vacated by a navy captain. It was a rambling Quonset hut, actually two large huts joined together, fronted by banana plants and poincianas.

Inside, jute fiber rugs covered most of the polished native hardwood floors, which Joseph learned was regularly chewed up by termites and had to be replaced each year. There was rattan furniture throughout the house. As Joseph was checking out the quarters, two Filipinos girls knocked timidly on the front door. Nina and Anita had been employed as maids by a navy family recently transferred. They wanted to stay on with Joseph's family. Officers and staff NCOs received allowances for domestics. Joseph chatted with the two who offered several references from previous employers. Poor little Nina had a cocked eye, the legacy of a blow from a Japanese rifle butt suffered as a child during the Japanese occupation. Anita was from the Visayan Islands and spoke a different dialect, one of some 400 spoken in the Philippine archipelago.

Both spoke broken English but between themselves conversed in Tagalog, the prevalent and official dialect of the Philippines. Anita was tall, for a Filipina, and fairly attractive. She carried herself erect and did not hang her head or avert eye contact when spoken to.

Joseph had not the time nor the inclination to begin shopping for maids, so he hired the two on the spot, Nina as the cook and general housekeeper and Anita as the *lavandera,* or laundry girl.

Next he went grocery shopping at the navy commissary and returned with a fine assortment of food, including choice cuts of beef which he stashed in the deep freezer. From the officers' club, he bought a bottle of champagne. Cara loved the bubbly stuff.

Driving a Marine Corps van, he met the plane at Clark, accompanied by Captain Davis, whose wife, Margaret, and two children were also aboard the flight. Driving through the many barrios along the route could be time-consuming. The road was always cluttered with pigs, chickens, dogs, carabaos, children, and if paved, women drying their grain on the concrete. The only remedy for drivers was to lean on the horn.

"You never drove like this before," said Cara, uncomfortable at the apparent ugly American manners of her husband.

"It's the only way unless you want to spend the night on the road," Joseph replied.

Annie's first view of the Third World was a culture shock. She was embarrassed at the sight of small children playing in their yards wearing only shirt tops. It was the way Filipino babies were potty-trained.

"They should wear panties instead of tops," Annie suggested.

Tired and hungry after the long flight, Cara and Annie freshened up after arriving at their new home. Nina had the plates and silverware set on the polished mahogany table and, following Joseph's instructions, lit a pair of candles. Joseph had not prescribed a menu for the occasion. The only instructions he had given to Nina beforehand was that he wanted a special welcome dinner for his family. He popped the cork on the champagne and poured a Coke for Annie.

They spread their napkins and waited with anticipation for the dinner. Nina emerged from the kitchen with a steaming platter and set it on the table.

"Meat loaf?" a startled Joseph exclaimed to himself, thinking of the standing rib in the freezer.

He and Cara exchanged glances. Meat loaf was something Cara never made. Nina hovered expectantly at a distance, her hands smoothing her apron. She noticed the looks between Cara and Joseph as they began eating.

"I make all the time for the other family," she said apologetically. "They like very very much. They favorite. You don't like?"

"Of course we like it," Cara and Joseph chimed. "It's very good."

It wasn't that they hated meat loaf, only that they didn't like it. After that, Cara made sure Nina wouldn't make a habit of cooking her specialty without hurting her feelings. She bought ground beef sparingly and always specified how it should be used.

Annie hadn't finished her sliced mango when her head began nodding. It had been an extra long day for the youngster, and Cara tucked her in bed. They talked and finished the champagne, and soon it was their bed time. They cuddled contentedly and listened to the singing of crickets and tree frogs beyond the screened windows. The electric fan on the wall hummed softly, and they soon dropped off to sleep.

Cara's travel alarm buzzed at six o'clock. She was expected in the classroom at 7:30. The school term started on the fifth of July, the beginning of the "cool" season.

Right on time, Cara greeted twenty-five bright-eyed fifth graders. They were the children of military personnel and of employees of the giant Pomeroy-Bechtol Construction Company, which was building new facilities, including an air station. There was a smattering of Filipino children whose fathers were civil service workers.

The marines maintained a small detachment on Grande Island which straddled the seaward side of the bay midway between the towering Redondo headland and Bataan Peninsula. Ostensibly, they were there to guard an ammunition dump. But there was only one ammunition bunker on the island; the main navy magazine was at Camayan Point across the bay.

A mysterious outfit civilian outfit from the State Department, known only as SJP-80, the initials apparently standing for "special joint project," had their headquarters on Grande in a rambling two-story wooden building. Joseph boarded a small boat for the ten-minute ride to the island. He inspected his men and their living quarters, but everything else in the building was off limits.

"What's with this SJP-80 outfit?" Joseph asked Colonel Williams upon his return.

Williams gave him a disapproving look.

"Don't even ask about them; it's not our business," he replied in an irritated voice.

They had the finest family quarters on the base on Kalayaan Heights overlooking the bay. It was a community of two-story concrete buildings at the edge of the jungle, better than the accommodations offered senior naval officers. Joseph's colleages conjectured among themselves that SJP-80 could have been a CIA operation keeping an eye on Red China across the South China Sea. In fact, Admiral Donaho, the base commander, said nearly as much to Captain Davis one day.

"They're nothing but a bunch of damned spies, and I'm sick and tired of them," he blurted out in an exasperated tone.

Before long, quarters more appropriate for a marine captain became available, an upstairs apartment in a Butler building. It was an all-metal structure put together with nuts and bolts and welding torches. The quarters were adequate but much smaller than the big Quonset. It soon became apparent that the kitchen was too crowded for Cara with two maids underfoot. There is an old saying not to shed tears for the housewife with maid problems.

Cara wasn't looking for sympathy but was rapidly becoming frustrated, particularly with Anita. In doing the laundry, she had used a ten-pound box of All in one week, and the collars of Joseph's new shirts were suddenly becoming frayed. Anita was not going to tolerate ring-around-the-collar, even with unsoiled shirts. When Cara found her scrubbing the collars with a Brillo pad, that was the end of it. She was let go. With an increase in her pay, Nina gladly took over all the household chores, including the laundry.

At Baguio, high in the mountains of central Luzon, the air force maintained Camp John Hay, a recreation camp for military personnel. After six months in the sweltering lowlands, servicemen and their families were eligible for a one-week stay in a cabin. The cool alpine air was an invigorating balm.

Nina had made several trips to Baguio with former employers and provided timely tips on road directions and dealing with natives on the way. Road projects along the sixty-mile route were frequent, seemingly none of them ever completed. Lane closures were marked, not with rubber cones but with menacing spikes sticking up from two-by-fours placed on the ground. The remains of broken bridges lay rusting over mountain streams, where the armies of Japan and the United States had retreated.

Their cabin at Baguio had a fireplace, and Nina built cheerful fires in the evenings when the temperatures dropped. They took most of their evening meals in the officers' club.

Camp Hay had a riding stable, and Annie was soon riding ponies. There was also a golf course, where Joseph was introduced to the game. As he was checking out a set of clubs and buying balls, a young, barefoot Filipino caddy came up and volunteered his services. They headed for the first tee, where a starter put him in a group about to begin play. Having hit several buckets of balls on the driving range, he was not totally unfamiliar with the golf swing. With the help of his cheating caddy, who worked for tips—the lower the score the higher the tip—he managed a respectable round for a beginner. Sliced balls that disappeared in the jungle were almost always recovered by his young caddy. Finding the errant ball, he would grasp it between his big and second toes and walk slowly back to the fairway with his head down. Reaching the light rough, he would suddenly step back and yell, "Here it is, sir," and Joseph would arrive on the spot to find a beautiful lie, equivocally speaking.

In the mysterious way of a neophyte, he was able to hit his best shots with the 2-iron, which for experienced golfers was the most difficult club in the bag. On a short par 3, the caddy handed him the 9-iron, which he hated. He gave it back and reached for the 2-iron. The caddy rolled his eyes as Joseph smashed a drive that never rose higher than six feet off the ground, sailed over the flag stick and disappeared into the jungle so deep that his caddy refused to go look for it. Only one hole on the course, number 18, had a grass green. The others were sand on which caddies dragged rubber matts to smooth over footprints in the line of putts. Number 18 had the only sand trap on the course, a monstrous hazard on the right side of the green.

Playing the 18th, Joseph had hit a respectable drive, leaving him with a mid-iron to the elevated green. The moment he struck his second shot, the ball began curving to the right. "Lord, don't let it be in the trap," he cried out. But even divine intervention couldn't straighten out that banana.

What made the trap on 18 so forbidding was the clubhouse that overlooked the green. It had a wide veranda always occupied by onlookers drinking gin and tonics. They perversely enjoyed the comedy of hackers trying to extricate their balls, an event that produced laughter and derisive comments. They placed bets on the number of strokes a victim would take in getting the ball out. Joseph spotted Cara sitting at a table with another couple and dreaded the thought of embarrassing her.

With trepidation and pounding pulse, he approached his ball at rest at the bottom of that hell pit and knew how the Christians must have felt as they were pushed by the Romans into the arena of waiting lions. The caddy handed him the hated 9-iron.

"Take a full swing, keep your head still, and hit down behind the ball," he whispered.

Joseph dug his crepe-sole loafers into the loose sand. A hush fell over the veranda as he addressed the ball which, mercifully, was not embedded. He took a tight grip, contrary to what his caddy had been preaching, swung mightily with the clubhead aimed straight down behind the ball. He kept his head lowered so long, he had no idea where the ball had gone until he heard a commotion on the veranda. From the bottom of the trap he could barely see the surface of the green, but there was his ball at rest ten feet from the flagstick. He vowed to say a Hail Mary when time permitted.

With that shot, which was rarely destined to be repeated, he was hooked on the game. Later, while spending a weekend at Clark, which had a golf course and pro shop, he bought a complete set of Tommy Armour MacGregors and a pair of golf shoes.

Joseph and his family made the trip to Baguio every six months. The first time they went in the DeSoto, which had arrived from Oakland. The rock-strewn mountain road nearly tore up the transmission and all but shredded the tires. From then on, Joseph would check out a navy station wagon from the base recreation department.

They made one memorable trip to the highlands, where the rice terraces on steep mountainsides rank among the wonders of the world. They stayed overnight in the village of Bontoc in a rustic hotel operated by an elderly Turkish immigrant.

Friends who had previously made the trip advised taking food for the evening meal, so Cara packed steaks in an ice chest. Mr. Gabriel, the host, prepared the meat to their satisfaction and served it with his fried sweet potatoes. They slept in one room on the second floor in rough wooden bunks draped with mosquito netting. Night creatures nesting in coffee bushes below kept them awake with exotic noises. In the barnyard below, pigs squealed and dogs barked. It seemed they had barely gotten to sleep when the crowing of a rooster announced the start of a new day.

They returned to Subic in time to experience a typhoon, which lashed the island of Luzon. Roads were flooded and Olongapo was under water. Children swam and splashed in the muddy waters and fishermen paddled their outrigger bancas through the streets.

Pomeroy-Bechtol Construction Company completed the first set of permanent quarters on the hilltop of East Kalayaan Heights. It was given the mundane name of Replacement Housing, and Joseph was assigned a unit in a two-story duplex. The buildings were constructed of precast concrete slabs joined together with mortar. The seams were not tightly mortared, and water leaked through. One morning after a rainy night, they awoke to find two inches of water on the floor. The contractor remedied the problem by drilling holes in the sides of the walls to drain the water.

About that time, SJP-80 pulled up stakes and left, under circumstances as inexplicable as had been their tenure on the base. Their cushy family quarters on West Kalayaan were promptly taken over by the navy, and Joseph's family moved for the fourth time to a comfortable two-story duplex. Adjoined to the dining room was a screened lanai, which would have been called a family room in the States. They were by far the finest accommodations Joseph and Cara enjoyed at Subic Bay. Joseph's fellow marine officers moved in quarters down the street, which facilitated after-hours socializing. Annie learned to swim in the pool two blocks away.

On Cubi Point, across the bay from the main base, the Seabees were putting the finishing touches on the naval air station, Farther south near the head of Bataan Peninsula, an ammunition magazine at Camayan Point, capable of storing nuclear weapons, was completed. With the increased need for security, the platoon-size marine guard unit at Cubi was increased to a company, and Joseph was assigned as company commander. His company of 200 men moved into a new concrete barracks building.

The navy was concerned about the reported presence of Hukbalahal guerillas. The HUKs were guerilla allies during the Japanese occupation but had fallen out of grace with the U.S. and Philippine governments when their ideology took a leftist lean. The HUKs presented fewer problems for Joseph's marines than did Filipino timber thieves illegally harvesting hardwood trees on the naval reservation.

Late one night, Joseph headed his jeep for an isolated guard post on Camayan Point to check on the lone sentry on duty. A shower had just drenched the jungle and the dripping foliage glistened in the headlights of the jeep. Rounding a curve on the Seabee-built coral road he suddenly hit the brake. Another object was glistening in the lights, a huge python slowly making its way across the road. The road was at least twenty feet wide, and the snake's head disappeared over the embankment before the tail had worked its way out of the jungle to the road. Joseph waited all of five minutes for the reptile to cross, probably on its way to make a meal of some unfortunate sleeping monkey.

On another occasion, Joseph arrived at an isolated guard post surrounded by coconut trees. A frustrated sentry was standing in a clearing littered with green coconuts and rocks. He had just been pelted by a screaming pack of monkeys in the trees.

"I didn't start it, they did," he lied. "Can I shoot the damn things, Captain?"

"No, I have a better idea," Joseph replied as he moved to the radio in his pickup truck.

He contacted the guard guardhouse and instructed the sergeant of the guard to bring out a riot shotgun and several rounds. When the sergeant arrived with the weapon, Joseph had him fire three shots in the air. Meanwhile, the monkeys had received reinforcements, and the treetops were teeming with screeching shifty-eyed simians. At the first shot, they leaped straight up from their perches and went flying through the jungle canopy, screaming like Tasmanian devils.

"Cease firing, they won't be back," he said to the sergeant. "And don't throw any more rocks at them," he admonished the sentry.

In the 1950s, American society was experiencing the beginnings of juvenile delinquency. Elvis Presley's rock-and-roll style of music was captivating the youth culture while a cadre of so-called "beat generation" writers was popularizing an existential way of life.

Young people began questioning traditional authorities and showing signs of rebellion. The corps was feeling the movement and Joseph could sense it in his men. Young marines who had not been through the crucibles of World War II and Korea were less dedicated and harder to handle. Discipline became more difficult to maintain. Senior NCOs complained that the Marine Corps was "going to hell in a hand basket." "Accidental" discharges of weapons by sentries were more frequent despite the increased emphasis on firearm safety and training. Drag-racing "cowboys" regularly tore up new pickup trucks used by roving security patrols.

One tragic incident had a sobering effect on the guard company. A sentry going off duty after a four-hour stint shot his relief. Details were sketchy, but apparently he was clowning around with his quick draw and accidentally chambered a round in his .45, pointed the gun at Private First Class Benjamin Bolt of Seattle, Washington, and shot Bolt squarely in the forehead. The pistol apparently had been pointed at an upward angle, and the bullet followed the inside of Bolt's skull and lodged at the base of his head. Miraculously he lived. Joseph headed for the base hospital and arrived as medics were taking Bolt into surgery. A Filipino neurosurgeon from Manila was flown in to perform the operation. A metal plate was inserted inside the man's skull, and it appeared he would recover.

But it was not to be. Word came back from the States after he was evacuated that he had died. Bolt was a clean-cut young man, always neat in appearance and quiet in demeanor. The perpetrator, whose name is best forgotten, was quite the opposite of Bolt in all respects. He gave the usual lame excuse that he didn't know the weapon was loaded. He showed no remorse and even adopted a cocky attitude. When Joseph got word through the gunnery sergeant that Bolt's friends were talking of avenging the shooting, he had him transferred out for his own safety. At that time, it was assumed that Bolt would survive.

Another member of the guard company was rumored to have brought back cocaine from his R&R leave in Hong Kong. Joseph reported the incident to the naval intelligence agency at Subic.

"Give him another leave to Hong Kong, and we'll check him when he returns," the agent, a civilian, advised.

Leaves to Hong Kong were scarce, but slots became available when eligible men not interested in going could trade their places.

When word went out that there was a vacant slot, the suspect bit and applied for a leave.

His request was granted, and when he debarked from the returning plane, the agent searched his bag and found several packets of cocaine. He pleaded innocent on grounds that he had been set up and that someone else had planted the drug in his bag. His general court martial board didn't buy the story, and he was dishonorably discharged.

The formal commissioning of the Cubi Point air station in July 1956 was a major event for Subic Bay. Ranking U.S. Naval commanders, including Admiral A. W. Radford, chairman of the Joint Chiefs of Staff, along with high ranking military and civilian defense officials of the Philippines, were invited. Among them was Philippines President Raymon Magsaysay.

Joseph was in charge of the honor guard to render military honors for the visiting dignitaries. Forming the honors platoon, he selected his best men and NCOs and rehearsed the ceremony until it was perfected. They turned out to await the arrival of the dignitaries, looking sharp in crisp khakis with white covers on their visor hats, white gloves, and white belts. The routine called for the guard to form on the tarmac near the arriving planes. As each official deplaned, he was greeted by Admiral Donaho and escorted to a position directly in front of the guard. A navy band played ruffles and flourishes for the flag officers and the Philippine national anthem for Filipino officials.

Joseph would draw his sword, lower it to the carry position, face about, command PRESENT ARMS, do another about face, and execute the sword salute. He would again face about, command ORDER ARMS, face about to the visiting official, and lead him past the three ranks of the honor guard for the ceremonial inspection.

Six times that day the ceremony was executed, each in a flawless manner, despite the heat reflecting from the tarmac that raised the temperature beyond one hundred degrees. President Magsaysay, wearing a double-breasted white jacket and dark trousers debarked from his presidential plane. He approached as Joseph flashed his sword in a salute, placed his hand on Joseph's shoulder, and with a nod of his head, said thank you.

Observing the ceremonies in the background was a large audience of military personnel, wives, families and Filipinos. Joseph had never felt so proud of his marines or of being one.

Tragically, the charismatic Magsaysay died in a plane crash on Cebu seven months later, plunging the country in mourning and creating anxiety among U.S. military leaders, who feared turmoil in the succession process given the unstable political climate of the Philippines. Magsaysay had been a staunch ally of U.S. military policies in the Philippines, but rumblings had already begun among dissident Philippine politicians wanting to abort the treaties of 1945 that had guaranteed U.S. military bases in the islands for ninety-nine years.

The fears were groundless. Vice-president Carlos Garcia moved into Malacanang Palace without any turmoil.

A major cold-war flash point in the Far East was the disputed islands of Quemoy and Matsu in the strait of Formosa held by the Chinese Nationalists. Red China had shelled the islands, but the Nationalists held on, bolstered by the Eisenhower administration's veiled threat of using nuclear weapons to prevent the islands from being taken by the Communists. Thereafter, any Chinese movement among the islands of the South China Sea was met with extreme apprehension by the U.S. military. One day, naval intelligence reported Chinese activity on an atoll midway between the Philippines and the mainland. The news set in motion a crisis at Subic Bay. Joseph was ordered to prepare a rifle company for an assault on the island. Meetings with naval intelligence agents provided meager information about the target, not even a map. One feature that stood out was the estimated size of the atoll; it was barely 500 yards wide and not much longer. The navy promised supporting fires from destroyers, but it appeared the only ground support weapon capable of firing on such a truncated target was the 60-millimeter mortar. A heavier caliber weapon would fire across the island into the sea on the opposite side.

The Subic Marines had the mortars but no ammunition. Joseph, with the support of Colonel Williams and Major Lee Bennett, the executive officer, insisted on the mortars, so the navy flew in a load of shells from Okinawa. It wasn't the job of the marines to second-guess the navy brass, but Joseph wondered aloud why a combat-ready unit from Okinawa wasn't used for the mission. Joseph shared the feeling among his fellow officers that the whole thing was either overblown or an outright hoax. Still, no report of aggression could be dismissed where the Chinese were involved.

With the arrival of the mortar shells, equipping the assault unit was completed. Joseph took his troops to Mount Redondo across the bay for a living firing exercise. A navy carrier arrived and docked. In the midst of preparations, a meeting was called aboard the carrier.

The navy commander, giving a briefing, read a radio dispatch sent from a U.S. destroyer that had cruised around the island. The ship reported that the only activity observed was a fleet of Chinese junks carrying off guano from the island.

Major Bennett raised his hand.

"What's guano, sir?" he asked.

"Bird shit, Major," the commander replied curtly.

It was an apt description of the whole quixotic episode that had been triggered by the report of a hysterical Vietnamese corvette captain. With a sigh of relief, Joseph passed the word to his would-be warriors who, following the expression in the Corps, "took off their packs."

To relieve the tension of the previous week, Joseph, Cara, Annie, and Nina, loaded their suitcases in the DeSoto and took off for a weekend in Manila. Joseph was given use of the admiral's guest cottage in the U.S. Embassy compound. Civilian accommodations in the city were nearly nonexistent and extremely expensive. The Manila Hotel, then, as today, was the showplace of the devastated city with room rates starting at fifty dollars, a fortune at that time.

The embassy grounds were on the waterfront, and offshore lay the rusted hulks of U.S. and Japanese ships which were being cut apart and salvaged. For ample reasons, the Filipinos still hated the Japanese, a circumstance that lent more irony to the fact that, lacking the know-how, the Filipino government had to hire a Japanese salvage company to remove the ships.

Manila was the third most devastated city of World War II, and, in 1956, still resembled itself eleven years earlier when it was wrested from General Yamashita's army in brutal house-to-house fighting that left some 100,000 civilians dead.

Occasionally the navy took families on sight-seeing trips to Corregidor fifty miles down the Bataan coast. The day-long trip was made aboard an old gunboat converted into a passenger ship. Little had changed on the battered island fortress since it had been recaptured from the Japanese in 1945. They debarked on the shell-torn dock where in 1942 General MacArthur had boarded a PT boat for his historic flight to Mindanao and thence to Australia. The skeletal remains of the prewar Army barracks stood like a ghostly tombstone overlooking the desolation of "the rock." The giant coastal guns and mortars stood rusting in their casemates.

Leaving Annie under the care of Nina and the watchful eye of a neighboring marine family, Joseph and Cara boarded a navy transport for a week's visit in Hong Kong. Children were not allowed to go. For the two-day cruise, wives were quartered in a separate compartment from their spouses and got a taste of troop life, sleeping on tiered canvas bunks. Making shore in Kowloon, couples headed for modern hotels. The U.S. dollar was worth five Hong Kong dollars, bringing the priciest hotels and restaurants within the budget of the Americans. After months of subsisting on commissary food at Subic Bay, the international cuisines of Hong Kong were a gastronomic adventure. They enjoyed one festive seven-course dinner aboard a floating restaurant in Aberdeen, reached in a sampan propelled by a young woman swinging a long pole paddle back and forth. The boat also served as home to the woman, her husband, and a small child.

One of Joseph's collateral duties at Subic was as exchange officer, in charge of the marine PX. The major supplier of Chinese merchandise in Hong Kong was T.Y. Lee and Company. Mr. Lee and jeweler Valley Kwok knew in advance of Joseph's visit. They took Joseph and Cara to dinners and on sightseeing trips. A German-made van with chauffeur was parked near the hotel, at the service of Joseph and Cara. On one shopping venture, they were driven to a clothier whose warehouse was stocked with bolts of the finest British woolens. As Joseph and Cara made their selections, a tailor whipped out his tape measure. The next day their made-to-order clothes were delivered to the hotel in cardboard suitcases.

At Mr. Kwok's jewelry store, Cara had a wedding band crafted of Burmese rubies and diamonds, along with a string of plump pearls. The standing joke at Subic was that wives returning from Hong Kong debarked from the ship wearing homemade cotton dresses adorned with strings of the finest pearls.

Next they went to a furniture factory on the outskirts of Kowloon. It was a long, ramshackle, unpainted wooden building surrounded by a high barbwire fence. Hanging from the ceiling and stacked high on all sides were bundles of black-stained furniture sections all elaborately carved and inlaid with mother-of-pearl. The customer made a choice, and the sections were slapped together with glue. The system made for quick and efficient assembly. Imagine the expression on the face of the Chinese artisan when Cara produced her own design for a chow table and matching end tables to be made from natural golden teakwood, with no carving or inlay.

He shook his head and jabbered excitedly in Chinese at Mr. Lee who had taken them. Joseph interpreted his gesticulation to indicate "no can do." Cara maintained a disappointed but uncompromising attitude. Still, the furniture maker had to respect Lee's explanation that these were not ordinary tourists but esteemed purchasers for a Marine Corps PX whose business was valued. As Captain Davis often mimicked the Chinese way of lavishing favors on valued customers, it was custom, system, business. Waving his arms in protest, the cabinet maker explained that he would be hard pressed to find enough kiln-dried natural teak for the order, primarily a twenty-four-by-fifty-four inch plank for the chow table. Joseph watched from a distance as he went from stack to stack of weathered lumber in the cluttered yard.

When he returned, Joseph read his expression as "can do." However, his acquiescence came with a warning that the order might not be finished by sailing time, three days hence. They departed with the cabinet maker staring at Cara's designs and shaking his head. They were also risking the possibility that the completed product would not be as Cara envisioned or that the furniture would be made of green wood that would split and crack before it got to the States.

Their ship was anchored in the stream that separated Hong Kong, an island, from Kowloon, and tons of merchandise purchased by the visitors were being manhandled by longshoremen into lighters and ferried out to the ship. On the day of departure, Joseph and Cara arrived at the dock in time to see a large crate with their name stenciled on the sides lowered into a boat. They breathed easier.

Mr. Lee took them on a sightseeing trip in the countryside, all the way to the frontier of Red China. They passed rustic fishing villages, where junks squatted on mud flats waiting for the next rising tide. In verdant farm lands, women goaded pigs and flocks of ducks across the roads. It rained on and off all day, and they took lunch under an umbrella on the patio of a Buddhist temple. It was a far more pleasant China than the one Joseph had experienced at Tientsin.

No visit to Hong Kong was complete without seeing the Tiger Balm Gardens, a garish attraction of Chinese pagodas with tile roofs of glistening blue ceramic, concrete dragons, artificial caves, and ponds of golden carp. The Disneylike theme park on a barren hillside portrayed in tableaus the layers of hell depicted in Chinese mythology. The garden was created by the maker of the renowned Asian medicinal salve of camphor and menthol reputed to cure all ailments.

At the entrance, they were ushered by Mr. Lee into a house whose every furnishing was decorated with pure jade. Never had they seen jade in such opulence. The walls were inlaid with the stuff. A two-foot artificial tree with leaves of jade stood in the center of one room on a table inlaid with jade. Giant urns of pure jade stood in corners. Items of all descriptions carved of jade adorned the walls. Every object in the house contained jade.

On the way home, their ship skirted the fringe of a typhoon, but the passengers were either too seasick or attempting to sleep off the rigors of their Hong Kong vacation to be concerned.

Back in Subic, their custom-made furniture was delivered to their quarters. Joseph and Cara held their breaths as they carefully pried upon the crates. It was like unwrapping a Christmas present. The last protective cushions of burlap came off, revealing three perfectly matched pieces of honey-colored furniture glazed with lacquer over beautifully grained surfaces that reflected like a mirror. In the weeks afterward, they kept a watchful eye on the furniture for any signs of cracking. It never happened. Cara felt so confident that she ordered a lamp table of the same design.

After twenty-eight months in the Philippines, Joseph got new orders. This time there was no friend in Washington to help him avoid Camp Lejeune, North Carolina, his next destination.

There followed a series of *despedidas*, farewell parties, which combined food, drink, and emotional camaraderie. The depths of friendships were realized. On the day of departure, Nina followed them to their cabin on the U.S.S. *Sultan*, weeping as she hugged her adopted family good-bye.

How many families had she lost in her years of service in military households? Too many, she would say. She wanted to follow them. Couldn't the captain arrange it so she could go to the States with them? Nina had indeed become a loving part of the family—faithful, reliable, and trustworthy. They would never forget her.

Joseph was going to miss the "poochies" (poached eggs) she cooked for breakfast, the ambrosial native custard she made with the jellied meat of unripened coconuts—*macapuna* she called it—and, of course, her meat loaf. Nina also made supurb *lumpia*, an hors d'oeuvre of finely-diced shrimp, pork, vegetables, and carabao cheese wrapped in rice paper and deep fried. Whole platters of lumpia representing hours of Nina's preparation would be devoured within minutes at Joseph's and Cara's cocktail parties.

They had been warmly received on two visits to her family home in the village of San Marcellino, on the coast north of Subic. It made Nina proud and happy to show off her American family. Her real family were gentle and friendly Filipino folk, who honored them with native dinners of pork and chicken.

Seventeen
Camp Lejeune: Farewell to the Corps—1959–1960

The *Sultan* slowly pulled away from the dock and the knots of friends sadly waving farewells. After a couple of days, it put in at Guam to take on more passengers. The ship would remain in port for some twelve hours, allowing passengers to debark for sight-seeing. Joseph spotted a marine lieutenant on the dock who was stationed on the island.

"I landed here in 1944 with the Third Division, and I would like to show my wife and daughter the battlefields," he said. "Is there any chance of getting transportation?"

"It's parked right over there, Captain," the lieutenant replied, pointing to a jeep at the foot of the dock. "Just get it back to me in some piece."

It was the standard courtesy of marines looking after marines—*semper fidelis*. With Annie in the backseat and Cara up front, Joseph headed the jeep along the coastal road from Apra Harbor to the old beachhead between Asan and Adelup Points. He showed them where his battery had come ashore amid mortar fire and pointed out Chonita Cliff just ahead where the Third Regiment had suffered so many casualties. There being no road to the hilltop where he had directed artillery fire in support of the 21st Marines, Joseph headed the jeep across the island to picturesque Talafofo Bay, where a small whitewashed chapel stood beneath the coconut palms. It had been spared from gunfire during the recapture of the island. Joseph turned off the coast road and followed a rough, rock-strewn trail. It ended on a hilltop overlooking the ocean at an ancient stone monument commemorating Magellan's brief stop on his way to circumnavigate the earth in the 15th century.

"I'm much obliged to you, Lieutenant," Joseph told his benefactor. "This has been a special day for me and my family."

"My pleasure, Captain," the lieutenant replied.

After crossing the Pacific, the eighth time for Joseph, the *Sultan* put in at Port Hueneme in Southern California to offload a returning battalion of Navy Seabees. Then they steamed northward for San Francisco, riding the coastal ground swells famous for causing seasickness.

When Joseph had returned from Korea aboard the *Meigs* in 1953, an army band on the Fort Mason dock played martial tunes, and entertaining celebrities sang patriotic songs. This time there were only friends, but their enthusiastic welcomes made up for their smaller numbers. They stayed with Ray and Arlene Steffins, she being a longtime chum of Cara's. Ray drove Joseph to the DeSoto dealership in Palo Alto, where he picked up a new car previously ordered from the Philippines. Then they set out for a cross-country trip to North Carolina via Louisiana and Florida in their new crème and maroon sedan that had the longest tail fins of any car on the road.

In a celebratory mood free of worries, with the car radio pouring out the sing-along tunes of Pat Boone, Patti Page, Perry Como, and Elvis Presley they headed eastward. A continent of happy trails awaited Cara. Their festive mood no doubt would have been dampened had they known that their DeSoto was already a dinosaur. There would be no more DeSotos manufactured from that year.

They went through Sacramento, past the historic California gold rush country and into the Sierras. They crossed the Nevada desert to Las Vegas and on to the Grand Canyon, anxious to show Annie nature's most awesome creation. They crossed the Rockies and made for the Carlsbad Caverns in New Mexico, where they watched clouds of bats swarming out at nightfall.

In Lake Tarsa, they were reacquainted with Clarissa's Cajun cooking and Ornas's barbeques. His bar and drive-through package store was thriving. Mae, Joseph's sister, and her husband Maurice had opened a grocery store and were prospering.

Annie was now old enough to show some interest in seeing where her father had grown up. Joseph took them to the old Pomeroy place, where his father had struggled bringing in rice crops during seasons of drought and intrusions of salt water from the nearby lake used for irrigation. The house was gone, as was the barn where young Joseph kept a pigeon loft.

Joseph was reminded of his dog Bobby. It was a mixed bulldog who shared his instincts between herding cattle, where he bloodied the noses of uncooperative animals by hanging on with his teeth until they went his way, and of being a lovable pet for the children.

Joseph had never forgotten that hot summer day when, as a five-year-old, he was on the back porch of the farm house playing with his father's wooden decoy ducks. He was suddenly frightened by the shouting of his mother who had him by the shirt collar dragging him through the screen door into the kitchen. A strange black dog, panting, and with froth coming from his mouth was trotting at a fast pace toward the house.

In a flash, Bobby tore out from beneath the wagon parked in the yard, where he had found shade, and attacked the stranger. The two went round and round in a cloud of dust snarling in a vicious dog fight until the intruder finally turned tail and headed back to the road.

Ornas and Uncle Felix, who had been working on a tractor in the barn, heard the commotion and came running as the fight broke up. News had spread of a rabid dog on the loose in the countryside. He belonged to Owens, a black sharecropper who lived in bottom land near the irrigation canal.

"Bobby's been bitten," Ornas said. "We'll have to kill him," he added sadly.

Sensing his brother's remorse, Felix went into the house, returned with the shotgun and prepared to do the deed. Poor Bobby, his duty heroically done, was back under the wagon licking his wounds.

He stared curiously at the gun barrel aimed point blank at him. Joseph watched in horror as the full load of birdshot tore into the dog's head, killing him instantly.

"It had to be done," his father said, 'Or else he would have been a mad dog, too. He gave his life for us."

At the end of the road from Pomeroy was another old family homestead on what was called Goose Island. It wasn't really an island but rather the last vestige of solid ground on the fringe of the great Louisiana salt marsh that constitutes the southern part of the state.

It was at the terminus of the great Mississippi Valley flyway for migratory water fowl and got its name from the teeming number of Canada geese that wintered there. On cold mornings, Ornas would take his shotgun off the rack, creep silently to the marsh nearby, and return within the hour with a pair of mallards for dinner.

Their nearest neighbor was the Blanchard family. Aunt Amelia was Ornas's oldest sister. Louis, her husband, was given to occasional drinking binges, on one of which he rode his horse through the open door into the house. The open door was also an invitation for the goats to enter and raid the family's rice supply stored in an open twenty-gallon crock in one corner of the front room. Louis eventually gave up farming and moved his family to Biloxi, Mississippi, for jobs in shrimp and oyster canneries.

Mae attended a one-room country school three miles off, walking all the way with the Blanchard children along a muddy road and frequently fleeing from wild cows.

Near Goose Island, the arable land yielded to the vast salt marsh, a treeless wetland of tall reeds, palmetto scrub, cane brakes, pickerel weed, and lotus ponds. It was crawling with alligators and the habitat for a variety of fur-bearing animals.

Near the gulf coast in Cameron Parish was Grand Chenier, an isolated community of fishermen, trappers, and ranchers clinging to a narrow elongated shelf of ancient dunes and shell mounds that stretched east and west for several miles. Weather-beaten clapboard houses hugged the precious high ground on isolated hummocks among stands of gnarled oaks. Herds of scrawny, longhorn cattle roamed the muck lands and palmetto scrub, surviving parasites and hordes of mosquitoes.

It was here that one of the fiercest hurricanes in history made landfall on June 27, 1957. With winds of one hundred miles an hour and twenty-foot waves, its twelve-foot storm surge engulfed everything for miles inland killing 526 people. Joseph and Cara had read news reports of Hurricane Audrey while aboard the *Sultan* and arrived in Lake Tarsa barely three weeks after the disaster. The ravaged area to the south was still staggering from the tragedy. Among the victims were names that Joseph had known. Horror stories abounded, including that of a woman and her baby rescued on a floating mattress crawling with moccasins and water snakes. All along the causeway road to Grand Chenier, as far as the eye could see, the marsh was littered with white kitchen appliances—stoves, refrigerators, freezers, and washing machines—borne by the storm surge and deposited miles inland.

Continuing to Florida, Joseph followed the coast route past Pensacola. The Emerald Coast was pristine with sand the whiteness of sugar, blue-green water, and stands of sea oats on the dunes that bent with the gentle gulf breezes. Motels were scarce, and no one would have imagined that in a few years high-rise resort hotels would sprout shoulder-to-shoulder along the beaches, blotting the ocean view from the highway. Although long favored for summer vacations by natives of the Panhandle and Alabama, the strip along the highway had not yet succumbed to the trashy, carnival trappings that would make it known as the "Redneck Riviera."

With a few exceptions, Florida's highways in the fifties were two-lane roads. President Dwight Eisenhower's plan to span the continent with a network of multilane interstate highways had only been approved by Congress in 1956. One could drive through rural Florida for miles with a better chance of encountering unfenced livestock on the road than of meeting another car. Accidents were frequent, particularly with out-of-state visitors not familiar with the loose sand on the road shoulders. A car veering off the pavement at high speed invariably met with tragic results.

Florida was still in an age of innocence, so to speak. Highways in the central peninsula were hemmed in on both sides by groves of citrus trees fragrant with blossoms in the spring. Daytona Beach was a popular destination where people came to drive their cars on the sand.

Tourist attractions were unsophisticated: Silver Springs in Ocala, where schools of fish were viewed through glass-bottomed boats and showman Ross Allen drew milk from the fangs of rattlesnakes. There were the Parrot Gardens in St. Petersburg and Miami. Bok Tower and its carillon in Lake Wales, and Cypress Gardens in Winter Haven where comely maidens promenaded in colorful antebellum hoop skirts. Marineland in St. Augustine was the first of many tourist aquariums that would be copycatted across the country. Miami's art deco look was yielding to neon and high rise. Roadside restaurants hung out signs advertising all-you-can-eat Florida lobster tails for four dollars. Restaurant menus in Key West featured green sea turtle steaks and soup.

Of historical interest were the ornate hotels built by early railroad tycoons Henry Flagler and Henry Plant in St. Augustine, Tampa, and Palm Beach to serve the rich and famous of the Gilded Age.

Cara's mother Millie was now widowed and living in Orlando. From San Francisco, she had returned to her native roots. She was born in Miami, where her father had homesteaded along the banks of the Miami River on land that became the heart of the city. Julia Tuttle had not yet enticed Henry Flagler to extend his railroad south to Miami. The only available transportation to cities and towns north along the coast was by sail or steamer, unless you were the barefoot mailman who raced along the beaches keeping his appointed rounds.

Millie's photo album was a treasure of Miami history. She had attended school with Helen Merrick, whose brother George would go on to develop Coral Gables, and the Burdine boys whose father had founded the city's first department store. At sixteen, Millie worked as a cashier in the store. From her station in a wire cage on the mezzanine, she was on the receiving end of the little baskets carrying cash and sales slips that flitted about the store on wire pulleys. Millie would deposit the money in a cash register and return the change in the basket to the sales person on the floor.

She went on to marry a young engineer. Cara's father was employed by the Corps of Engineers dredging canals to drain the Everglades. Upon his death, years later in San Francisco, Millie moved to Orlando and lived on the income from two rental duplexes she bought.

After a brief remarriage to a Michigan businessman, she was again widowed. She had always yearned for a place of her own, and when she returned to Florida, it was to build a house on Lake Whipporwill, among the orange groves away from the hubbub. An indomitable soul, she did all the lifting on her plot, gracefully landscaping her yard and tending to her small citrus orchard. She lived contentedly until cancer claimed her at age eighty-two. She had sold her property before her death, and several years later, Joseph and Cara visited the place.

They were not prepared for what they found. The yard was overgrown with weeds and the azalea bushes were dying from neglect. Rusting parts of old machinery were strewn about. Underbrush obscured the little dock on the lake that Millie's son Bart had built for her. Vines and cobwebs encased the house. It was a heartrending scene.

A large German shepherd poked his head through the door, followed by a woman holding his leash. Joseph identified himself and told her the purpose of their visit. They chatted briefly with her. A fairly attractive woman nearing middle age, she had been recently widowed when her aviator husband died in a plane crash. The rural area around the lake, once a safe and peaceful haven, was now unsafe from the criminal elements that roamed and preyed on the unending supply of victims from Disney World and the many other tourist attractions that the Orlando countryside had succumbed to. It seemed no place in Florida was safe to live in.

* * *

Reporting to Camp Lejeune, Joseph was pleasantly surprised. His lasting image of the place had been the flimsy little green plywood huts in the virgin pine forest where the Third Division had formed and trained in 1942. Now, the entrance into the base was a handsome four-lane road carved through the virgin pines and neatly landscaped with azaleas, camellias, and evergreens. Colonial style, three-story brick buildings, offices, and troop quarters rose everywhere like a college campus. In the shuffling of combat units following Word War II, the 2nd Marine Division, which was formed in San Diego, was now based at Lejeune. The 1st Division, originally from the East Coast was at Camp Pendleton.

Joseph deposited Cara and Annie in the officers' guest house and reported in to the 10th Marines. He liked his new C.O. from the start. Colonel Bert Davis was also a native of Louisiana. An affable, laid-back career officer, he spoke of his passions for hunting and fishing and following the fortunes of the LSU Tigers. He assigned Joseph as C.O. of H Battery; 105s again.

As usual, there was a waiting list for family quarters on the base, so they went house-hunting. They were fortunate to find a little two-bedroom bungalow on Banks Street in the town of Jacksonville. Their furniture and household belongings had already been transported across country and was in storage on the base. They settled in with a minimum of difficulties. A neighborhood school was within walking distance. Cara took on a part-time job as a substitute teacher. Annie enrolled in the fourth grade. Joseph made the daily four-mile commute to his new outfit, which was spending a lot of time on maneuvers in the wilds of the 110,000-acre military reservation.

Annie got her long-awaited puppy. "Nipper" was a black and tan female of coon hound parentage. By now they had moved into quarters on the base, a neat Cape Cod frame house on the river. Their next-door neighbor, a warrant officer, who was a tournament skeet shooter and avid hunter, was admiring the half-grown dog.

"I'll bet she'll make a fine hunting dog," he said to Joseph. "I'd like to take her squirrel hunting tomorrow."

Joseph and Cara discussed it with Annie, and it was agreed that Nipper would benefit from the experience.

The following afternoon, the warrant officer and his young son loaded their station wagon and off they went with Nipper in the back. It was nearing darkness, and they had not returned. Joseph and Cara became concerned. Finally, as Cara was putting supper on the table, the station wagon pulled in next door and Nipper came bounding up the back steps to the screen door.

"You must have shot a lot of squirrels, as late as you are," Joseph said to the warrant officer.

"We didn't hunt one lick," the disgusted warrant said. "Spent the whole time rounding up your dog."

For some unknown reason, Nipper feared guns. At the sight of the shotguns being unsheathed from their carrying cases, she had bolted into the woods. The huntsmen dared not return without Annie's pet and had searched far and wide before finding her as darkness was enveloping the forest.

The division's field exercises evolved into a monotonous repetition of confronting an imaginary Red force that threatened the supply of oil in the Middle East. In 1958, the war games took on real meaning when the division sent a brigade force into Lebanon to protect U.S. interests against anti-American factions threatening to topple the pro-American government. By this time, Joseph had become the logistics officer for his battalion and was left behind with the rear echelon when it boarded transports for the Mediterranean at Morehead City.

Joseph's orders were to remain on call to bring the rest of the supplies and gear when the battalion set up camp in Lebanon. Day by day, Joseph waited for the call, which never came. It was nerve-wracking. He badly wanted to go over. After a month, the bulk of the brigade returned, leaving a reinforced infantry battalion floating on troopships in what was to become the trademark "Med cruises" of the Marine Corps.

Earlier that year, the division was ordered to send a rescue force for Vice-President Richard Nixon and Mrs. Nixon who had been stoned in Caracas by communist-instigated mobs while on a goodwill tour of South America.

A crack infantry unit of the division was hastily airlifted from the Cherry Point Marine Air Station. It arrived at the staging area in Puerto Rico ahead of an army ranger unit, but without their ammunition, which, in their haste, had been left behind on the tarmac at Cherry Point. With interservice rivalry at an all-time high in Washington, the marines were ridiculed at great length. It didn't matter that Nixon escaped Caracas safely without the intervention of U.S. troops. The Army played it up as proof that it was more reliable during emergencies.

The humiliation reverberated up and down the chain of command in the 2nd Division. Readiness became the mantra. Some commanding officers even had their men sleeping in combat uniforms with their packs alongside in their bunks. There were even a few who openly yearned for war, to accelerate their promotions. In five years, their prayers would be answered in Vietnam.

Slowly, Joseph's outlook on his military career became blurred. For the first time, he was unhappy. Toughness had never bothered him, but ridiculous orders did. Furthermore, he was a mustang, an officer promoted from the enlisted ranks, and held a temporary commission whereas the majority of the corps' commissioned officers came from college ROTC programs, officer candidate classes or the Naval Academy. Lacking a college degree not only handicapped his promotion to major, but made it a virtual barrier. Announcements of forthcoming promotion lists from Washington were invariably prefaced with notations that temporary officers would not be considered.

Joseph felt that he had proven, on the battlefield and in every peacetime assignment, that he could discharge his duties and measure up to the responsibilities of command as well or better than the majority of his peers having college degrees and permanent commissions. It irked him, and slowly frustration gnawed away at his attitude.

One day, he faced the truth. He had had enough, was fed up. Retirement beckoned. But what would he do in the civilian world without a college education? He would get one. He was barely forty. The words of the counselor in San Francisco after the war that is test scores weren't good enough for college still rankled him. He was consumed by the urge for knowledge, and the counselor's words became a challenge. If he had to spend all his waking hours studying, then he would do so.

Joseph had already begun work on a degree. Two nights a week he took off-campus courses from East Carolina College in Greenville and completed eight hours of English.

With Cara's encouragement, he made the decision. He would retire after twenty-two years at half-pay and enter college with the aid of the GI Bill. Cara was prepared to return to full-time teaching while he matriculated. The problem was what field of study would he undertake? He enjoyed writing and the words of his high school English teacher at Lake Tarsa still lingered.

"You really should go to the university and study journalism," Marie Gross had said to him.

He was further encouraged by his East Carolina professor in English composition, who read one of his essays before the class of some sixty students. Joseph had become inspired while writing a fictitious piece entitled "Airport."

Self-consciously, he squirmed in his desk. As the professor read, the others turned their eyes about the room searching for the author, who remained anonymous. When finished, the professor praised the essay, calling it imaginative and entertaining, and identified Joseph as the writer. The class of mostly officers, NCOs, and wives, applauded, and Joseph blushed with embarrassment.

When another teacher offered bonus grade points for any student memorizing the first twenty lines of *The Canterbury Tales*, Joseph did so and nervously recited Geoffrey Chaucer's ancient English tongue-twisting verse.

Most military retirees returning to college took courses in business administration then went into insurance or real estate.

"Why journalism?" Joseph was asked time and again when discussing his plans with friends. Secretly, he savored the idea of doing something exciting. The thought of selling insurance or real estate or crunching numbers as an accountant had no appeal. Making money was not as important as doing something he would enjoy. Entering the field of journalism, known for paying low salaries, having to compete with young, energetic reporters would give Joseph all the challenges he needed.

He had always figured he would retire in California, the fastest growing state with unlimited opportunities. But Cara yearned to be near her mother, still living in Florida. It wasn't a hard decision to make. Millie had formed her own opinion of Florida, then a medium-sized southern state better known for its boom and bust days of the past.

"Florida is different," Millie had said. "There's not much in the way of jobs here. You have to have a racket."

"A racket? Like what?" Joseph asked.

"Well, like renting out beach chairs or fishing tackle," Millie responded.

It was Millie's apt description of a service economy. But no one would then predict the enormous demand, not just for beach chairs and fishing tackle but for retirement homes, shopping malls, golf resorts, and tourists attractions that were to bring the ultimate growth boom.

Joseph checked out the brochures of Florida colleges and universities. The University of Florida in Gainesville offered a degree program in journalism as did the University of Miami. Florida State in Tallahassee had a program in communications that didn't appear to have what Joseph had in mind. He submitted his letter of retirement to Headquarters Marine Corps and took a week's leave of absence. Leaving Annie with a family of friends at Lejeune, Joseph and Cara set out for Florida. Gainesville was the first stop.

Joseph parked the DeSoto on 13th Street in front of Tigert Hall, the administration building. He conferred with the registrar, a friendly fellow who suggested he go to the journalism school and talk with the director. The School of Journalism and Communications, as then known, was housed inside the stands of the football stadium.

The vacant space had recently been converted into modern classrooms and laboratories. Primarily, it was air-conditioned, a comfort most of the older classroom buildings on the campus lacked.

The office secretary led him into an empty classroom to meet the director. A heavy-set, round-faced man in shirt sleeves with wavy blondish-red hair was moving typewriters about. Joseph noticed that his right arm was withered from the elbow down.

"Rae Weimer," he said with a toothy grin, extending his left hand. "What can we do for you?"

Apparently he had mistaken Joseph to be a sales representative or visiting fireman, but didn't bat an eyelash when Joseph told him he wanted to attend journalism school.

"We'd be happy to have you," he said after Joseph had told him he was in the process of retiring from the Marine Corps. "Come back when you're ready. We'll hold a place for you."

Joseph and Cara toured the campus and then headed for a look at the city. Driving aimlessly westward in the suburbs, they went by a couple of new subdivisions, taking no particular notice of the aging gray Cadillac parked car on the narrow roadside. But as they continued driving slowly past the developments, the Cadilac followed them at a distance. When they pulled over to look at a new house, the Cadillac followed suit. A man of about Joseph's age with blond features walked up and introduced himself.

"Howdy, folks," he said cordially. "I'm Clark Butler. Can I show you around?"

Butler was the developer of three new subdivisions in an area bounded by the Millhopper Road and Southwest 16th Avenue. He showed them several houses in various stages of completion and offered to take them to lunch. The Gainesville Golf and Country Club was not far from the campus with the dining room overlooking the first and eighteenth fairways. Joseph was impressed. They ordered martinis as Butler explained that Alachua County was dry, but the country club was a legal "bottle club." When he learned that Joseph played golf, he promised to introduce him to the club if they decided on Gainesville. Their amiable host offered them houses in several price ranges. Joseph stated their preference. If they bought, it would be one of the little tract houses in Sunnybrook Estates.

"We would only plan on staying here while I went to school," he explained. "We wouldn't want to be burdened with an expensive house that might be hard to sell."

Houses in Sunnybrook were selling for $13,500 with modest mortgage payments.

With warm, positive feelings about Gainesville, they, nonetheless, continued on to Miami where they were impressed by the university's modern campus in Coral Gables. They were cordially welcomed by the dean of the journalism school. For lunch they went to the school cafeteria, where they were shocked by the table manners of the students. The floors and tabletops looked like there had been food fight. It left a lasting impression.

They found a real estate office in Miami and inquired about housing near the campus. Several agents sitting at desks eyed each other with puzzled looks. Apparently they were in the business of selling acreage and not single houses. At length, an elderly member of the staff grabbed his hat and offered to show them a couple of places. They looked at two houses, one of which had a canal in the backyard. When they showed no interest, their agent didn't appear to be the least bit disappointed.

Joseph and Cara made their decision. They beat it back to Gainesville, called Clark Butler, and placed a down payment on a three-bedroom, two-bath house in Sunnybrook Estates.

On returning in December 1959, Joseph applied for admission to the University of Florida's spring semester. He provided the necessary high school records, along with transcripts of his off-campus English credits from East Carolina. Still, he would have to pass the university's admissions test. He took the test in the university's old Seagle Building and anxiously awaited results. In the Marine Corps, he had passed the college equivalency test required of officers, so it never occurred to him that he might not qualify. He had bought a house and moved his family to Gainesville under the assumption that his admission would be a routine matter. His bridges were burned, and now he had to sweat it out.

Finally the letter came, informing him of his admission. Elated, he checked out the course requirements for journalism majors, bought the necessary textbooks, and began reading a month before the spring term convened. When the semester began, the university's enrollment was just over 10,000 students.

The only catch to his admission was that the university refused to accept him as an in-state student, no matter that he was a property owner and registered voter. He would have to pay the fees of a nonresident. In the eyes of Tigert Hall, he was a Gator but not a Florida Gator. Not that it was any hardship—the GI Bill covered most of his tuition, he had his retirement pension and a nest egg in savings, and Cara had secured a teaching job—but he felt like an outsider. In his twenty-two years in the Marine Corps, he had never had a permanent residence, and now that he had finally set down roots, he was being discriminated for being a nonresident.

An arcane regulation provided that after a full year, a nonresident could petition for residency through the state board of control, which then governed the university system. His request was finally granted. Joseph always considered the nonresident rule an insult to any person who had chosen to retire in Florida and was in every respect a citizen of the state.

Joseph was prepared to accept the oddity of being a forty-one-year-old freshman. Students his age were all in postgraduate studies.

The teenagers in his first C-course class (C as in comprehensive) took note of his tailored Hong Kong clothes and stared at his cordovan officer's chukka boots. He soon adjusted and felt at home, though he would have preferred not to be addressed as sir by the young folk. It made him feel older. Often, while walking to and from classes on the campus, he would be mistaken for a professor and asked for directions to certain buildings.

When the weather warmed to Florida's subtropical summer temperatures, he was taken aback by coeds sitting in adjacent desks wearing provocative shorts. Some students even wore rubber shower slippers to classes. In a math class, a young man sitting nearest Joseph read paperback novels throughout the lectures. If there was a pop quiz at the conclusion of the session, the young man took all of two minutes to solve the problems before taking off for his next class—probably to continue reading his book—while Joseph and the majority of his classmates stayed past the bell feverishly calculating quadratic equations.

Joseph's classmates represented the cream of Florida's high school classes. This placed him at a disadvantage in that he had graduated twenty-two years earlier from a high school that didn't, for example, teach biology. He had to make up for the inadequacy by relying on his life experiences and long hours of studying. Once he learned the tricks professors used in phrasing test questions, he often "set the curve," as the expression went, by making the highest score. A high leading score on a test raised the percentile for passing grades for the entire class.

"That marine did it again," he once overheard a sophomore remark sourly to others while scanning the scores of a geology test posted on the bulletin board.

Journalism majors were required or encouraged to take a smorgasbord of elective courses to broaden their overall knowledge. Joseph especially enjoyed the humanities, history, and earth sciences. In economics, he came away with the knowledge that pork and applesauce were tandem products—as the price of one went, so went the other—and that when the federal government was short of cash, it simply turned on the presses and churned out more certificates.

In a basic art class that was supposed to instill news editors with creative ideas in making up pages, Professor McIntosh quickly unveiled Joseph's rigid mind-set.

"Your military experience shows in your art," he said. "Look how severe your designs are. Loosen up."

Joseph's political ideology was neutral. Although he had been a Democrat since Truman's election in 1948, he had not voted since. From the view of marines, politics were for civilians who never ceased squabbling over their differences. He was unprepared for the zealotry exhibited by a few liberal professors and offended when a teacher in international relations ridiculed President Dwight Eisenhower's intellect. The fact that no black people were to be seen in classrooms was not unusual. The navy and marines had reluctantly become integrated under the prodding of President Harry Truman by the time of the Korean War. So, the "Colored" sign over the drinking fountain outside the old Victorian brick courthouse on the town square set off a dissonant ring in Joseph's mind. The issue of civil rights had not yet been fully raised, but the unfairness of racial discrimination had begun to bother him. Although professors unabashedly trumpeted their pet sociological reforms, integration was seldom mentioned.

In his first journalism course, he learned the basics of news writing from Jo Ann Smith, a young graduate of the University of Minnesota. She demanded clarity and made cliches and triteness the enemies of good writing.

After that, he was ready for H. G. "Buddy" Davis and his class in basic reporting, or at least he thought he was ready. Davis was the most demanding teacher in the school. His patience was reserved for students who worked hard and showed the most interest—Joseph among them—but he had zero tolerance for sloth. Outspoken and critical, he pounded his lessons home. "Blurt it out!" he would shout while critiquing weak story leads that failed to seize the importance of the event in the first sentence. "Grab the reader," was his slogan.

He kept records of students who had failed to complete assignments. Near the end of the semester, when minds were focused on examinations, Davis would announce the winners of his award, the "Crown of Thorns." It was for those unfortunates who had thought their missed assignments were forgotten. To remove the crown and earn a passing grade, a student had to research a lengthy list of esoteric topics and write reports on each, tasks no less demanding than the labors of Hercules.

Davis had no love for sports and considered sports writing a waste of talent. He made life miserable for the few sports "stringers" in the class who earned a few bucks from newspapers around the state by reporting on Gator athletic events.

Joseph discovered how tenacious and passionate Davis was about teaching when assigned to look into a report alleging the abuse of prescription drugs obtained from the student infirmary. Amphetamine-popping was becoming widespread, and the rumors were that the medical staff at the infirmary was more than generous in dispensing "feel-good" pills.

Joseph sought out the medical doctor in charge and asked for an interview on the subject. To his surprise, the doctor not only agreed, but invited him into his home, a short walk off the campus, and gave him a candid overview of the problem. Yes, he acknowledged, students who came in complaining of psychological problems were frequently given pills, and the control of drugs was an ongoing problem.

As faculty advisor to the *Florida Alligator,* Professor Davis routinely passed on the best stories of his assignments to the campus newspaper. The evening after Joseph had handed in his story, the phone began ringing at home in Sunnybrook Estates. The first call was from the dean of students urging him not to write the story.

Apparently, the doctor had second thoughts after the interview and wanted the story killed. Administrators in Tigert Hall feared the wrath of politicians in Tallahassee, who controlled the purse strings of the universities. A critical report, especially where the well-being or morality of students was concerned, could meet with dire consequences in the next appropriation.

"The story is already written and turned in," Joseph replied.

"Well, tell Professor Davis you don't wish to have it published," the dean implored.

"I didn't know it was to be published," Joseph confessed.

The next call came from the president of the university, Dr. J. Wayne Reitz. Politely, he repeated the dean's request that the story be quashed. Nervously, Joseph explained that the story was in the hands of his professor.

Damn, he said, after hanging up the phone, what had he done? He only wanted to earn a degree, and here he had stirred up an academic dogfight.

Next, the heat was shifted to Davis. When the director of physical education, who was responsible for the dispensary and, to a degree, all athletic facilities, asked Davis to kill the story, Davis came up with one of his classic retorts.

"How would you like it if I scattered broken glass all over your football field before the next game? That's what you're doing to this student."

Davis was already a bête noir with the athletic department, having failed a star football player and making him ineligible for the coming season.

Poor Rae Weimer again was caught in the middle. He had had to intercede in the football player's behalf when Davis refused to change his grade. 'You'll have to change it yourself," had been Davis's response. With not only the university administration to deal with, Weimer faced the wrath of the football boosters whose members included a few state legislators.

Rarely did a dean or director go over a teacher's head to change a grade, but that was what Weimer had done. Now he was, in effect, being ordered to retrieve the story from the *Alligator*'s editor, a journalism student, which he eventually did.

Mr. Weimer was no pushover. His withered arm was the legacy of a fall from a horse while herding cattle on his father's Nebraska farm in his youth. He was a product of the school of hard knocks. Without benefit of a college degree—"call me Rae, I'm not Dr. Weimer," he would frequently protest—he had risen to become managing editor of the first, and only, newspaper that accepted no advertisements. The *P.M.*, a pioneering, news-only daily in New York published by Marshall Field, failed but became widely acclaimed in journalism circles.

As peacekeeper among feuding teachers, Weimer acted in the best interest of the school while maintaining the respect of his faculty, including Davis.

Joseph's incipient venture into investigative reporting had taught him the lengths authority figures would go to prevent the boat from being rocked. It also taught him the fallacy of their intransigence. The *Alligator*'s eager student reporters, alerted by the dust-up, and probably by Davis, pounced on the amphetamine story with renewed gusto and eventually brought about a shake-up in the dispensary staff.

Davis taught another class on the history of journalism, in which he projected a more jocular personality. He regaled his students with stories about the early pamphleteers, the penny presses, muckrakers, infamous hoaxes, yellow journalists, and crusading publishers. He breathed life into the dry fabric of newspaper history, making it pliant and relevant. Before teaching, Davis has paid his dues as a political reporter in the Tallahassee bureau of the *Jacksonville Times Union,* an experience that provided him with endless grist on Florida politics.

Hugh Cunningham, who taught feature writing, was the antithesis of Davis. Where the latter's style evoked a love-hate relationship with students, Cunningham's class was a port in a storm. The calm, self-effacing Texan seldom got riled, though he was capable of being pushed to exasperation. His easygoing tolerance concealed a sternness that left no shades of gray to be interpreted. Where Davis's class was more of a nuts and bolts education in news gathering and reporting, Cunningham's took the student into the real world. A visit to a working farm could provide any number of story "angles" to feature on agriculture. Attendance at local court trials and government meetings brought students face to face with the realities of endless social problems to be explored and dissected.

While teaching journalism at Sam Houston State, a small East Texas school, one of his students was Dan Rather, a fact that the modest Cunningham never mentioned until the celebrated CBS anchor man himself brought it up in a national magazine interview. Rather idolized Cunningham and, in lectures and interviews, seldom failed to credit his old mentor for having turned him on to news reporting. Cunningham's only regret was that Rather's career had veered to the liberal side of politics.

"That's one thing I can't take credit for," Cunningham would say wryly, himself a staunch conservative.

Joseph was racing through his course requirements nonstop, taking loads of up to twenty hours in some semesters. It so happened that in a summer session, when he was taking photojournalism, Cunningham was a fill-in for the regular teacher. After apologizing at length for his lack of experience as a news photographer he proceeded to instill in students the importance of good news photos. Students took pictures with a variety of cameras, processed their film in the darkroom and printed out photos. It was the only course in Joseph's rugged curriculum that he could call "fun."

On one assignment, Joseph took his turn with a small 35-millimeter camera whose flash reflector was a fragile set of metal leaves that opened and closed like a fan. Often the reflector collapsed before the shutter went off. The battered little box bore the scars of abuse from impatient students. Of all the cameras Joseph had experimented with, including the bulky Speed Graphic, this one presented the worst problems.

One Sunday afternoon, Cara and Joseph joined their next-door neighbors on a trip to the little Gulf Coast fishing village of Cedar Key for a seafood dinner. Joseph took his school camera, just in case. As they arrived in town, Joseph observed a crowd of people on the dock.

"I'm going to see what it's all about," he said to the others as they proceeded to the restaurant. "Somebody probably caught a big fish."

It turned out to be a boatman who had been adrift in his disabled twenty-foot cabin cruiser for fourteen days and reported missing. A party fishing boat had found him twenty miles out and towed him in. Joseph, sensing the importance of the moment, began snapping pictures. To his relief, the cantankerous flash unit was working.

The boatman, who had been en route from Clearwater to Panama City, across the gulf, when his engine quit, had a pair of Boston terriers aboard. He had shared his meager supply of food and water with the dogs.

"Hold them up, please," Joseph called excitedly, all the while fearing other photographers would arrive on the scene.

After the boatman provided details of his survival, Joseph hastened to rejoin his friends.

What should he do with his film? Joseph tossed the question back and forth to his dinner companions as they ate. He had been the only photographer on the scene. Professor Cunningham would know. Gathering a fistful of coins, he made for the pay phone on the dock, reached Cunningham in his home, and related the story. Calmly, Cunningham thought the problem through aloud while Joseph fed coins in the pay phone.

The best bet, Cunningham finally ventured in his Texas drawl, was the Associated Press, but the nearest AP bureau with a photo transmitter was in Tallahassee. The question was how to get the film to them. Cunningham suggested Joseph get back to Gainesville, wrap the film and take it to the bus station to be put on the next bus to Tallahassee.

"When you've done that, call the AP, tell them to watch for your film, and dictate a story to them," he instructed. It was past midnight when Joseph had returned to Gainesville, shipped his roll of film, and called the AP.

By the time the AP had received the film, processed it, and put the photo on the wire, it was well past the deadlines for the Monday morning papers. Having no morning classes on Tuesday, Joseph was sleeping in. Cara crept into the bedroom with a copy of the *Florida Times Union*. On the front page was his photo, sharp and dramatic, of the boatman holding a terrier under each arm.

By the time he had reported for his next class, he had seen his photo on the news racks of the *Miami Herald*, *St. Petersburgh Times* and *Orlando Sentinel*. It not only appeared in Florida but in many national newspapers including the *Chicago Tribune*.

At the next meeting of the photo class, Cunningham held up copies of several newspapers with the photo.

"I guess I have no choice but to give him an 'A' for the week," he said dryly, while suppressing a smile.

Joseph savored the moment, unlike the accolade from his East Carolina professor who had read his essay to the class.

At last, Joseph had "been published" as the expression went for neophyte writers. But he wanted more for the resume he would need when he graduated.

The campus news bureau, as then known, hired students to do part-time work, and Joseph applied. Allen Skaggs, the PR director, gave him a job. It involved interviewing professors and researchers and writing feature stories on their work. "Puff" pieces, they were called. Joseph's copy would be closely edited, sometimes rewritten by a staff member, and routinely returned to the source for approval.

Professors were always fearful of being misquoted or embarrassed before their peers. The final product would be reproduced in mass and mailed out to dozens of papers in the state. Skaggs always scanned the large papers for one of his stories. A clipping would be posted in the glassed information board outside the building, a cachet attesting to the news bureau's importance to the university.

During the football season, Joseph was put to work designing and laying out the football programs, a magazinelike publication that featured stories about the academic side of the university, along with team rosters, player biographies, and photos. Joseph was complaining about the boring aspect of the project one day, when a female office staffer said, "Hey, there's 60,000 people in the stands reading your copy."

"Yeah, 500 professors reading my stuff and the others reading the football statistics," Joseph moaned.

By the second year, Joseph was invited into Sigma Delta Chi, the national professional journalism society, and was quickly shanghaied into being the chapter president. Professor Davis was chapter advisor and an enthusiastic torchbearer for the national organization. As such, he arranged to bring working newsmen in Florida into the fold. The chapter officers would pile into Davis's VW van for the trip to the target newspaper, Joseph carrying the sacred black kit containing the paraphernalia required for the ceremony. It held a black tablecloth bearing the society's logo, black robes for the officiating officers, two votive candles, and a manual of the society. Joseph humorously joked of it as being the Eucharistic kit and of himself as a high priest. Usually meeting in empty newsrooms,

Joseph's officers would light the candles and douse the lights. Joseph would read passages from the handbook of SDX: "Seek ye the truth and the truth shall set ye free," he'd quote from the creed of Sigma Delta Chi and the scripture of St. John. They had perfected the ritual so that hardened newsmen—no women in the society then—were visibly impressed.

"I think they liked the snake oil," Joseph once joked out of Davis's hearing.

From the typography class, taught by the soft-spoken John Webb, Joseph got a smattering of rotary presses, slugs, matrices, Cheltenham, Bodoni, and the endless number of typefaces loaded into the fonts of hot lead linotype machines. Webb would joke that no one could pass his course without learning the meaning of "eatain shrdlu," gibberish letters typed onto a spoiled slug by a disgusted machine compositor.

At the far end of the lengthy corridor of the JM school under the stadium, opposite the unseen concrete bleachers and south end zone of Florida Field, was the cluttered office of Professor John Paul Jones. A veteran newsman and teacher, he conducted a seminar for seniors and graduate students, which dwelt mainly on the business end of publishing, but his main activity was as secretary of the Florida Press Association. Jones's wife Marian, who was also his secretary, toiled from a desk surrounded by yellowing stacks of newspapers from around the state, mainly rural weeklies.

In the summer of his senior year, Joseph applied for internships in several state papers and was accepted by the *Daytona Beach News-Journal*. It was an evening paper on weekdays, with morning editions Saturdays and Sundays. He rented a beach cottage in nearby Flagler Beach. With Cara and Annie out of school, the three combined a summer of work and vacation. While his women splashed in the surf and worked on their tans, Joseph trained under Steve Pappas, the veteran managing editor of the *News-Journal*.

In his first day on the job, Pappas sent him to cover a statewide convention of the Florida Education Association. The news from the event wasn't going to be anything to shout about until late in the morning session when one of the officers offered a motion to endorse Fred Karl as a gubernatorial candidate. Routine, Joseph reflected, as Karl represented Volusia County and Daytona Beach in the state legislature. Moreover, his pro-education record in Tallahassee had earned him the title of "darling of the teachers." But surprisingly, another member objected to the motion.

"Please," he implored, "don't do this to Fred Karl."

The motion passed after a lengthy debate which turned out to be revealing and prophetic. The FEA was becoming a strident lobby in the state, and its support of a candidate promised to be controversial. Joseph's report, with his by-line, got front-page play.

Newspapers thrive on controversies, and a few days later, Joseph was in the middle of another one while covering a meeting of the Port Orange city council. A fierce argument, which nearly erupted into a fist fight, broke out over a motion to have the suburban community annexed by Daytona Beach.

The *News Journal* also owned a radio station, which had a reporter broadcasting news flashes from the newsroom. The radio announcer was stationed next to Joseph's desk. From time to time he would turn the microphone in Joseph's direction. The idea was to capture the sound of typewriters clacking away, creating a sense of immediacy to the newscasts. In rushing to meet his noon deadline, Joseph had forgotten to make a carbon copy of his story for the radio man. When his first "take" on the story was finished, the assistant city editor grabbed it from the typewriter and raced to his desk to edit it. The radio man was left to ad lib his lead story, after which an argument ensued between the two. Several choice words were exchanged, none suitable for the air or for print.

Pappas departed to cover an extended legislative session, leaving an assistant by the name of Gallant in charge. Each day about noontime, only minutes before deadline, Pappas would phone in his report from Tallahassee. Other reporters made good pretenses of working on deadline stories, leaving Joseph to take the report from Pappas. With the phone wedged between his ear and shoulder, Joseph would strain to hear the voice on the other end above the racket in the newsroom. He banged the keys on his old Remington, vainly trying to keep up with Pappas's rapid and erratic dictation, making mistakes galore. Not to worry, Gallant would yell. "Just type it, and I'll do the editing."

Instead of individual sheets, the rollers of the typewriter were threaded with a continuous web of copy paper that fed from a cardboard box on the floor in front of the desk. After every three or four paragraphs, Gallant would impatiently rip the paper out of the machine, leaving Joseph to connect a blank space on the paper. The journalism school had not prepared him for this. Somehow, Gallant rendered the copy printable, and the story would be finished before the press began to roll. Pappas's late-breaking report would appear in a boldface box near the bottom of the page. Joseph would stumble down the stairs a nervous wreck and head for a downtown lunch counter. Such was the routine of an evening paper, racing the clock all morning and in the afternoon idly searching for feature material.

Joseph commuted to the paper in a boxy little British Ford Anglia he had bought in Gainesville as a second car. On his way home one afternoon, he was caught in a fierce summer thunderstorm. He had taken a little-traveled side road between the beach and the Intracoastal Waterway. The up-and-down roller coaster ride across the dunes was a relief from the monotony of the crowded beach road. The area from Daytona Beach westward to Tampa is well known as "lightning alley," and this one lived up to the name. Streaks of lightning lashed the sky, some so close, he could smell the air burning. For whatever reason, lighting storms hover directly over the beach, and as it streaked and cracked above, the Anglia splashed through a depression between dunes and conked out.

Joseph watched as the low spot he had stalled in slowly became a torrent making its way to the ocean. Water began seeping in below the doors of the car. He drew some consolation from the thought that a car is said to be somewhat insulated from lightning hits. But what if his little European car got washed out to sea? He raised his feet above the floor and parked them on the dashboard opposite the passenger seat. After an hour, the storm moved away and the water on the road receded. Apprehensively, he turned the ignition key and the engine coughed and sputtered to life.

"We were worried about you," Cara greeted him at home. "It was really bad here."

"Yeah, I wished I had been here instead of there," Joseph cracked as he reached for the bourbon bottle under the kitchen sink.

The summer passed quickly, and in late August, Joseph prepared to return to Gainesville for his final semester of school. Pappas offered him a permanent job.

"You'll get other offers, but don't forget we gave you a chance," he said, contributing to the guilt complex already festering in Joseph's mind.

The *News Journal* people had gone out of their way to make him feel among friends and had treated him more as a permanent addition to the staff than as an intern. Still, he was hoping to work for a bigger paper.

Cara resumed teaching at Stephen Foster Elementary and Annie prepared to enter Gainesville High School.

After his internship experience, Joseph felt like a pro among amateurs. *The Gainesville Sun* invited him for an interview. William Pepper, Sr., the scholarly publisher of the paper, wanted him to come to work immediately. Joseph expressed his appreciation but declined. He did not want to drop out of school one semester short of his degree.

"We'll arrange your schedule so you can continue to attend classes," Pepper persisted. "We have reporters now who are still working on their degrees."

Although the pay wasn't what Joseph expected, he was flattered by the offer. On the other hand, he did not feel up to working full-time while studying for his degree. He respectfully declined.

Following an uneventful final semester, in mid-December, Joseph donned his black graduation gown and mortar board with the black-and-white tassel denoting the journalism degree. On his right shoulder he wore the braided orange and blue fourragère indentifying him as an honors graduate. The graduation class sat in collapsible chairs on the floor of Florida gym, hearing speeches filled with moral imperatives. Cara, her mother, and Annie watched from the stands. Eventually, he made the walk up the stage to receive his degree and handshake from President Reitz and became the first member of his extended family back in Louisiana ever to receive a college degree.

Eighteen
A Time in the Sun—1962–1985

Joseph felt like a marathon runner at the finish line. He was exhausted, listless, and mentally drained. He had crammed four years of college studies into three. Cara always had that feeling at midterm of her teaching semesters. She and Annie were off from school for the winter holiday season, so they all packed a few things and set out for Tampa to visit their former neighbors. Dan and Helen Faulkner were the ones who had gone to Cedar Key with Joseph and Cara when Joseph lucked upon his photo of the rescued mariner. Dan was a fun-loving guy always ready with a quip. After the photo episode in Cedar Key, he annoyed Joseph by calling him "Scoop." A sales rep for a cement company, he had been moved to the Tampa office. One of his perks, which he proudly displayed as a token of authority, was a key to the executive toilet.

Among the many guests at the Faulkners' New Year's Eve party were Don and Helen Gilbart, whom Joseph and Cara had met in Gainesville when Don was working on a graduate degree. The party was getting a bit wild, and Joseph joined the Gilbarts, who were newly married, outside for a breath of fresh air. As the three lit up cigarettes, the conversation centered on their respective smoking habits.

"I've been smoking way too much," Joseph began, "staying up late and studying. I feel beat."

"These things are really bad," Helen said with a distasteful look at the ember of her cigarette. "I don't know why we do this to ourselves."

"Amen," Joseph added. "We called them coffin nails in the Marines."

"Well, then, why don't we quit," said Helen, always ready with a suggestion.

"It's not so easy," Don added. "I've tried it before."

"So have I," Joseph said. "I tried tapering off. Limited myself to five a day, then cut down to three. Something would always come up, like a crisis, and soon I'd be puffing away as usual again."

"We need a reason to quit," Helen insisted. "If we had a good reason, we could do it."

"Name it," said Don.

"Okay," Helen responded. "How about this? We'll make a New Year's resolution never to smoke again."

"Starting when?" Don asked.

"Tomorrow," Helen said emphatically.

They clasped hands as if to cement the vow and rejoined the party, with Helen the only one really believing the compact would be taken seriously.

Driving home the next day, Joseph thought about it. He had never been a heavy smoker in the marines, but had become one during the long nights studying for his degree. In the morning he would wake up with a raw tongue and a vile taste in his mouth.

"I've got to try," he said to himself, "but I'll keep quiet about it."

It didn't take a doctor or the surgeon-general—who had yet to issue his report on the health hazards of smoking—for Joseph to realize that if nicotine could stain his fingers and teeth, lord knows what it was doing to his lungs.

After each graduating class, Weimer would send out lists of his graduates to newspapers around the state with comments on their potential. Joseph was considering job offers from the *Jacksonville Times-Union, Tampa Tribune,* and *Orlando Sentinel.* The trophy jobs were with the *Miami Herald* and *St. Petersburg Times,* the best-paying and most distinguished newspapers in Florida. He also had an offer from the *Atlanta Journal* and *Constitution,* but the beginning salary was so poor, he could barely have afforded an apartment in the city. *Miami* hadn't shown any interest but the *Times* invited him to St. Petersburg for an interview. The editors expressed an interest in Joseph, but there wasn't an immediate opening. They gave a vague promise to let him know if a reporting job became open.

After so many moves in the marines, Joseph and Cara dreaded another. The poor woman even had nightmares that she was packing endless barrels of household items for another move. She'd wake up exhausted after a night of bad dreams. They had adjusted to their little house in Sunnybrook Estates, and Joseph decided to put off a decision. There was a job open in the publications department of the College of Engineering. He took it.

Rachel, his new boss, was a veteran in editing and producing various publications. She welcomed him flatteringly.

The engineering school published a variety of pamphlets and newsletters on applied sciences that went to industrial businesses in and beyond the state. Joseph's job was interviewing professors and researcher engineers and writing articles. The subjects were dry and technical. If Joseph attempted to lighten up subjects or inject a bit of humor, he would be met with stern disapproval.

The boredom of his new job didn't make his vow with the Gilbarts any easier, but he had made up his mind. No more cigarettes. Cara's mother, who was staying with them while building her own house in Orlando, had taken over most of the housekeeping while Cara taught school. She kept the house spotless. One day after checking the ashtrays, she asked Cara, "What's he doing with his cigarette butts? The ashtrays are always empty."

When confronted with the question, Joseph sheepishly answered that he had quit. He had been reluctant to talk about it for fear that his will power would fail him. Now he had even more incentive not to resume, and he made it stick. On a shelf in a clothes closet across the room from his bed was a half-finished carton of filter-tipped Kents. It was the first object that caught his eye as he headed for the bathroom upon arising, when he habitually lit up his first smoke of the day. The Kents remained for weeks, until he mustered the courage to give them away. Helen Gilbart also stuck to the vow, but Don fell off the wagon. With much encouragement from Helen, and some prodding, he, too, finally rejoined the ranks of the reformed.

An event that was to have a major impact on the city of Gainesville and shake it to its foundations had taken place. The *Sun*, owned for many years by the Pepper family, was sold to the Cowles Corporation, publishers of *Look Magazine*, the *Minneapolis Star-Tribune*, the *Des Moines Register*, and several lesser dailies. They had recently bought a couple of small papers and a radio station in South Florida.

Within weeks, the persona of the Gainesville newspaper underwent a transformation that magnified the ideologies of the community. Subjects that had been taboo with the Peppers, like racial segregation, began appearing in the paper. The Pepper family had been no different than the typical family-owned newspaper publishers in the South. They downplayed news that their readers disliked. But the Cowles people were outsiders with liberal ideas, a zest for reform and no one to please but themselves.

Gardner Cowles, the corporate publisher, brought in his son-in-law to run the *Sun*. John Harrison was a brash young executive, a product of the elite Phillips Exeter prep school and the Harvard business school. Urbane, aloof, and often imperious, he wore garish combinations of shirts and ties, attributed—according to one local haberdasher—to color blindness. If he was color-blind in the literal sense, he was even more so figuratively in his racial outlook.

The new publisher had little tolerance for the old Gainesville power structure but courted the mercantile community, some of whom had pulled their ads. He turned to the university, primarily the journalism school, for advice. Rae Weimer responded enthusiastically, and before long, the *Sun's* editorials were written by Professor H. G. "Buddy" Davis. From his bully pulpit, Davis attacked the local government power structure, the Gainesville Police Department, anything that smacked of corruption, racial segregation, Republicans, conservatives, and intransigent bureaucrats and politicians.

Harrison opened the op-ed page to letters from readers, most of which were critical and vitriolic. Revealing his limited experience as a publisher, he frequently added his personal comments at the bottom of critical letters in light-face type. At the end of one particular disagreeable letter, he rejoined weakly with a quote from Thomas Jefferson: "If I had to choose between newspapers and government, I would rather have newspapers."

The "new" *Sun* was the talk of the town, and Joseph was enjoying the conflict. Then one day, he got a call from Ed Johnson, the paper's new executive editor. Johnson wanted to talk to him about a job.

"I'll hear what he has to say, but I already turned down one job offer from the *Sun* and I already have a job," Joseph confided to Cara.

They met in the student cafeteria at the university and discussed the offer over cups of coffee.

Johnson was a bright, young journalist who had been hired from his job as features editor at the *Tampa Tribune*. Joseph liked him from the start. Johnson blended his intelligence and friendliness with a keen sense of humor.

"We want you to be our education specialist," Johnson began. "Nothing else. We feel the university has been overlooked by the old paper and we want it covered thoroughly.

"Our coverage of the public schools needs improving," he continued. "From what I've learned, you are just the man we need."

The salary was no better than most beginning offers Joseph had received, but he was dying to accept. Still, there was the matter of his loyalty to Rachel and his commitment to the engineering school. He asked Johnson for time to think over the offer.

Inadvertently, Harrison had chanced upon a way to free Joseph from his obligation in a conversation with Dr. Joseph Weil, dean of the engineering school. Weil, like several other administrators and deans, was making the most of Harrison's open ear with the university community. The state legislature was approaching its biennial session, and the talk was all about the University of Florida's budget requests. Previous legislative appropriations from Tallahassee had been far from meeting expectations. The University of Florida, knowing there would be no significant across-the-board budget increase, adopted a strategy. Putting its eggs in a single basket, so to speak, it would focus on what was perceived to be its greatest strength, engineering.

Harrison had promised support of the cause with a vigorous series of articles and editorials designed to catch the eyes of politicians in Tallahassee.

It never was clear to Joseph how his name entered the picture, but apparently Harrison had mentioned the *Sun* was waiting for him to become its education writer. Weil's ears must have perked up at the prospect of having one of his own employees on the newspaper staff.

Soon after his meeting with Harrison, the cagey old dean summoned Joseph into his office.

"Aren't you going to take the job with the *Sun*?" he asked bluntly.

"If you're wanting to get rid of me, I will," Joseph replied. "But I thought I had a commitment to work for Rachel."

"No problem," Weil shot back. "You can do us more good with the newspaper. Take the job."

Joseph could hardly believe his ears. He was being encouraged, actually pushed, to leave his job and join the *Gainesville Sun*.

Weil apparently figured he would have his own publicist at the newspaper. But he was not about to be a hack for the engineering school, Joseph thought, as he floated on air back to his desk to call Johnson.

"I'm free, Ed," he said. "When do I start?"

"Whenever you're ready," came the response. "The sooner the better."

Poor Rachel exploded when Joseph broke the news, carefully making the point that Weil had urged him to take the newspaper job.

"Damn, that old so-and-so," she steamed. "He's always doing things like that to me."

She never bore a grudge with Joseph, and they remained friends long after he joined the *Sun*.

Cowles, Inc. had committed to making the *Sun* a respected part of the community, and soon the decrepit old two-story building on South East 2nd Place was being gutted and remodeled. As an evening paper, the workday for the production department and a few editors began at daybreak.

On walking toward the employee entrance on his first day, Joseph's ears caught a sound from the open windows that he would always associate with the printing of the paper. It was the metallic clatter of brass letters in linotype machines trickling from type fonts through chutes on the way to be imprinted on hot lead sticks.

When climbing the creaking wooden stairs to the newsroom on the second floor, he was not prepared for what he would see. The wall along the west side of the building had been ripped out, exposing the newsroom to the open air. Johnson pointed him to a desk perilously close to the opening, thirty feet from the street below. A single two-by-four was nailed between studs as a safety measure. Sitting at the desk shoved against Joseph's work station was "Buzz" Mixson, the area editor.

Buzz was a likable, self-effacing individual, tall and lanky, with an ever-present cigarette between his fingers. He greeted Joseph in the drawl characteristic of the rural folk in his native Levy County. He was frequently absent from his desk, working his beat in the small towns and farms to the west of Gainesville. Joseph would automatically answer his telephone. So it turned out that his first story at the *Sun* was not on education, but about the decomposed remains of a body discovered in the drainage ditch of a road in Gilchrist County. The report came from a deputy in the sheriff's office.

As Joseph surveyed the newsroom, Johnson apologized for its unkempt appearance. The conditions were only temporary, he said assuredly. Grimy desktops were cluttered with typewriters, paste pots, and wicked steel spikes reporters used to impale duplicates and stories ripped from the AP teletype machines to be held as references. At the head of the room, there was a long desk occupied by the news editor and one or two assistants. Their job was to edit stories selected from the AP machines and from reporters in the newsroom, write headlines, and arrange them on "dummy" form sheets that represented page make-ups. Behind the news desk was a small room with a glass front containing a half-dozen clacking teletype machines.

Joseph wasn't prepared for the men's room. It begged for a thorough Marine Corps "head" detail. The floor was littered with trash and old newspapers. In lieu of toilet tissue, there was the remnants of a roll of newsprint near the commode.

Sooner than Joseph had expected, the renovation was completed, making the newsroom a clean and agreeable workplace. Joseph plunged into his new job with eagerness. In his trusty little English Ford, he regularly made the rounds of the university, the school board offices, and the county schools.

He so enjoyed the job that he could hardly wait to get to work in the mornings. He was never wanting in story material. Johnson regularly by-lined his copy and marked it for the front page. Any good local story is better on the front page than a wire story, Johnson reasoned.

At home, the mail brought a letter from the St. Pete *Times* with an offer. Reluctantly, Joseph turned down the trophy job. At times he would second-guess his decision, but in the end, he bore no regrets.

Keeping the *Sun*'s commitment to the university and the engineering school, Joseph was assigned to interview state senator Charlie Johns, an influential member of the senate appropriations committee. Johns was despised by a majority of the university faculty for his recent probes into the alleged homosexual activities of some professors. The notorious Johns Committee, as it came to be called, operated much in the style of the infamous Joseph McCarthy committee on un-American activities in Washington a decade earlier. Any one who protested the committee's intrusions was labeled a suspect. Johns was not noted for his erudite phrases.

Joseph recalled a story told by Professor Davis, going back to when Davis was a political correspondent in Tallahassee and Johns was acting governor. During his brief tenure as governor, Johns was pressed into the limelight with news conferences after which he routinely criticized the press corps for misquoting him. According to Davis, reporters sometimes "cleaned up" his comments but did so to clarify the governor's muddled answers and correct his fractured English.

Stung by the criticisms, the reporters retaliated by quoting Johns verbatim, pointing to his solecisms with the snide, parenthesized "sic."

A secretary ushered Joseph into the cramped office in Starke, where the senator conducted his insurance business and which served as his base away from Tallahassee.

As a reporter for a liberal newspaper, Joseph was surprised to be greeted so courteously by the curmudgeon politician. Johns was more than willing to espouse his support of the university. As Joseph scribbled answers and comments in his notepad, he was reminded of Davis's story. The senator's grammar would need polishing and buffing.

The story appeared in the Sunday edition under a 24-point headline that proclaimed the senator's commitment to help the University of Florida. Joseph expected to be criticized for misquoting the senator. Instead, the senator sent a flattering letter to Harrison approving of the story.

"You got his folksy way of talking down pat without making him look bad," Harrison joked.

In Tallahassee, a prestigious outside consulting task force appointed by the governor was readying a blueprint that was to have a major impact on the state's higher education structure. Several new universities would be created. The University of Florida, long assumed to be the state's flagship institution, felt its position threatened by Florida State University in Tallahassee and, perhaps, by the new schools. Joseph was dispatched to Tallahassee to cover the presentation of the final report. At that historic meeting, he also discovered the competitive nature of the news business. With the *Sun*'s deadline at hand, he rushed to a telephone to dictate his story on the report. Johnson took the call on his phone.

"The story ran an hour ago on the AP wire," Johnson told his surprised education reporter. "Someone must have leaked the report."

Joseph was crestfallen. The "someone" turned out to be Martin Waldron, a veteran Saint Petersburg *Times* political reporter in Tallahassee. Waldron had obtained a copy of the report the evening before from a politician anxious to curry favors with the *Times*.

The *Times* broke the story the following morning before the report had been made public. The AP had then picked it up and put it on the state wire. Pushing his deadline to the last minute, Johnson skillfully blended Joseph's version with details from the AP report and gave Joseph a byline. It was an act of loyalty and face-saving that did not go unnoticed by the *Sun*'s new reporter.

Johnson was running the editorial side of the paper much like a weekly country editor, supervising reporters, editing copy, managing the personnel side of the news staff, and dealing with production and circulation problems. One day he called Joseph into his office.

"I need a city editor," he began. "Do you think you could take on that job and continue with your education beat. We can give you a raise."

Joseph agreed. Johnson was borrowing from the publisher's management style, which he often lampooned: If it takes two people to do a job, the *Sun* will do it with one.

Not counting his own responsibilities, Joseph had only four full-time reporters. One covered city government and another county government, both staples of the daily local news diet. There was a police reporter, and a general assignment reporter who sort of freelanced it. Joseph also assigned the two staff photographers to special events. His mornings were occupied with assigning and editing stories. After the paper had been put to bed and he had grabbed a bite of lunch in a drive-through or at the lunch counter of a greasy spoon up the street, Joseph would be off pursuing education stories. It was a hectic routine, but he preferred it to sitting around at his desk, answering the phone.

One warm November day, Joseph had just returned from lunch and was idly scanning the day's newspaper when his phone rang. Phil Emmer, a young developer, was on the line.

"The television is reporting that President Kennedy has been shot. Do you have anything on it?"

"Hold the line. I'll check our wire," Joseph responded, thinking the report was a hoax.

He raced across the newsroom to the wire room calling out to Jim Redden, the news editor. The two hovered over the national wire machine that had just begun to move the story.

"*Dateline Dallas . . .*" it began, then hesitated before starting the lead. "*President John F. Kennedy has been shot.*" The machine stuttered, like it was in a catatonic state before resuming. Agonizingly, the two newsmen watched the story grow word by word. The president was dead. It was Friday, November 22, 1963.

Redden ripped the paper from the machine, dashed back to his desk, and called down to the composing room to stand by for a major remake. Joseph went back to his phone to confirm the bad news with Emmer and await other calls.

The AP had been badly beaten by the rival United Press. Radio and television were off and running with the assassination story before AP had anything to report. In the days following, the *Sun*'s newsroom was in a wake. A stream of grieving readers came in to drop off letters and to talk with reporters about the tragedy. Students and town folk crowded into the university gym for a memorial service. The events following the assassination filled the pages of the *Sun* with riveting news accounts.

Lyndon B. Johnson was sworn in as president, and Harvey Lee Oswald, the assassin, was shot and killed by Jack Ruby, a town character that hung around the Dallas police station. Each day, history was being made and reported. The scenes of Jacqueline Kennedy and her two young children in the capitol rotunda where the president lay in state, and the funeral itself played out before a grief-stricken nation. They were news events of a magnitude never before reported by the new *Gainesville Sun*.

Jean Marshall, a young reporter, transferred to the *Sun* from the *Lakeland Ledger,* a sister paper in the Cowles Florida chain. A graduate of the UF journalism school, Jean was bored in Lakeland

and yearned to rejoin the social life around the university. Aggressive and intuitive, she covered city hall and wrote Sunday columns.

One morning on her way to work, Jean noticed hearses pulling out from the parking lot of a funeral home that occupied the same block as the *Sun*. At that time, hearses doubled as ambulances, there being no emergency rescue service. Jean followed the hearses to the airport where a plume of black smoke at the end of the runway still hung over the site of a major tragedy. A twin-engine Beechcraft commuter plane of the South Central Airlines had plummeted to the ground soon after taking off for Tallahassee, killing all eleven passengers and the pilot.

"Buzz" Rummel, the general assignment reporter, joined Jean Marshall, and the two began phoning in pieces of the story. The commuter line's agent refused to release the passenger list until the next of kin had been notified and the airline had authorized him to do so. The two *Sun* reporters had identified some of the victims in interviews with grief-stricken family members and friends who had remained at the airport after dropping off passengers. The deadline had already passed, but Johnson held the final edition. The complete and official passenger list was crucial to the story. It was past 1:00 P.M. when Marshall and Rummel returned to write their final version of the crash.

Joseph grabbed a notepad and raced for the airport. He reached the passenger terminal just as a company representative was about to issue a statement and release the passenger list. As Joseph waited, along with several other reporters, the coroner's jury passed through in single file, bearing gruesome body bags oozing with burnt flesh. A juror turned aside to vomit.

"My God, was that . . .?" he called a friend's name to another juror.

The passenger list included several university staffers and the parents of "Buddy" MacKay, a young state legislator from Ocala who would later become lieutenant governor. Joseph rushed to the phone to call the names to Johnson. The *Sun*'s final edition was late, but carried a complete and thorough story of the tragedy.

Civil suits filed by families of the victims alleged the design of the original aircraft had been altered to accommodate added weight and wing lift. After years of litigation, the airline settled and filed for bankruptcy.

Marshall, who later became Mrs. Jean Chance, witnessed the new president's style at first hand when covering the ceremonial ground breaking for the controversial Cross-Florida Barge Canal. Reporters, including an obnoxious contingent of the national press, gathered in a cow pasture near Palatka, where President Lyndon Johnson would trigger an explosion of earth, marking the eastern terminus of the canal.

The president was late arriving, a habit he relished to keep the press waiting, and it began raining. With Joseph sitting near his phone as the deadline approached, Marshall could only run to a nearby phone and call in snippets of the coming event, mostly a description of the mob scene of reporters. Well past deadline, and with Ed Johnson again holding up the final edition, the president arrived. After extolling the commercial benefits the canal would bring the people of Florida, he finally pressed the button. The bang threw up mud and left a hole in the ground that was never to become part of the canal. After years of protest by Florida environmentalists, Congress deauthorized the canal project and cut off its funds.

One local political figure who consistently kept his name in the paper was Claude "Red" Franks, the county's tax assessor. He constantly dueled with taxing authorities of the city and county, using the *Sun* as a conduit. Franks resented that he would get the blame for any tax increase on real property. So he routinely delayed his property valuations from elected governing boards, who needed the figures to determine their millage rates. The school board was fretting about the approaching deadline for the annual budget with no information from Franks.

When Joseph called the controversial tax appraiser about the situation, his response was, "Tell the school board I'm sending over a beer truck and then I'll padlock the doors to the toilets."

Once Franks called Jean Marshall and told her he was placing a bomb under the *Sun*. He was joking, but Harrison wasn't so sure. Obsessed with the idea of showing up the elected officials as tax-and-spend politicians. Franks ultimately was charged with malfeasance and removed from office by the governor.

Jack Harrison pecked away editorials on his shiny Remington typewriter. Amazingly, in 1965, he was awarded a Pulitzer Prize for a series of tersely written pieces calling for a housing code to improve substandard living conditions in the city's black community. His writing bore a striking resemblance to the style of "Buddy" Davis.

Johnson, who regularly had to shoot down the publisher's off-the-wall ideas, was at a loss for words. Johnson wasn't jealous but was in a state of disbelief. The news staff resented Harrison's meddling and considered him a novice. Now he possessed the holy grail of journalism.

This is not to say that the award was undeserved. The city's black neighborhoods lacked sewers and paved streets. White slumlords were loath to maintain and improve dilapidated rent houses, and the city government was dragging its feet.

It didn't take a genius to note that the liberal Pulitzer board based at the Columbia University School of Journalism was partial to any Southern newspaper that championed the cause for racial equality. An editor from the Deep South who went against the grain of his segregation-minded readers was likely to be highly regarded by his peers in the East.

It wouldn't have mattered with the Pulitzer board that the city had, in fact, begun laying sewers and paving streets in the black community before Harrison's editorials had been published.

In 1966, a Republican attorney from Palm Beach County, Claude Kirk, was elected governor of Florida in a major upset, becoming the state's first GOP chief executive since the post-Civil War days of Reconstruction. The Democrats were stunned, as was the *Sun,* which had staunchly supported the Democratic nominee, Miami mayor, Robert King High.

The day following the election, Ed Johnson was dismayed and crestfallen.

"Cheer up, Ed," Joseph said to him. "Look at it this way. Kirk is a newsmaker, and that's what we're all about. He'll be good copy."

Johnson glumly agreed. And Kirk did not disappoint. Soon after taking office, the flamboyant Kirk began baiting and nagging at the Democrats, particularly the rural dinosaurs of the party known as the "pork chop" gang, who controlled both chambers of the legislature. Buddy Davis was not lacking grist in attacking both Kirk and the pork choppers in his editorials.

Coinciding with Kirk's election, the Florida Education Association was becoming more vocal in its complaints. Poor salaries, crumbling schoolhouses, and shortages of classroom necessities were but a few of the teachers' complaints.

The FEA replaced its long-time executive secretary and lobbyist in Tallahassee with a militant young firebrand named Phil Constans. A confrontation with the Republican governor was inevitable even though the Democrats, who had held the reins of power in Tallahassee for decades, were no more inclined than Kirk to accede to the FEA's demands.

Constans blustered and threatened a teacher strike, only it would be called a walkout. His ultimatum was that the FEA's 50,000 members would resign en masse. Kirk finally called a special session of the legislature to deal with the problem. Joseph sat in the press section of the house chamber and witnessed firsthand the bitterness of the political enemies. In introducing the governor to the assembled lawmakers, the wrinkled, white-maned, Democratic speaker of the house insulted the governor with a feigned slip of the tongue:

"Honorable members of the legislature . . . Governor Claude Quirk—er—Kirk." The Democrats chuckled with glee while the handful of Republicans scowled and applauded Kirk.

As fast as relief bills were passed for the teachers, Kirk vetoed them. Finally, Constans set a date for the walkout. Cara was a member of the FEA, and she had made up her mind "to walk." In fact, on that gray, drizzly Monday morning in February, she was working the phone, talking with her colleagues who couldn't make up their minds to join the walkout.

It was a chaotic scene in Alachua County schools that morning. Volunteers shepherded crying first graders back to their buses. Principals herded students into auditoriums to be entertained with films. At the school board, a tearful teacher representative of the FEA handed in bundles of resignations. The superintendent declined to accept them.

During the day, the teachers sequestered themselves in a downtown theater to hear inspirational speeches and reassure each other of their determination. The scene continued for twenty-one days. Constans had predicted that 40,000 teachers statewide would join the walkout, but it was closer to 25,000.

In some counties, the strike was hardly felt while in others, Alachua County among them, the walkout had a crippling effect. Untrained and unscreened teacher volunteers flocked to earn a few bucks as scabs. Baby-sitters, they were called. Gradually, a trickle of teachers began returning, those who were breadwinners in their families.

Meanwhile in Tallahassee, appropriations bills for education were fluttering back and forth between the legislature and the governor. After the first week, it was a foregone conclusion that the strike would fail.

Joseph had to straddle a thin line covering the story. His sympathy was clearly with Cara and the teachers, and he had to battle his emotions to present a clear picture of the conflict. At times he failed. In the third week with a majority of the teachers having returned to their jobs—Cara not among them—a compromise bill was passed, ending the debacle. Neither side could claim victory. Teachers got token raises, and schools some needed funds for classroom supplies. But when Joseph carefully evaluated the legislation, he saw it was the county administrators, not a single one of whom had put their jobs on the line, who were the big winners. They got healthy raises, and a batch of new supervisory jobs had been created.

Cara went back to work, proud and not the least humbled. Her principal had been a silent supporter of the teachers, and he expressed admiration to his returning faculty for fighting for what they believed was right.

For his stories, Joseph received the first of three annual awards from the FEA for "distinguished news coverage in the field of education." At the presentation in the Jacksonville Coliseum, Joseph occupied a chair on the stage next to the evening's featured speaker, Drew Pearson, the renowned political pundit whose columns appeared in hundreds of newspapers nationwide under the title of "Washington Merry-Go-Round."

Pearson captivated the audience with stories of his recent visit to the Soviet Union, where he had interviewed Secretary Nikita Khrushchev. The two had gone for a swim in the Black Sea in the nude.

"For all of his blustering, I found him to be a lot like us," Pearson said with a chuckle.

Previously, a lighthearted feature on the community's flower lovers had won Joseph a first place award from the Florida Press Association. Known to only a few, a bed of rare trilliums grew in a wooded area across from the university's golf course on 34th Street. Trilliums are not tolerant of hot, humid climates and botanists at the university believed this was as far south as any of the species were known to exist.

Enter a developer who began building apartments on the corner that posed a threat to the plants. An alarmed garden club began secretly alerting its members. The flowers had to be rescued and moved to safer locations. Motorists on 34th Street were mystified by the furtive movements of women lugging cardboard boxes from the woods to their cars. A curious caller asked Joseph, "What's going on?"

Joseph, through Cara, already knew what was going on. But he was not supposed to blurt it out and cause a stampede in the surviving trillium beds. Only when the rescue operation was nearing completion and most of the plants were already in safe beds did he write about it.

"Congratulations, here's your cheese board," Johnson said with his typical humor as he handed Joseph a walnut plaque with a colorful tile in the center that portrayed magnolia blossoms, not trilliums.

Cara had carried out her own box of trilliums, which she tenderly pressed into the moist black soil under the oaks on their newly-acquired four-acre wooded lot west of the city, where they would one day build their dream house.

Nineteen
The Turbulent Years—The Sixties

In the mid-1960s, national news events that would eclipse the Kennedy assassination exploded almost simultaneously. The budding sexual revolution resulting from the availability of the birth control pill blossomed with the flower children and their hedonistic hippie lifestyles. Almost as a single issue, the civil rights movement and Vietnam War protests burst upon the national scene. Combined, the moral issues of sex, war, race, and drugs were compacted into a powder keg that blew up with devastating social and political consequences. To top it all off, Watergate soon followed.

On a summer afternoon just before the fall term, Joseph sat in a back row of the auditorium at the University of Florida, where President Wayne Reitz was addressing his faculty. He had just returned from a visit to Central America. Marxist revolutionaries had shut down the university Reitz had gone to observe.

He described in detail the sadness of seeing a beautiful campus devoid of students. Joseph recognized the graduate student sitting one row ahead as the leader of the local Students for a Democratic Society. Before long, the SDS and assorted student protest groups would attempt to shut down the University of Florida.

The student rebellion began with an assault on campus rules that stymied their lifestyles. They wanted to do at school what they weren't allowed to do at home. *In loco parentis,* in the place of a parent, became the target of protest against university administrators. Before long, students had their way when separate dormitories for the sexes became coeducational.

The University of California at Berkeley was spearheading the student rebellion starting with its Free Speech Movement. Campuses around the country joined in. The University of Florida considered itself in the vanguard and wanted to be known as the "Berkeley of the South."

Meanwhile, blacks in Gainesville, led by juveniles immune from imprisonment, were staging sit-ins at downtown drug store lunch counters and at the Manor Motel restaurant on 13th Street. White civil rights sympathizers besieged the school board with demands to integrate schools as desegregation suits were being filed in federal courts.

When finally the school board acted, it enraged the black community with an order closing the black Lincoln High School and moving its students to all-white Gainesville High. Lincoln students overturned lockers and desks, vandalized their school, and took to the streets in protest.

A shaken Sheriff Joe Crevasse appeared in the *Sun* newsroom. His squad car had just been surrounded and rocked back and forth by an angry mob of students as he passed Lincoln High.

"I ask you," Crevasse said in a pleading tone, "if the sheriff of this county isn't safe in a marked car, who is?"

Good question, Joseph pondered sympathetically.

Several days later, Joseph visited Gainesville High School, where daily gang fights between whites and blacks were common occurrences. Four black students, arm in arm, rudely forced him off a walkway. Returning to his car in the parking lot, he found several surly black youths draped around it. Forcing a smile, Joseph said, "Excuse me, this is my car." With hostile glares, they grudgingly gave way.

Why weren't they in class? Joseph wondered as he drove back to the office.

Millions of dollars were being spent in their behalf on lawyers and in federal courts to give them a better education. Joseph's writing had been outspokenly in favor of desegregation and civil rights. The incidents didn't change his resolve, but left him with a different perspective on racial integration.

Of all the county's elementary schools, a single black youth was assigned to Stephen Foster, where Cara was teaching one of the three, fifth-grade classes. Gravely, the principal gathered his fifth-grade teachers to decide which would "have to take" little George Kimbrough. Cara immediately relieved his anxiety by asking that the youth be assigned to her room.

An indication of the hostility that existed about blacks in white schools was the white cafeteria worker at Stephen Foster who resigned, saying she "would never serve a nigger."

The resourceful Cara dedicated the school year to the theme of citizenship and the qualities of being a good person. George was a bright kid and a model student, in addition to being athletic. Soon he was the center of attention in the class, and white students boasted to other kids in school about having him in *their* class.

Ironically, the county's first soldier to be killed in action in Vietnam was a young black infantryman.

As a member of the National Education Writers Association, Joseph joined a group of journalists on a tour of public universities in several states. For miles along the Ohio Turnpike, their chartered bus passed group after group of young people from across the midwest hitchhiking to Washington for a mass protest against the war in Vietnam. Among them were socialists, anarchists, radicals, Marxists, pacifists, draft protestors, and ordinary students out for a good time.

Along with the Pentagon and the Lyndon Johnson administration, corporate America was at the center of protest, especially companies producing war materials, like Dow Chemical. That weekend, parts of Washington burned.

Administrators at Kent State University proudly escorted the writers through a new state-of-the-art academic building. In keeping with the school architecture of the time, the building featured carpeted, split-level hallways, many short stairs and lots of nooks, crannies, and alcoves. Joseph thought it would have made a dandy kindergarten. Along the way, the visitors frequently had to step over lovers sprawled out on carpeted stairways entwined in hot embraces. A professor lamely apologized for the inconveniences, offering the information that Kent State's students were drawn predominantly from blue-collar families in nearby Cleveland. Two months later the nation was shocked by the news that the Ohio National Guard had opened fire on war protestors at Kent State, killing four students and wounding eleven.

The war protest heated up at the University of Florida. Rampaging students blocked University Avenue and 13th Street, the city's two main thoroughfares. A platoon of law enforcement officers finally broke up the mob with tear gas. Some streets on the campus were barricaded by protestors. As serious as the situation was, Joseph was amused by one roadblock of timbers and barrels on top of which posed a shirtless redheaded youth wearing a white headband. No doubt he envisioned himself as another Che Guevera, the revered Cuban revolutionary.

Joseph could never understand how closing the university would stop the war in Vietnam. Neither could Stephen C. O'Connell, the university's pugnacious new president.

O'Connell had stepped down from the bench of the Florida Supreme Court to take over the reins from President Reitz. He was not about to succumb to the urgings of a few liberal professors and give in to the radicals.

A hundred or so of the more militant students forced their way into O'Connell's office for a sit-in. His patience expended, O'Connell called in the police who tear-gassed Tigert Hall, forcing everyone to evacuate. Tigert Hall was temporarily closed but not the University of Florida.

Abbie Hoffman, the national icon of the counterculture, appeared on campus for a lecture. From an outdoor platform on the quadrangle, he urged students to rebel against their parents, reject the Protestant work ethic, and experiment with drugs and sex. While delivering a litany of foul jokes, he sucked from a bottle of red wine. Four crew-cut students, probably engineering, walked by, carrying a "Bomb Hanoi" sign.

Reporting such an event in a serious vein posed a problem. Hoffman's off-the-wall comments couldn't be taken seriously as straight news, so Joseph wrote it up as an analysis, under a logo that allowed a degree of journalistic license. The article contained as many expletives deleted and bleeps as it did serious thoughts. It also brought a flock of letters to the editor from campus militants denouncing the *Sun*'s treatment of their icon.

Joseph had mixed feelings about the war. On the one hand, some of his former marine acquaintances were fighting in Vietnam. He hoped for a successful military conclusion of the conflict, but with the way it was being conducted, he sympathized with the youths who were being drafted and sent to die for a lost cause. It was obvious that the United States, with its reliability on aerial bombardment, would never root out the Viet Cong from the jungles.

Joseph often thought of Annie, who was away attending a girls' college in Georgia, and he was thankful he did not have a son of draft age.

At the outset of the war, there was a half-hearted degree of patriotism on the campus. Student government leaders attempted to drum up support for the military by entertaining four decorated Green Berets recently returned from Vietnam. On a weekend, they were wined, dined, and provided with cute sorority dates for a big dance. A year later they would have been jeered and spat upon.

Joseph's reporters at the *Sun*—he now had eight or ten—gleefully covered every demonstration. They were young and sympathetic with the protests. He was frequently at odds with them as his own liberal views slowly eroded. He was weary of protest stories dominating the local news.

At the completion of a semester, Buddy Davis occasionally entertained students with a poolside party at his residence, a customary practice with faculty members. Often included among the invitees were "VIPs" from the *Sun*. On this occasion, Joseph was in attendance along with Ed Johnson and Bob Tartaglione, the *Sun's* circulation manager. The guests stood around the pool deck, sipping frothy beer from a keg and watching the swimmers, mostly students.

Suddenly, eyeballs popped when two statuesque coeds pulled themselves from the water like mermaids, casually removed their swimsuits, and proceeded to towel off in full view of the guests. They chatted nonchalantly as though alone in a girls' dressing room. With towels wrapped around their midriffs they padded off to the changing room, presumably to dress.

Joseph happened to be talking with Marjorie Davis, the hostess. She lowered her eyes and mumbled. "They sure are different these days." Her statement needed no response.

More women reporters were filling jobs in the newsroom, until they accounted for half of the staff. Editors disagreed among themselves about the trend, some fearing a male minority would create an unhealthy balance. Joseph found little difference in the performances of males and females. Some women wrote better than men and were no less aggressive in pursuing their assignments. Others were ordinary writers who needed constant prodding.

After Watergate, every new graduate of the journalism school aspired to be a investigative reporter like Bob Woodward or Carl Bernstein. A few considered their talents wasted when assigned to write obituaries.

Gerald Ford, the Republican minority leader in the U.S. House of Representatives, visited the campus to address a small group of Young Republicans in the student union. Had he tried to speak to a larger assembly, he would have been shouted down, as had happened to every conservative invited to speak on campus. Although the term had not yet been popularized, political correctness at the UF was already in vogue. Ford's remarks were rather innocuous, given the level of rhetoric of the time and the fact that he was a hawk who often criticized President Johnson for not pursuing the war more vigorously.

After his remarks, Joseph approached him, notepad in hand with a few questions. Of all the politicians Joseph had interviewed, he was most impressed with Ford's earnestness and candor. His eye contact was unwavering and his presence reflected a man of dignity and integrity. He gave this impression despite his sponsor, a zealous Republican congressman from St. Petersburgh, who kept interposing himself between Joseph and Ford, as though he were a bodyguard shielding his leader. Ford was plainly annoyed with his escort and forthrightly answered Joseph's questions, which had to do with the Vietnam War.

Not long afterwards, Ford was picked to be vice-president by Richard Nixon after scandals had forced Spiro Agnew to resign. When Nixon himself was toppled by the events of Watergate, Ford became the nation's thirty-eighth president. Joseph never believed Nixon deserved the pillory he received from Democrats and the national media. Joseph saw him as a victim of the war, as had been Lyndon Johnson. He had heard Nixon speak during his student days at UF and was greatly impressed with the then–vice-president's acumen and intellect.

President John F. Kennedy had tacitly authorized the invasion of the Bay of Pigs and then pulled the rug from under the Cuban patriots by withholding U.S. military support. Yet he not only escaped criticism in the press for the debacle, as well as for his well-known sexual escapades, but he was idolized by the media.

Joseph routinely covered meetings of the Board of Regents, which met monthly on various campuses of the state's seven universities. On the evening before a meeting, the university presidents usually gathered for dinner in the hotel. On occasion, members of the press were allowed to join the group with the understanding that any information gleaned from conversations was for background use only and not for publication. No one was to be quoted.

During one of the dinners, Joseph silently twirled his wine glass on the tablecloth as the rotund president of a Miami area university offered his impressions of newspaper journalists, unaware that he was sitting next to one. His discussion attempted to explain why reporters were so often liberal in their views and critical of persons of authority. His comments are annotated with Joseph's thoughts at the time:

"To begin with they are underpaid," he said. *Right on target.*

"They resent people of wealth." *Some do, some don't.*

"They are overly suspicious of officials, elected or appointed, and always look for motives in their actions." *Quite true.*

"They are always out to get someone." *Not always; only when there's smoke.*

As the university president was giving his impressions of the Fourth Estate, the others around the table who knew Joseph lowered their heads in embarrassment. When he had finished with his assessment, Joseph spoke up. "That was a good analysis. You really should tell it to the journalism students in your school."

In April 1971, the *New York Times* acquired the *Gainesville Sun* in a merger with Cowles Inc. Reporters rejoiced at the prospect of pay raises and staff increases from the nation's largest and most prestigious newspaper.

"Don't expect much difference in salary," Ed Johnson cautioned. "But," he added, "the *Times* employee fringe benefits rated top among the major corporations." These included complete health insurance that continued through retirement, stock purchase options, and a supplementary retirement investment plan.

Times executives began sending young family members down from New York to gain experience. Among them was Sidney Gruson, whose father was a *Times* vice-president. Young Gruson was a willing learner, cheerfully accepting any and all of Joseph's assignments. It wasn't long before he returned to New York as a *Times* reporter.

John Harrison was moved to Lakeland to run the *Times* Regional Newspaper Group, replaced by Bill Ebersole, longtime advertising manager of the *Sun*. In spite of his ties with advertising clients, Ebersole was a popular publisher, maintaining a strict separation of the news and advertising departments. Occasionally Ebersole would drop in to the newsroom and discreetly offer a news tip. But he never exerted the slightest pressure on the news and editorial staff.

Soon after the barbaric massacre of 504 Vietnamese civilians at My Lai by U.S. troops under Army Lieutenant William S. Calley, it was learned that Calley's sister, married to a university professor, was quietly living in Gainesville. Soon the sidewalk and street in front of their house were crowded with reporters and TV trucks. The besieged Calley sister refused any and all comment. She would have been asked about her brother's character. Had he been Eagle Scout, an altar boy, or a juvenile delinquent with a police record? As a boy, was he mean? Did he play war games or cowboys and robbers? What was his father like? And his mother? Had she talked to him since the My Lai incident, and what had he said? Where was he now? However intrusive, these were standard questions in news gathering.

Calley was a public figure, and although not yet court martialed or proven guilty, his name had gained notoriety. Calley's sister made it plain she wasn't going to make any statements about her brother or give any interviews. She pleaded to be left alone.

Stacy Bridges, a bright and conscientious young female journalist, joined the vigil. A crestfallen Stacy returned to the newsroom. Calley's sister had cracked the door open and, for the umpteenth time, pleaded with the mob to be left alone.

"She called us a bunch vultures," Stacy said. "And you know what? That's what I felt like. I'm not going back."

In April 1971, the *Sun* won its second Pulitzer Prize for a series of editorials by H. G. "Buddy" Davis in support of the peaceful desegregation of Florida's public schools. Rarely, if ever, in the history of the coveted award had a newspaper the size of the *Sun* won two Pulitzers. It had been less than a decade earlier that publisher John R. Harrison had pecked out his award-winning editorials calling for improved living conditions in Gainesville's black neighborhoods.

During the same period, several obscure Southern newspapers had been lifted into literary prominence by the Pulitzer award for championing the cause of desegregation. To express it snidely, the racial issue was a meal ticket for editorial writers. Scruffy beat reporters would argue that their daily coverage of the civil rights movement from the trenches had more effect in bringing the injustices to blacks before the public eye than editorialists in their paneled offices. A dainty female reporter from the *Charlotte Observer* stated it succinctly in a journalism seminar while relating how the *Observer's* reporters teamed to do an investigative series on brown lung disease among coal miners. The series won a Pulitzer in 1981 and focused national attention on the plight of coal miners.

"Did you follow up the series with editorials?" came a question from the audience.

"Didn't need to," responded the dainty female writer. "Editorials are no more than a fart in a whirlwind."

Joseph believed his own writing had contributed to the founding of Santa Fe Community College or, at least, provided the needed impetus.

A stalemate had developed between adherents of a community college and the school board, which leaned toward a vocational school. Commercial interests needed mechanics to repair automobiles and air conditioners. Why build a junior college when the University of Florida was here? they argued. University administrators, believing a second college in the area would dilute dollars for higher education, were lukewarm.

Joseph attended a national conference on community colleges in Williamsburg, Virginia, to gain knowledge on the issue. He returned convinced that a community college would not only produce mechanics but also nurses and medical technicians needed in Gainesville's rapidly developing health care industry. Through the academic curriculum, students could complete two years of college programs, becoming more employable, or they could transfer their credits to a university and continue toward a degree.

Armed with this knowledge, Joseph wrote a three-part analysis on the merits of the community college. Call it advocacy journalism. Shortly thereafter, the county's legislative delegation introduced an enabling bill that authorized planning to begin for the community college.

At the height of the cold war, Joseph accepted an offer to visit the USSR. It was with another academic group, the Research Center for the Study of Socialist Education. It was headed by Dr. Gerald Read and based at Kent State University. Joseph had not met Read while visiting Kent State. Through the efforts of Dr. Glen Hass of the University of Florida, Joseph received a partial grant from Read's group to cover half his expenses. The *Sun* agreed to kick in the other half.

In late November, the group, made up of college professors, public school administrators, and a few teachers, landed at Moscow's Sheremetyevo Airport. Though well briefed by Dr. Read, who had led several other groups through the Soviet Union, they were not prepared for the scrutiny by hostile customs agents.

Unsmiling young officials in army uniforms pawed clumsily through suitcases sifting for contraband among the underwear. Bibles, carried by one or two members of the group, were confiscated. One member had bought a photography magazine at the airport on Copenhagen. It, too, was confiscated because it contained one or two artistic photos of partially nude women.

It was during the regime of Premier Leonid Brezhnev when missiles with atomic warheads of each country were aimed at the other. As the lone newspaper journalist in the group, one working for a *New York Times* paper no less, Joseph felt his every movement observed by KGB agents.

Cause for his unease was the recently published book, *The Russians,* by the *New York Times'* Hedrick Smith who had recently been bureau chief for the *Times* in Moscow. Smith's book, a best seller, was critical but objective. It was an accurate description of the Russian people with humorous accounts of Americans in the Soviet Union trying to cope with Russian customs and the state bureaucracy.

But the Intourist guides assigned to the U.S. education group were in no laughing mood and constantly badgered Joseph about the unfairness of Smith's book.

Nellie, the head guide, was a veteran. She had served as a translator during Richard Nixon's state visit. One evening in Samarkand, as they were having tea in the hotel courtyard, Joseph was accosted by two of the female guides wanting to discuss the book. After hearing their complaints, it was plain that they had not read it.

"Have you read the book?" Joseph asked.

They looked at each other and nodded.

"I mean the whole, unabridged, book," Joseph prodded.

"We read excerpts," one admitted.

"Put out by your government?" Joseph continued. "Is the complete book available in your libraries or book stores?"

They stammered that they had only read transcripts, but that was all they needed. Obviously, the transcripts had been issued by the Soviet propaganda agency. And it was also obvious that the book was banned in Russia, as was Boris Pasternak's *Doctor Zhivago*.

"I don't see how we can discuss the book if you don't know the whole of it," Joseph said, sipping the last of his tea and excusing himself. The subject of *The Russians* did not come up again.

Joseph's arrival at the Rossiya Hotel, a humongous building on the Moscow River next to Red Square, had been as stressful as the customs inspection. On leaving the bus, Joseph forgot his camera bag in the luggage rack above his seat. He quickly left the line at the registration desk to return to the bus, but a hotel attendant blocked his way to the door. "Go back in the line," he said sternly, ignoring Joseph's pleas.

Nellie came from where she was supervising the registration procedure and translating for the Americans. She bolted for the door when Joseph told her he'd left his camera bag on the bus.

She returned empty-handed and made for a telephone in the lobby. She was furious.

"The bus has already gone back to the garage on the other side of the city. They will look for your bag there."

By the time Joseph had registered and tendered his passport, Nellie returned.

His camera bag had been found and was being returned. Joseph breathed a sigh of relief, but he still faced Nellie's wrath. She berated his carelessness at length despite his apologies.

"I would have been responsible if your bag had been lost," she steamed through uneven front teeth, one capped with a gold crown. "From now on, you had better hang on to your belongings."

Saying that it was her responsibility meant that if Joseph's cameras had been stolen, it would have cast Nellie and the government in a bad light. Theft was not tolerated in the Soviet Union. The people were short on individual freedoms but there was law and order.

The Americans were ushered through schools where children in black and white uniforms sat rigidly at their desks. In an English class, a young girl stumbled while giving a translation. Rebuked by the instructor, she sat down blushing with embarrassment. It was a moment when all of the American visitors felt her shame and longed to console her.

School administrators in Joseph's tour group brought American books as gifts for Russian students. Joseph shared a large dormitorylike room with three others, including the principal of a small school in Illinois. He had brought a collection of paperback books including some by Mark Twain and Jack London, favorites with Russian readers. As Joseph was idly looking at the books, one title caught his eye. It was *Animal Farm,* George Orwell's scathing satire on Communism.

"Do you really intend to give them this book?" Joseph inquired of the principal.

"Yeah, it's a children's book that my teachers picked out," he answered naively.

"I wouldn't be caught in Russia with that book," Joseph said and then proceeded to explain that Orwell ridiculed communism with a pig who organized the animals in the barnyard and appointed himself commissar.

Convinced that he had a damaging piece of contraband in his possession, the shaken principal eyed the trash basket in the room.

"Not in our room," said Joseph, "or we'll all wind up in Lefortova prison or some gulag. You know they examine every piece of writing we discard. Don't even throw it away in this hotel. Put it in a trash container in the street."

The shaken principal secreted the book in his overcoat and reached for his hat.

Joseph could picture him on a street corner furtively looking in all directions, like a character in a spy thriller, before depositing the incriminating document in a trash can. Joseph also wondered if the principal's "helpful" faculty was also ignorant of *Animal Farm,* or had they deliberately set him up. There would be some explaining to do when he returned to Illinois.

In some high schools, the hallways displayed patriotic reminders of Russian battles in World War II. In a glass case, one school had a diorama of a battlefield with pieces of shrapnel and barbed wire gathered from the Moscow front where Hitler's army had been turned away from the city's walls. Red lights flashed on and off and muffled cannon thundered on a sound track creating a realistic illusion. Back home, students were burning the Stars and Stripes.

At Moscow State University, dominated by a Stalin-era "wedding cake" high-rise academic building, Joseph's group chatted with university students eager to practice their English. In the cavernous library room with an ornate, cathedral-like ceiling, the visitors found the periodicals section wanting in American newspapers and magazines. A student, reading a magazine, confided that there was one copy of the daily *New York Times* kept at the reference desk. Only professors and authorized graduate students could check it out.

Keeping visitors guessing and off balance was an art form with the Russians. Schedules constantly changed, and events were announced at the spur of the moment. The Americans were to visit Akademgorodok (Academic City), a research complex and scientific think tank in Novosibirsk, Siberia. As directed, early one evening, they assembled in the lobby of the Rossiya with their baggage. Two hours later the buses arrived. At the airport, they were led to a boarding station at the end of a winding concourse.

It was a freezing night, and they huddled around a potbellied stove to await boarding. At 2:00 A.M. they were herded out to a four-prop Aeroflot Tupelov 114 parked forlornly on the tarmac. Its wings drooped under the burden of a foot of snow. The passenger cabin was unheated and remained so for most of the flight. Joseph was wedged in a cramped seat that allowed little movement. The seat to his right was occupied by a young Russian soldier who sat erectly and stared straight ahead. Joseph managed to fish out his flask of brandy from his carry-on bag. He took a healthy sip and offered the flask to the soldier, who shook his head with an emphatic "*nyet.*"

Four hours into the flight over the Urals and across the vast Siberian taiga, an endless collage of snow and evergreen forests, a buxom, rosy-cheeked stewardess brought out breakfast trays. They held two slices of cold roast beef, frozen peas that eluded the fork like ball bearings, a slice of sausage, a roll, lukewarm tea, and an apple. After the all-night wait for the flight, Joseph wolfed the cold food.

The first evening in Novosibirsk, they were bused to a modern opera house for a Shakespearan performance. After a sleepless night and a journey past four time zones, Joseph nodded and dozed through the performance.

At the university, they heard esoteric lectures so complex and boring that only the most learned professors in the group derived any meaning from them.

On their departure after a two-day stay, their flight was delayed an hour when one of the Americans was detained by the police for snapping a picture of a couple walking through the snow.

Back in Moscow, the group joined a serpentine line in Red Square waiting to enter Lenin's tomb. Citizens from the far-flung republics of the USSR shuffled silently through the snow. Like maps, their faces reflected dozens of ethnic nationalities that made up the Soviet Union.

The world's most famous Communist resembled a wax figure in his sealed coffin under glass. Vladimir Lenin had lain there since his death in 1924. The Soviet Union was an atheistic society, but the idolatry of Lenin was a religion in itself. His likeness in huge portraits and bronze castings throughout the city was seldom out of sight of the citizens.

Intourist guided them through the usual ideological exhibits, including the air museum where a model of Sputnik hung from the rafters. At the historic Bolshoi Theater, they enjoyed a memorable ballet performance of *Giselle*. The Russian circus was unlike any the Americans had ever witnessed—two hours of madness in a red-carpeted ring featuring wild animals, clowns, dancing bears, yaks, and daring acrobats. It was the only time the visitors had seen Russians laughing.

They boarded the overnight express to Leningrad, the last leg of the tour. Laced with a network of canals, the city on the Neva River was sometimes referred to as the Venice of the north. It was prettier than Moscow and its people friendlier. In Moscow, the citizens of the capital suffered a martyr complex, bearing the burden of Communist ideology. People were more relaxed in Leningrad, less politicized, and in their minds, more cultured. Joseph was reminded of San Francisco, which thought of itself as more cultured than Los Angeles. That was before the hippies took over. Now it's a toss-up.

Joseph had gathered enough material on the USSR for a book. "How much do you want?" he asked Ed Johnson.

"Just write the story, impressions and all, we'll find the space," was Ed's reply. The story, with Joseph's photos, some taken at the risk of being handcuffed by the KGB, appeared in two parts, each two full pages in length. Joseph cringed with embarrassment at the 36-point headlines: A RUSSIAN JOURNAL and OUR MAN IN MOSCOW.

When asked how good a story was, Joseph's mentor in journalism school, Hugh Cunningham, used to say, "If you like it, then it's good. You are the best judge." Joseph was pleased with his report.

From the standpoint of the *Gainesville Sun*, the events of the sixties and seventies had produced the most news of any other epoch. Joseph considered himself lucky to have been a journalist during the period. By contrast, the 1980s were a letdown, though a welcome one. University students cut their hair and concentrated on careers. It was time to get to work. A few diehards condemned the boredom of the post-protest years and mourned the passing of the Age of Aquarius.

Joseph had seen the paper's circulation grow from about 10,000 when he joined it to 60,000 in the mid-1980s. Bob Tartaglione was the circulation manager and Joseph's frequent golfing partner. He had experienced the frustrations and tribulations of growing the paper in the rural regions of North Florida where the *Sun*'s liberal leanings clashed with hostile, conservative folk. During the height of the Vietnam War protests, his newspaper racks in the small towns were routinely vandalized. Bundles of papers were stolen from vending machines and strewn along the roadsides. Carrier trucks with the *Sun* logo on the sides were even stoned.

Through it all, the *Sun* had evolved from its old linotype machines and letterpress printing to offset printing and ultimately to photo composition and computer production. The old teletype wire machines disappeared, replaced by computers linked to the various state and national wire services.

Eventually, the *Sun* abandoned its old downtown building and moved to a modern facility south on 13th Street. The newsroom was on the second floor with box planters on a balcony overlooking an atrium with ficus trees on the ground floor. Reporters worked in cubicles, and a thick carpet muffled the noisiest of high heels in the passageways. Compared to the old newsroom where Joseph had begun, the atmosphere was more like a library.

Propelled by the whirlwind events of the two decades, Joseph's journalism career had been a fleeting one. Where most journalists had not yet attained their productive peak after twenty years, his time with the newspaper had been a second career and a short one. Working alongside reporters half his age had been a tonic that kept him current with the times and helped him avoid the mindset of an old fogy. In the final years, Joseph devoted his full time to being city editor and writing occasional columns. Ed Johnson had unburdened him of his education beat and placed his name in the masthead as associate editor.

He enjoyed good health and still had his vitality, but the failing health of his aged parents placed new demands on his time with frequent trips to Louisiana. Moreover, Cara had retired, and he wanted to spend more time with her. So, after twenty-two years, about the same as his Marine Corps service, he submitted his request for retirement.

Rob Oglesby, the managing editor, wanted him to continue writing with a weekly column. Never having been one to fill space with trivia or personal idle thoughts, he declined. But with the indulgence of Diane Chun, the features editor, he would contribute articles on the numerous travels that he and Cara frequently embarked on.

Twenty
The Golden Years—1986

Spring brings out the best in Hoot 'n Hollow. The weather is what one wishes for all the time—warm and sunny days with cool nights. The yellow trumpets of Carolina jasmine on vines high in the treetops are first to signal the end of winter. The early blooming redbud and wild plum appear next. Soon the woods are white with flowering dogwood, and the azaleas all around the yard explode into a riot of red, purple, rose, and white. The air is fragrant with honeysuckle blossoms.

Wrens frantically stuff every nook and crevice in the garage with false nests before settling down to the business of laying eggs. Cardinals crack sunflower seeds on the bird feeder to carry back to their fledgings fluttering on unsteady wings among the branches. Above it all, the red-shouldered hawk screams warnings intended to panic and flush his prey. The black snake, its glistening body thick from a feast of rodents or baby birds, suns itself in the grass. His presence helps explain the absence of rattlers.

Early in his employment with the *Sun*, Joseph and Cara bought the four wooded acres nine miles west of the center of town. Hoke Kerns, director of information at the university and a friend of Joseph's, owned ten acres, where he kept a few head of cattle as a pastime. One day he invited Joseph to see his herd, while talking up the adjoining lots up for sale at bargain prices. The owners, an elderly couple, he being in ill health, were selling their farm land to pay for his hospital bills. This was just before Medicare had come into being. Joseph and Cara bought the four-acre parcel for $3,200. Even if they never built on the property, it might still be a good investment. They were happy at Sunnybrook Estates and in no hurry to build their dream house. Annie had left the nest to attend college in Georgia.

On weekends, they would put on old clothes and, with Nipper in the back seat, set out to explore their woodland. They would drive west a piece on Newberry Road and turn off on a trail that wound through a majestic grove of live oaks, later cut down to make way for a mall. Interstate 75 was under construction, and the trail took them across the overturned clay and limerock boulders that would become the road bed for four lanes of asphalt. Past the I-75 construction, the trail took them to Tower Road, an eponym for the tall transmission masts of the university's radio station nearby, to Southwest 24th Avenue, a sand washboard that severely tested the undercarriage of vehicles. Thence to 81st Street, a rutted dirt road that took them to their land on 28th Place. Mr. Howze, who had farmed the land, had graded the road to Joseph and Cara's parcel but it was overgrown with tall weeds.

The prospect of building out there was like pioneering. The nearest neighbor was a quarter-mile away by road. Joseph and Cara were city people and the thought of septic tanks and a water well was not enticing. They even considered trading their plot for one in the city. But their land was a lure. They liked trees and their property was a dense forest except for a small open field of about half an acre fronting the road. The forest was a profusion of sweetgum, four varieties of oak, hickory, loblolly pine, hackberry, wild plum, cedar, holly, and cabbage palm. Dogwoods were scattered throughout under the canopy of taller trees and there were even a few tung trees, survivors of a grove planted in the twenties when paint was made from oil extracted from their large round nuts that resemble green apples.

As they explored the land, seeking the stone survey markers on the four corners, the path was often blocked by thickets, and thorny greenbriar vines tore at their clothes. Occupied by Virginia creeper clutching at their ankles, they'd look up point blank into spider webs inhabited by menacing long-legged black and yellow arachnids. Old Nipper sniffed out scats of raccoon and fox, savoring the wildness of the scent. At the base of rotting pine stumps, they discovered old clay pots that had collected turpentine in years past. Cara saved them for flower pots. They made out the vague tracks of an old wagon road that one of the neighbors claimed was the trail to Fort Clark dating to the Seminole Indian wars.

The pristine parcel remained only a weekend pastime, and their plans were still vague and undetermined. That was, until a young married couple moved in next door and the man of the house put up a basketball backboard over his car port. Kids flocked from around the neighborhood to shoot baskets. Afternoons and evenings was a constant thump thump of dribbling balls on the concrete driveway, accompanied by a commensurate level of yelling and shouting. The driveway court was barely 60 feet from Joseph's bedroom window. One evening, he had just dropped off to sleep after a tiring day, when the outdoor floods went on next door and a late-night one-on-one game got underway. That was it.

Joseph and Cara made up their minds to build. The next day, they contacted G. W. Robinson, a recommended builder. GW, as he was commonly known, was making his mark on the home development market at Gainesville, just as Clark Butler, their old friend from Sunnybrook, would make it in a big way in commercial development. At first, Robinson was reluctant to build their house. He made bigger profits building "spec houses" on lots he owned. But finally he agreed, and they drew up a contract. Their budget was $60,000. No financing. Robinson set a date to begin. Now the weekend explorations of Joseph and Cara took on an urgent meaning.

They had to locate their property lines through the trees and decide on the exact homesite. Joseph eschewed a surveyor and borrowed a transit from Robinson. Relying on the faded memory of his artillery days siting gun positions, he set up the instrument on a corner lot marker and aligned the verticle crosshair with the visible stone survey marker on the opposite corner. He then swung off a ninety-degree angle and sent Cara through the tangles with a tall stake to align with the crosshair. At intervals, she tied ribbons to tree trunks to mark the line. Sometimes he would lose sight of her in the foliage, resulting in exchanges of loud shouting. Once she ran into a nest of wasps and was painfully stung. Gamely, she resumed the task. Cara usually packed a picnic lunch, and they would relax with cold drinks and sandwiches while sitting on a fallen tree trunk. Their efforts lent a new meaning to the term "sweat equity."

The arrival of a bulldozer signaled the start of construction. With a fury, it tore into a thicket that Joseph and Cara had settled on as the homesite some 250 feet from the road. It wasn't pretty seeing young trees falling and wild grape vines pulled down from high in the treetops. Before long, there was a circular clearing stripped of vegetation. A well digger drilled 120 feet down and tapped into a vein of cool, clear water. Clay Electric, a rural cooperative power company, stretched wires to a utility pole, providing electricity for the well and the contractor's power tools. The summer rainy season was at its height, and soon the driveway was turned into a quagmire. "Got to stabilize that road," Robinson said, calling in several dump trucks with crushed limestone.

Joseph and Cara had decided on an L-shaped design with four bedrooms and three baths. A swimming pool would fit inside the L immediately adjacent to the house. They watched with eager anticipation as their dream house slowly took shape. But euphoria turned to frustration when the interior was enclosed, "dried in" was the contractor's term. Subcontractors misplaced selections Cara had carefully chosen. What kind of front door do you want? Did you want wood paneling in the family room? What shade? The wallpaper you selected for the bathroom isn't waterproof. Joseph had deferred to Cara on the interior decorations, and she'd have to go through the selections a second or third time.

All ended well, and by the beginning of the new year, they had a house to be proud of. Their old house in Sunnybrook Estates had been sold, and they were ready to move. The movers arrived late, and the van got stuck between trees. It sat for the night with the furniture aboard. Joseph blew up an air mattress and they slept on the floor. At daybreak, they were awakened by the twittering and chirping of small birds in the trees that were probably gossiping about their new neighbors.

Tired of pushing a lawn mower in the old place all summer and hoping to retain the natural surroundings of the new one, Joseph opted for cypress mulch in the front yard instead of grass. Only in the back around the pool was grass planted. When the summer rains arrived, the first torrential downpour, a "frog strangler" in the Florida vernacular, washed away the mulch. That was when Joseph realized the house was built on a slope, the severity of which could not be detected before the vegetation had been stripped. He ordered another load of mulch, but with the next rain, it, too, was carried away among the trees beyond the yard.

There was more than just mulch to worry about. The rains were turning the ground near the house into a quagmire. In desperation, after carefully noting the direction of the flow, Joseph took a shovel and set about carving a gentle swale to divert the water away from the house. That done, he and Cara proceeded to plug in a lawn of St. Augustine grass. They added a clump of azaleas at the front near the driveway that soaked up more runoff, and later, Joseph built an elevated landscape planter across the front. Cara christened it, "The Ark." Robinson had not installed gutters, and sheets of rain water cascaded off the roof, adding to the soaking near the house. Joseph hired a contractor to install gutters and worked alongside him to cut down the cost of the job. Downspouts emptied the gutters into an underground drainage pipe that carried the water past the house into the woods.

When the lawn had grown in, Joseph surveyed the results of his hydraulics engineering with satisfaction. His efforts had paid off, but dreams of a labor-free yard were shattered.

One evening, just before dark, a small gray fox made an appearance near the house. It seemed to say, "I live here, too." After a moment, it vanished into the woods. Raccoons made nightly forays, washing their prey of frogs in the pool and leaving muddy footprints. The mess they made was nothing compared to the destruction of the armadillos rooting in the new lawn for worms. One night, Cara saw one digging near the front door. It was so preoccupied, it never moved as she approached and lowered a cardboard box over it. Like a shot it exploded straight up through the box, scaring the daylights out of Cara.

Finally, Joseph took to shooting them. A state wildlife officer had told him armadillos were not indigenous to Florida. They ate the eggs of ground-nesting birds and were a threat to the habitats of native animals, such as the skunk. "You are helping preserve native wildlife when you shoot them," the officer said. His conscience clear, Joseph swabbed the barrel of his 12-gauge Winchester automatic, not fired since he had given up quail hunting twenty years before. Armed with a box of double 0 buckshot, he awaited the opportunity. But 'dillers are nocturnal, and they didn't emerge from the woods until the late night hours. Their favorite feeding ground was outside Cara's bedroom window. A light sleeper, she would hear them rooting and awaken Joseph. He'd stagger sleepily out the bedroom, shotgun at the ready, and quietly open the front door. In the glare of the floodlights, they were easy targets. One blast of buckshot was all it took. Actually, the thumb-nail size shot was an overkill, but Joseph preferred that to the possibility of only maiming them.

Early in the morning, Joseph would have to dig an armadillo grave in the woods with a post hole digger. Slowly the critters disappeared, leaving only the raccoons as pests. Joseph wasn't about to shoot raccoons or the squirrels that hogged the bird feeder. He did trap raccoons in a wire cage. He'd put the cage in the trunk of the car and release them in the countryside. But others always returned, as did the armadillos. Joseph grew weary of the nocturnal killings and gave up. The shotgun blast would keep his ears ringing for hours, ruining a good night's sleep.

Cara was an avid birder, and her sightings were considerable. Hardest to see but unmistakable to hear were the owls. In the early evenings, particularly during the cooler months, they call back and forth with eight characteristic hoots. Rarely, one can be spotted sitting motionless on a limb. Joseph and Cara once observed a family—mother, father and baby—perched side by side high in a tree. Just as secretive are the summer tanagers and yellow-breasted cuckoos. The mournful cooing of doves brings a feeling of ennui, and in early summer evenings, the calling of the chuck-will's-widow evokes bucolic memories of yesteryear on the farm. Joseph accidently flushed one from its secretive ground nest deep in the woods. Startlingly, it darted out in a low, noisy flight, like quail flushed out by a hunting dog.

The red-shouldered hawk is a fixture, screaming in flight to frighten prey. Racous crows congregate by the dozens, incurring the wrath of smaller birds whose nests have been raided. As large as crows are the piliated woodpeckers. They work as a pair, flying from one decaying tree to another, squawking loudly while in flight. Each spring, fledgling wrens emerge from nests in the garage, the mailbox, the bed of Joseph's utility trailer in the carport, or seemingly any place but the trees. Not long after moving in, Joseph and Cara watched a pair of wrens bring forth a family in an empty shoe box on a shelf in the garage.

Cara was returning home one evening from visiting friends and as the car entered the garage, the headlights caught a rat snake in the nest *in fragrante delicto*. It had a lump in its belly and another victim in its mouth. Cara raced from the car, reached up and grabbed the snake by the neck forcing it to cough up the baby bird. She flung the snake out the garage and tenderly swabbed the saliva from the bird with a ball of cotton. Then she placed it into an empty packing barrel, where the mother later enticed it to fly out.

Joseph, who feared and loathed snakes, cringed when Cara told him of the incident.

"You actually grabbed that snake with your bare hands?" he said. The only time he'd ever touched a snake was by the very tip of the tail after killing it.

"How else could I get the bird from it?" Cara replied. "They're not poisonous snakes."

Joseph had had a similar experience saving a baby rabbit from a rat snake, but he handled it differently. By chance he looked toward the swimming pool one day to see an object he thought was a large leaf floating on the water. It was a baby rabbit swimming for its life. Following alongside on the pool deck was a striped snake of considerable size slithering back and forth waiting for the rabbit to emerge. Joseph raced out yelling and clapping his hands, but the snake was not the least deterred and continued following the movements of its prey. "Okay, buddy, I hate to do this, but you're asking for it," he said aloud, while reaching for a rake leaning against the house. After dispatching the snake, he fished the frightened bunny from the water with a leaf net and set it free in the bushes.

In both incidents, Joseph and Cara had instinctively reacted as caring humans saving baby animals but, in so doing, had interfered with the workings of nature.

Never having had one, a working fireplace was a must in the new home, not one of those decorative, nonfunctional things found in so many new homes. Theirs was lined with firebrick. The hearth and sides were finished with native stone unearthed when the pool was dug. On chilly evenings, the warm hearth was a source of contentment and relaxation after a long day at the office. The Gilbarts contributed a set of andirons in the shape of owls.

Joseph bought a chain saw and was never wanting for firewood. There was always a fallen tree to be cut up. He became adept with the saw, a maul ax, and a wedge. He enjoyed splitting wood. It was exercise put to a good purpose. He built a woodshed and stashed stacks of wood to cure and keep dry. Old pine stumps yielded fat wood for starting fires, and the plentiful supply of dried greenbriar vines made ideal kindling.

"Everyone should have a pool once in a lifetime," a playing partner of Joseph once said, sardonically, on the golf course. He had grown tired of maintaining a swimming pool and sold his house to unburden himself. "I've got one, and I'm damned glad I do," had been Joseph's response.

True, the pool was a demanding luxury, but well worth the care and maintenance in terms of the exercise benefits. Their pool was a rectangle, thirty-two feet by sixteen. It was purely functional, not a kidney-shaped plaything people built with the idea of poolside parties or idly floating about on a tube with a cold drink.

Six months of the year—the pool not being heated—Joseph swam laps for thirty minutes a day, covering nearly 1,000 feet; a mile and a half per week, 5.5 miles a month, thirty-four miles for the season. Halfway to Jacksonville. By the first of November, the water would be too cold for sustained swimming. Disconsolate through the winter, Joseph tried to make up the loss of swimming exercise by taking longer walks and splitting more wood. Finally, he joined a health and fitness center and swam in its heated pool until his own pool water warmed up in May.

One by one, the empty parcels of the old Howze farm had been developed. Five-acre lots were selling for upwards of $50,000, and eventually the old farm tract was occupied by 17 homes. The new residents included an engineer, two neurosurgeons, an orthopedic surgeon, an oncologist, a college dean, two research Ph.D.s, a stockbroker, a lawyer, a school board administrator, a college music teacher, a sculptress, and a surveyor. Accessed via a private road, it was an ideal retreat, quiet and crime-free, yet only nine miles from the city center. The old rutted lime rock road was paved, paid for by the residents, with a sign at the entrance that said, PRIVATE DRIVE.

With expensive houses being built all around, Joseph and Cara's low-budget dream home rose in value on the tax appraiser's rolls.

When they questioned the increased taxes, they were told, "The market value of your property goes up correspondingly with the value of adjoining properties."

"Yeah, great, but we're here to stay, not to sell" was Joseph's retort.

Greenbriar Estates, the nickname for the neighborhood as listed on the sheriff's crime neighborhood record, had become a Camelot for the cultured and affluent.

But then the epidemic struck. It wasn't a virus but had the appearance of being contagious. It must be something in the water, people said. The epidemic was divorce. Seven of them among the then-fourteen households within a period of eighteen months, a whopping fifty-percent rate. Joseph and Cara didn't take to drinking bottled water, but silently reaffirmed their vows. Finally, the outbreak had run its course. Some of the victims remarried; others remained "divorsees" and "divorsays."

Among the latter was the nearest neighbor who began reliving his gay bachelor lifestyle. This Lothario threw wild parties with music so loud, the trees trembled. The partying was especially heavy following Gator football games. Joseph's complaints were politely accepted with regrets and promises to lower the stereo. It wasn't just the stereo. The screams of women caused Joseph to wonder just what kind of game was going on in the swimming pool. Once, the party lasted through the night. After tossing and turning in bed all night, Joseph arose at 5:00 A.M., half an hour after "animal house" had finally fallen quiet.

I think they've finally crashed, Joseph thought as he dressed. From the garden shed, he took down his chain saw and headed for his woodshed, which wasn't far from the offending neighbor's house. Through the dim light of dawn, Joseph counted six or seven cars parked in the yard.

He jerked the lanyard, and the saw started instantly. Letting it warm up to the task, Joseph greatly squeezed the trigger until the engine reached a deafening crescendo. Like a virtuoso, he idled the engine then revved it to screaming, ear-splitting decibels. To add realism to his effort, he proceeded to cut up an old log. Sawing wood on a Sunday morning. Forgive me, Lord. When he finally allowed the engine to idle, he heard a commotion in the house. Not surprisingly, they were awake.

Soon, sleepy celebrants stumbled out to their cars. He would not have been surprised had John Belushi been one of them. It was now broad daylight. One of the guests took a few steps in Joseph's direction, glowering menacingly. Joseph stood his ground, holding the smoking saw. With an expression that might have indicated he'd seen the horror movie, *Texas Chainsaw Massacre*, the party boy turned back to his car, revved up his own motor and scratched out angrily.

It was not a neighborly thing to do, but it put a stop to the wild parties. Not long afterwards, Lothario sold the house and moved out. A young orthopedic surgeon moved in with his lovely wife and young daughter. Quietness returned to the woods. "You never appreciate good neighbors until you've had a bad one," Joseph liked to say.

Annie met Jack while home from college during the summer working as hostess in the Holiday Inn dining room. The courtship continued by long distance where she returned to Brenau in Georgia for her final term and Jack came calling from Fort Bragg, where he was stationed with the elite 82nd Airborne Division. Jack volunteered after dropping out of business school at the University of Florida and becoming fair game for the draft. After qualifying as a paratrooper, he was sent to the army's finance school and then assigned to the division's payroll section. There, he remained a fixture for the duration of his enlistment, too valuable to be sent to "the 'Nam."

They returned to Gainesville to be married. Jack resumed work on his business administration degree, and Annie, with her degree in sociology, went to work with the Florida Department of Health and Human Services. They moved to Orlando when Jack graduated and joined the accounting firm of Earnst and Earnst. Jack and three of his coworkers formed an investment partnership, dabbling in real estate. Among their investments was a condo at Sanibel Island on the Gulf Coast connected by a causeway to Fort Myers. It was called Loggerhead Cay. Appropriately, the partnership became known as the Lager Heads. After visiting their investment, Jack and Annie fell in love with the island. When an opportunity came to manage a vacation condominium complex, they left their jobs in Orlando, kicked off their shoes, and became permanent islanders. Eventually, Jack migrated into real estate, leaving Annie with the condo management job. They built their own home in the Dunes.

Annie loved dogs and, at one time, had three. Bogie, a stray, was a fun-loving mixed Russell terrier. He'd been corraled by the animal control people while chasing birds in the Ding Darling Wildlife Preserve. While he awaited his fate at the animal shelter, Jack and Annie claimed him. Unfortunately, he got careless while teasing a hungry alligator one night and met his untimely demise.

Later, Annie met Muffin in the shelter, and it was love at first sight. Muffin was a honey-colored mixed female terrier with a striking resemblance to Benjie the movie star dog. Trouble was, Muffin and Cricket, an established member of the household didn't get along. They marked territories in the house and fought at every opportunity. Annie couldn't bring herself to return Muffin to the shelter, so they brought her to Gainesville. After old Nipper had gone to the great kennel in the sky, Joseph and Cara decided there'd be no more dogs. They were traveling a lot and didn't want a pet to worry about.

Annie first pleaded her case to Joseph, who said, "I don't want a dog, but it's up to Mama."

Next she went to Cara, who said, "I don't want a dog, but it's up to Daddy."

Case closed. Throughout the brief but conclusive negotiation Muffin barked lustily as though to show she was an alert, healthy dog, ready and willing to protect her new owners.

"She's going to spend a lot of time in a kennel when we're traveling," Joseph announced in the way of a threat.

"Not to worry," Annie replied, "she's already used to that. She'll adapt." It didn't take Muffin long to ingratiate herself with her new owners. An intelligent dog, she was fiercely protective of her new domain. From her post inside the living room window, her barking announced the approach of anyone coming to the house or of delivery trucks on the road. The ringing of the door chimes sent her into a frenzy. She'd race to the front door, barking savagely and would have to be restrained until the caller had ben greeted as a friend. She had never bitten anyone but gave every indication of wanting to. One day as Joseph went to answer the chime, he cracked the door a bit too wide and Muffin tore out through the opening. She made a pass for the legs of a man standing on the doorstep, taking a bite of his pant leg.

"It bit me!" he hollered.

"I don't think so," Joseph said as he collared his misbehaving mutt. "She just pretends to bite. By the way, who are you?"

"I'm from the tax appraiser's office."

"In that case, the bite wasn't misplaced," Joseph answered jokingly.

His own humor was misplaced. The man, a young Hispanic, was irate.

"Let's see if you were really bitten, raise your pant leg," Joseph said.

There was no sign of a bite. Not even a red spot.

"Like I said, she wasn't trying to bite you. She just pretends to," Joseph offered, unconvincingly.

"It doesn't matter if I was bitten or not, I'm required to make a report," the visitor replied.

Three days later Joseph received a report. Muffin was quarantined. She was to be under control at all times and not to leave the premises until notified. In two weeks, an animal control inspector would call to check on the dog.

Two weeks later, a white pickup truck with government markings drove up. Joseph snapped the leash on Muffin and went out to meet the visitors.

"I'm here to see about your dog," the first guy said.

"Well, here she is, take a good look," Joseph said. With that he picked up Muffin, who weighed less than forty pounds, and held her face to face to the inspector.

Muffin hated being picked up and put on her best hang-dog look. Satisfied that the bureaucracy of the Alachua County government had been properly served, the inspector smiled sheepishly and drove off.

Muffin trotted alongside Joseph on his daily walks without a leash, seldom wandering out of his sight. He taught her to "stay" before reaching busy 24th Avenue, the turnabout point of the walk. She'd wait obediently for Joseph to complete the distance and return. From being a reject with her original owners in her puppyhood. Muffin inherited a perfect home, with boundless room to roam, squirrels, raccoons, and armadillos to chase and loving owners who never returned from their weekly nights eating out without a doggie bag of steak scraps.

When Joseph and Cara vacationed in the North Carolina condominium they co-owned as members of the Lager Head partnership, Muffin went along. She lived an idyllic life in Hoot 'N Hollow, until cancer claimed her just past her sixteenth year.

From his introduction to the game in the Philippines, golf had become a lifetime recreation for Joseph, although his playing was limited on the weekends at the Gainesville Country Club. He always looked forward to retirement days when he could play whenever he desired. Yet after he left the *Sun*, he continued to play only twice a week. His handicap remained in the vicinity of twenty strokes, but he managed to make four holes-in-one in his years of playing. Many golfers more skilled at the game play a lifetime without ever recording one ace.

Catering to Cara's appetite for traveling, Joseph sought out opportunities to visit unusual places. They went to Russia, his second visit. From Irkutsk, near Lake Baikal, they rode the Trans-Siberian Express into Mongolia. Cara was one of the intrepid few in the travel group who dared to sample the fermented mare's milk put on the table in the hotel at Ulan Bator.

Joseph booked passage on a Norwegian coastal steamer. In a cabin the size of a phone booth, they bounced around on the voyage over rough Arctic seas from Bergen to the North Cape.

In between, they flew to Europe three times, touring Great Britain and France in rented cars and revisiting the site of Joseph's old wartime camp in Iceland. Doing France on their own provided memorable experiences. Overnighting in cramped little hotels, they'd begin the day's travel shopping for their picnic lunch in the town square. They'd pick up a loaf of freshly baked French bread, a hunk of local cheese, cold cuts, and a bottle of the *vin du pays*. It was truly a moveable feast, to borrow from the title of an Earnest Hemingway diary.

In Scotland, they stayed several days at St. Andrews, where Joseph rented a set of clubs and played the New Course, the historic Old Course being occupied with the annual national amateur championship matches. He had previously bought a pair of golf shoes at Prestwick, planning to play there or at nearby Troon, but had been disappointed in not succeeding to get a tee time. He was more successful at Gleneagles. Cara never played the game but walked with him and helped with the search for stray balls in the thick rough. Joseph had lost two sleeves of balls and faced the prospect of having to cut the round short and walk in. He hailed a foursome of Scots playing in the opposite direction on the adjoining fairway and asked if any in the group had some old balls he could buy.

One chap in the group unzipped the pouch of his bag, drew out four experienced balls and tossed them over. Joseph fished out a note from his billfold and extended it, but his benefactor scowled and shook his head at the offer of payment. The word "Scotch," syonymous with thrift in American conversation, didn't apply to Scottish golfers.

When Joseph and Cara were introduced to Elderhostel, their journeys took on a new dimension. The program for seniors combined travel with learning. Elderhostelers stayed on college campuses or in affordable hotels. They attended lectures by college professors on the local culture, history, and environment. Meals were adequate but far from the gourmet variety. So far, Joseph and Cara have been on the eighteen Elderhostels from Vancouver in British Columbia to Verona in Italy.

On their first Elderhostel, they rode a ferry boat on the Alaskan Marine Highway from Seattle to Juneau while being educated on the ecological dangers of clear-cutting virgin forests. The travels provided Joseph with a variety of materials for articles in the *Sun*.

When Joseph retired from the Marine Corps, he completely severed the umbilical. He remained loyal to the Corps but had no desire to join the any veterans organization. He had no interest in sitting around shooting the bull about the war with other veterans. Forget about the military and concentrate on your new career was his creed. Influenced by the bungling in Vietnam and surrounded by liberals at the *Gainesville Sun,* his attitude bordered on being antimilitary. His commanding officer in Quantico, Colonel Alexander Vandegrift, Jr., whose father was the hero of Guadalcanal and later commandant of the Marine Corps, had said, "When you retire, forget about the Marine Corps and concentrate on being a successful civilian."

Years later, Joseph read of a forthcoming reunion of Iwo Jima veterans in Oceanside, California. Cara was eager to go. They hadn't been to California in almost thirty years. In a ceremony in the base chapel at Camp Pendleton, Joseph was moved to tears when he recognized Marlowe Williams lighting a candle symbolizing the bloody campaign of the Third Marine Division. Colonel Williams commanded a battalion of the 21st Regiment with which Joseph had fought.

After his name was published in the Third Division newsletter, he received a note from Sam Jones in Indiana. Jones had been a communications man with Easy Battery. After the war, he organized annual reunions of the battery's veterans, attended mainly by communicators and truck drivers. Joseph joined them in New Castle, Pennsylvania, reuniting with Andy Sabol, his trusted wire sergeant with the FO team on Iwo. The following year, the group gathered at Beaufort, South Carolina, where Jim Leffers had retired. Jim died of a brain hemmorhage three years later.

George Green, Joseph's counterpart F.O. on Iwo Jima and also an Iceland veteran, presided over a reunion group of the 2nd Battalion, 12th Marines. Joseph and Cara joined them in St. Louis, where Joseph met Captain McElroy and several other officers of the battalion. Green returned to Iwo Jima with a reunion group, bringing back a sack of black sand from the beach, which he bottled in miniature jars and distributed to his reunion group. Joseph's little jar of sand sits on the fireplace mantle next to his bronze replica of the flag raising.

Next, Joseph joined the Subic Bay survivors and their reunion in San Diego. He was reunited with Captain B. B. Davis, the barracks adjutant, Lieutenant Sam Houston, and several NCOs he had served with in the mid-fifties. Considerable quantities of San Miguel beer were consumed by the Philippine veterans in the way of showing their loyalty for Subic Bay. The desire to reunite with old Marine comrades slowly waned. Joseph exchanged Christmas cards with his old friends but no longer felt the urge to attend reunions.

Before his retirement from the *Sun,* Joseph got his first look at the Iwo Jima Memorial in Arlington, Virginia. He took Cara along while attending a newspaper seminar in Washington. They took a cab across the Potomac. En route to the statue, Joseph told the driver he was a veteran of the battle of Iwo Jima. As Joseph and Cara silently viewed the monument, the cabbie respectfully turned off the meter. "Take as long as you want," he said.

"I helped build it," Joseph said in a low tone, while recalling the troubled fund-raising history of the memorial built with donations from marines and friends of the Corps. Every payday, company first sergeants stationed themselves at the end of the pay table, collecting dollars from reluctant doners. It was shakedown. Units competed for the honor of outraising each other. The campaign dragged on relentlessly for several years. Near the end, Joseph employed a scheme designed to relieve the lower-ranked men of his outfit from having their paycheck diminished. He was then stationed at Twenty-nine Palms in the California desert, commanding a 155-millimeter gun battery. He composed a letter about the proposed memorial addressed to a dozen of the then-sexiest Hollywood movie actresses. Each was asked for a dozen cheesecake photos, which would be auctioined off to troops with the proceeds going to the Iwo Jima memorial fund.

"I know it's a crazy idea, but what the hell, it's worth a try," he told Lieutenant Mike Nunnery, his executive officer.

A couple of weeks later, packets of nine-by-twelve slick photos of stars and starlets in provocative poses began arriving from press agents. Responses came from the likes of Mamie Van Doren and Piper Laurie. One movie star even volunteered to make a personal appearance at the marine base. Joseph backed off. His idea did not have the endorsement of Marine Corps brass. But he did proceed with the auction when the battalion was in the field on a firing exercise. During a break for noon chow, Joseph's staff NCOs stood on ammunition crates holding up pin-up photos and barking out in imitation of auctioneers. News spread to other batteries that were in competition to see which would raise the most. The bidding became spirited, particularly for Jane Mansfield glossies, one of which sold for ten dollars. When the photos were gone, several hundred dollars had been raised.

Headquarters Marine Corps announced that the goal had been reached and plans were being made to begin construction. Time went by with no further word from headquarters.

A rumor spread throughout the corps that the custodian of the fund, a major, had absconded with a large chunk of the fund and lost it betting on the ponies at Pimlico. Headquarters hushed it up and once again the shakedowns resumed at the pay tables. Joseph felt betrayed. He was not alone.

* * *

Trips to Louisiana are an annual event, always in the spring, when the crawfish are succulent and the sweet Lake Ponchartrain strawberries ripen. It's also the time of the LSU spring football game, when visions of the team will carry over until the fall season. Poor Lake Tarsa is a dying town, surviving on life support. At high noon, Main Street is deserted; not a solitary soul is seen on the sidewalks along the boarded up storefronts. The old movie theater is gutted with only the walls of its sides standing. Further up the street, the elegant facade of the old drugstore still records its birthdate with yellow bricks—1914. Below the numbers, garish red letters spell out the building's new occupant, Sausage Factory. A bar and a hair salon appear to be the only viable businesses. Ornas's old saloon still stands, darkened on the inside.

The ancient old oak still presides at the end of the street where Huey Long ranted about making every man a king. A westerly wind blowing from Texas whips up a chop on the milk chocolate waters of the lake. Louisianans used to say about their bragging neighbors, "There's lots of big winds in Texas."

Joseph buys two fried crawfish "po boys" from the take-out stand at the corner near the stoplight on the Dennings highway. Reportedly it becomes the scene of frenzied drug activity after nightfall. They drive to the park on the lake front and enjoy their sandwiches at a picnic table. Silently they watch the waves dancing about the knees of the stately old cypress trees that stand off the shore. Joseph's thoughts are immersed in the dim past. The town has seen its better days, but the timeless movement of the Mamatau River on its way to the Gulf of Mexico remains immutable.

Adam, who was Joseph's best boyhood pal and remained a trusted friend, sits silently in a wheelchair in his spacious lakefront home. He survived parachute jumps behind enemy lines in Sicily and France with the 82nd Airborne, returned home safely, married Betty—they produced a fine family—and through hard work, prospered with his grocery store. Among the townfolk, he goes by the affectionate appellation of "Mr. Adam." After suffering a heart attack and the amputation of both legs, he resumed a normal lifestyle, driving his pickup truck, walking on artificial legs, playing poker at the VFW club, and enjoying breakfasts at Shoney's in Dennings with his cronies. Then came a devastating stroke that confined him to a wheelchair, unable to talk. Awkwardly, Joseph makes an effort of starting a conversation, but his old friend only stares, occasionally nodding in acknowledgment.

Adam and Joseph are among the surviving fossils of Tom Brokaw's "Greatest Generations." But they never thought of themselves as heroes. They grew up in the worst of times and made the best of it. The call to arms in World War II came as an escape from the deprivations of the Great Depression. They went to war in opposite directions of the globe and actually savored the excitement of surviving battles in faraway places they'd never dreamed of seeing. In Joseph's case, only the circumstances of war could have brought him to meet the woman of his life. Adam returned to Lake Tarsa to marry a hometown girl.

They quietly picked up the pieces of their lives and never dwelt on their exploits. Calling them the greatest of generations is perhaps a stretch, yet they leave a legacy that will be difficult to match. It's been a helleva ride.

Joseph, in his golden years, is blessed with better health than his old friend, but the gift is wearing thin. He maintained an active lifestyle that made the years pass fleetingly. He adapted to Social Security, Medicare, AARP, and visits to doctors. Early-bird dinners and senior discounts became rewards for being old. Cognitive clutter and senior moments were temporary nuisances to be quickly brushed aside and forgotten. Reluctantly, he joined his golf foursome when they abandoned the white tees and took to hitting from the senior tees.

Along the way there were occasional surgical encounters to repair worn body parts, and sojourns in the hospital. The road gets bumpier with each passing year, but, happily, life's journey lurches on.

Semper fidelis.